THREE YEARS' WANDERINGS IN THE NORTHERN PROVINCES OF CHINA (1847)

THREE YEARS' WANDERINGS IN THE NORTHERN PROVINCES OF CHINA (1847)

Robert Fortune

A General Books LLC Publication.

CONTENTS

1

SECTION 1

PREFACE

THE SECOND EDITION.

The Author has been much gratified with the favourable manner in which the first edition of his work has been received by the public. It has been suggested by his friends, that it would be desirable in a new edition to enter more fully into the subject of Tea. He has therefore given some statistical information, tending to show the quantity of this production which is consumed by the Chinese themselves, as well as what they could spare for the European market, in the event of a greater demand arising from the reduction of tea duties. Attention has also been directed to our dominions in the north-west of India, which seem to possess all the requisites of a tea country.

These, and some other additions which have been made to the work, will, it is hoped, render it more interesting.

Chelsea, Aug. 12. 1847.

INTRODUCTION.

When the news of the peace with China first reached England, in the autumn of 1842, I obtained the appointment of Botanical Collector to the Horticultural Society of London, and proceeded to China in that capacity early in the spring of the following year. In laying my travels and their results before the public, I beg to say at the commencement, that I have no intention of writing or " making " a " book on China." By this I mean such books as have often been issued from the press, professing to give a faithful and true account of the history of the Chinese from the earliest ages, and their earliest kings down to Taouk-wang and the present day, of the arts, sciences, religion and laws, and the social and moral condition of the people; whose authors, with true Chinese " *Oula Custom,*" stand manfully by what the writers of other days have told them; and faithfully hand down to posterity, by the aid of the scissors and the pen, all the exaggerations and absurdities which have ever been written on China and the Chinese.

This celebrated country has been long looked upon as a kind of fairy-land by the nations of theWestern world. Its position on the globe is so remote that few|at least in former days|had an opportunity of seeing and judging for themselves ; and besides, those few were confined within the most narrow limits at Canton and Macao, the very outskirts of the kingdom, and far removed from the central parts or the seat of the government. Even the Embassies of Lord Macartney and Lord Amherst, although they went as far as the capital, were so fettered and watched by the jealous Chinese that they saw little more than their friends who remained at Canton. Under these circumstances much that was gleaned from the Chinese themselves relating to their country, was of the most exaggerated description, if not entirely fabulous. They from the highest Mandarin down to the meanest beggar are filled with the most conceited notions of their own importance and power; and fancy that no people however civilised, and no country However powerful, are for one moment to be compared with them. As an instance of this I may mention the following: | When the first steamer visited the coast of China, the Chinese in Canton and Macao did not exhibit the least surprise, but merely said, " *Have got plenty, all same, inside,*" meaning that such things were quite common in the interior of their country. Moreover, they cannot appreciate statistical inquiries ; but always fancy that we have some secret motive for making them; or that the subject cannot be of the slightest importance, either to ourselves

These remarks do not apply to such works as those of Davis, Staunton, Medhurst, and Jocelyn, which contain correct and valuable information on those subjects which came under the observation of their authors.

INTRODUCTION. IX

or others, and consequently do not trouble themselves about obtaining correct information.

I have been often much annoyed with this propensity of theirs during my travels in the country; and have had frequently to travel many a weary mile, merely because they did not think it worth their while to give me correct information. In fact, latterly I made a practice of disbelieving every thing they told me, until I had an opportunity of seeing and judging for myself.

Shut out from the country, and having no means of getting information on which we could depend, (for independent of Chinese statements, the accounts written by the Jesuits were in many instances much exaggerated,) it is not to be wondered at if the works in our language were more remarkable for the exhibition of the imaginative power of their authors, than for facts concerning China and the Chinese. We were in the position of little children who gaze with admiration and wonder at a penny peep-show in a fair or market-place at home|We looked with magnifying eyes on every thing Chinese; and fancied, for the time at least, that what we saw was certainly real. But the same children who look with wonder upon the scenes of Trafalgar and Waterloo, when the curtain falls, and their pennyworth of sights has passed by, find that, instead of being amongst those striking scenes which have just passed in review before their eyes, they are only, after all, in the market-place of their native town. So it is with " children of a larger growth."This mystery served the purpose of the Chinese so long as it lasted; and although we perhaps did not give them credit for all to which they pretended, at least we gave them much more than they really deserved.

Viewing the subject in this light we have little difficulty in accounting for the false colouring which has been given to every picture drawn by authors who have written on this country, and who have extolled to the skies her perfection in the arts, in agriculture, in horticulture, the fertility of the soil, the industry of the people, and the excellence of her government and laws. But the curtain which had been drawn around the celestial country for ages has now been rent asunder; and instead of viewing an enchanted fairy-land, we find, after all, that China is just like other countries. Doubtless the Chinese were in that half-civilised state in which they are now, at a very early period, and when the now polished nations of the West were yet rude savages. It is long since they discovered the art of making the beautiful porcelain, lacquer-ware, and silks, which have for centuries been so much admired in Europe; but these very facts | their civilised condition, their advancement in the arts, and even their discovering a magnetic power in nature, which they could convert into a compass for the purpose of navigation | instead of telling in their favour as an active and intelligent people, do the very reverse when we consider what they might have been now and what they really are.

INTRODUCTION. XI

A great proportion of the northern Chinese seem to be in a sleepy or dreaming state, from which it is difficult to awake them. When a foreigner at any of the northern ports goes into a shop, the whole place inside and out is immediately crowded with Chinese, who gaze at him with a sort of stupid dreaming eye ; and it is difficult to say whether they really see him or not, or whether they have been drawn there by some strange mesmeric influence over which they have no control; and I am quite sure that, were it possible for the stranger to slip out of his clothes and leave a block standing in his place, these Chinese would still continue to gaze on, and never know the difference. The conduct of the Chinese peasants during the war was very remarkable in this respect. I have been told by some of the military officers, that, when the whole fleet of sailing vessels and steamers went up the Yang-tse- Kiang in 1842, many of the agricultural labourers on the banks of the river used to hold up their heads for a few seconds, and look with a kind of stupid gaze upon our noble fleet; and then quietly resume their labours, as if the thing was only an every day occurrence, and they had seen it a thousand times before. When the " Medusa " steamer went up the Shanghae river for several miles above the city, the river became so narrow that they had some difficulty in finding a place wide enough to allow the steamer to come round. A peasant was standing on the bank smoking his pipe, and looking on with the most perfect unconcern, when, the helm being put down, the little vessel in coming round shot right across the stream, and came in contact with the bank, just under the very feet of the Chinaman. The shock was of course considerable, and the man who all at once seemed to awake from a trance, set *off* in the utmost terror, like an arrow, across the fields, without once looking behind him; and as Captain Hewitt, who related the story, remarked, for any thing he knew, the man was running until this day! Many of the Chinese are of course very different characters from those I have just described, and are as active men as you find in any part of the world: but the above are striking features in the character of the inhabitants of the northern parts of the country which I have had an opportunity of visiting.

In the knowledge and practice of agriculture, although the Chinese may be in advance of other Eastern nations, they are not for a moment to be compared with the civilised nations of the West. Perhaps more nonsense has been written upon this subject, than upon any other connected with China; and we can only account for it by supposing the writers to have been entirely unacquainted with the subject, and led away by the fancies and prejudices above alluded to. How ridiculous, for example, for them to speak in such glowing terms of the fertility of the land, when we bear in mind that they judged from what they saw at Canton and Macao! Had they seen the glorious scenery amongst the mountains at Tein-tung near Ning-po, or the rich plain of Shanghae, then indeed they

INTRODUCTION. X1U

might have written in the most glowing terms of the fertility of Chinese soil; but what terms could they have found to describe it, after giving the barren soil of the south such a character ?

Although it is not my intention to devote any part of these pages to the history and government of the Chinese, I must still notice, in passing, what has been so often said about the perfection of their government and laws. And here, too, I must differ from those who have such high notions of the Chinese in these respects. I think no country can be well governed where the government is powerless, and has not the means of punishing those who break the laws. China is very weak in this respect, compared with European nations, and the only thing which keeps the country together is the quiet and inoffensive character of the people. Everybody, who has travelled in China, knows that, wherever the natives are enterprising and bold, they set the government at defiance whenever it suits their purpose to do so. For example, what can the government do if the natives on the coast of Fokien, la bold and lawless race I choose to disobey its mandates? Positively nothing. Even further north, where the mandarins are more powerfull in Shanghae for examplelthe Chinchew men, as they are called, often fight pitched battles with firearms in the streets and in open day; and the mandarins, with all their soldiers at their backs, dare not to interfere. Surely no government worth any thing would tolerate this state of things. The system of apprehension and punishment is so

curious, and so characteristic of the Chinese government, that I must not omit to mention it. The belligerents are allowed to fight as long and as fiercely as they choose, and the soldiers never interfere: but when the weakest side is overpowered, and probably a number of lives lost in the affray, they come down in great force and seize and carry off to punishment the most defenceless: and, in circumstances of this kind, they are not over particular about seizing the most riotous, or those most implicated in the disturbances, provided those they seize are the weakest and least able to resist. Such conduct in the Chinese government I have been an eye-witness to, again and again, in the north of China; more particularly in Shanghae. What should we think if such a state of things existed in England ? and yet this is a specimen of the government which has been considered so perfect, and which has been so highly eulogised.

There can be no doubt that the Chinese empire arrived at its highest state of perfection many years ago; and since then it has rather been retrograding than advancing. Many of the northern cities, evidently once in the most flourishing condition, are now in a state of decay, or in ruins; the pagodas which crown the distant hills are crumbling to pieces, and apparently are seldom repaired; the spacious temples are no longer as they used to be in former days; even the celebrated temples on Poo-too-San (an island near Chusan), to which, as to Jerusalem of old, the natives come from afar to worship, show all the signs of having seen better

INTRODUCTION. XV

days. It is very true that these are heathen temples, and the good in every land will hail with delight the day when these shall give way to others which shall be erected to the true God: but nevertheless such is the fact, that these places are not supported as they used to be: and from this I conclude, that the Chinese, as a nation, are retrograding rather than advancing.

Although I have considered it necessary to expose in this manner the prejudiced opinions which have been from time to time given out to the world by authors on China, I am far from having any prejudice against the Chinese people. On the contrary, in many respects they stand high in my estimation. During the last three years I have been continually among them; wandering over and among their hills, dining in their houses, and sleeping in their temples: and from this experience I do not hesitate in pronouncing them a very different race from what they are generally supposed to be. The natives of the southern towns, and all along the coast, at least as far north as Chekiang, richly deserve the bad character which every one gives them; being remarkable for their hatred to foreigners and conceited notions of their own importance, besides abounding in characters of the very worst description, who are nothing less than thieves and pirates. But the character of the Chinese as a nation must not suffer from a partial view of this kind: for it must be recollected that, in every country, the worst and most lawless characters are amongst those who inhabit seaport towns, and who come in contact with natives of other countries: and unfortunately we must confess that European nations have contributed their share to make these people what they really are. In the north of China, and more particularly inland, the natives are entirely different. There are doubtless bad characters and thieves amongst them too: but generally the traveller is not exposed to insult; and the natives are quiet, civil, and obliging. And although they are not entitled to the credit of being equal to, much less in advance of the nations of the West in science, in the arts, in government, or in laws; yet they are certainly considerably in advance of the Hindoos, Malays, and other nations who inhabit the central and western portions of Asia. Besides, the manners and customs of the people, and the strange formation of the country, are indeed striking when viewed by the stranger's eye;|the pagodas, like monuments to departed greatness, towering on the hills; the strange dresses and long tails of the men, and the small deformed feet of the women. Added to which, this is the land of tea,|a beverage which in the eyes of Englishmen is enough to immortalise any country, had it nothing else besides. But I must again assert, that the great secret of the popularity of China, and the Chinese people, lies in the manner in which foreigners allowed themselves to be treated in former days, and in the mystery with which the Chinese, from principle, enveloped every thing relating to their country.

LIST OF ILLUSTRATIONS.

2

SECTION 2

THREE YEARS' WANDERINGS
CHINA.
CHAPTER I.
FIRST VIEW OF CHINA, AND THE IMPRESSIONS PRODUCED.
CONTRASTED WITH JAVA. LAND AT HONG-KONG DESCRIPTION OF ITS
HARBOUR. TOWN OK VICTORIA. I CHINESE
TOWNS, STANLEY AND ABERDEEN. DESCRIPTION OF THE
ISLAND. EFFECTS OF RAINS. " HAPPY VALLEY " NOTICED.
CHINESE MODE OF "STOPPING THE SUPPLIES." VIEWS
FROM THE TOPS OF MOUNTAINS. CLIMATE. BOTANY OP
THE ISLAND. FEW ANDMALS INDIGENOUS. UNHEALTHINESS
OF THE SETTLEMENT ITS CAUSES. CHARACTER OF THE
CHINESE POPULATION. MIXED CHARACTER OF FOREIGNERS.
REMARKS ON THE SETTLEMENT AS A PLACE OF TRADE.

On the sixth of July, 1843, after a passage of four months from England, I had the first view of the shores of China: and although I had often heard of the bare and unproductive hills of this celebrated country, I certainly was not prepared to find them so barren as they really are. Viewed from the sea, they have everywhere a scorched appearance, with rocks of granite and red clay showing all overtheir surface: the trees are few, and stunted in their growth, being perfectly useless for any thing but fire-wood, the purpose to which they are generally applied in this part of the country. A kind of fir- tree *(Pinus sinensis)* seems to struggle hard for existence, and is found in great quantities all over the hill sides; but, what with the barren nature of the soil, and the Chinese practice of lopping off its branches for fuel, it never attains any size, but is merely a stunted bush. Was this, then, the " flowery land," the land of camellias, azaleas, and roses, of which I had heard so much in England ? What a contrast betwixt this scenery and the hills and valleys of Java, where I had been only a few days before! There, from the sea-shore to the tops of the highest hills, the whole is clothed with the most luxuriant vegetation; and when the sun rises in the morning, or when his last rays scatter themselves over the lovely landscape, deepening the tints of the foliage of all hues, the scene presented to the view may well be called grand and sublime. But, as the poet sings, I

"Tis the land of the East, the clime of the sun."

After a few hours' pleasant sailing amongst the islands, we at last reached the beautiful bay of Hong-kong, and anchored opposite to the new town of Victoria. Hong-kong bay is one of the finest which I have ever seen; it is eight or ten miles in length, and irregular in breadth; in some places two, and in others six miles wide, having ex-

Chap. I.] TOWN OF VICTORIA. 3

cellent anchorage all over it, and perfectly free from hidden dangers. It is completely sheltered by the mountains of Hong-kong on the south, and by those of the main land of China on the opposite shore; land-locked, in fact, on all sides; so that the shipping can ride out the heaviest gales with perfect safety.

The new town of Victoria is situated on the north side of the island, along the shores of this splendid bay, with the mountain chain rising precipitously and majestically behind it. When viewed from the sea in 1843, it had a curious and irregular appearance; but as the plan of the town becomes more developed, and better houses are built, it will really be a very pretty little place. When I left China, at the end of December, 1845, it had made most rapid progress; new houses and even new streets had risen, as if by magic. Some noble government buildings were nearly completed, to be used as barracks for the soldiers; excellent and substantial houses were erected, or in the course of erection, for the merchants; and a large Chinese town had been built to the westward, for the principal part of the Chinese population. A beautiful road, called the Queen's Road, has been formed along the shore for several miles; and this was lined with excellent houses, and many very good shops. Many of the Chinese shops are little inferior to those in Canton, and certainly equal to what used to be in Macao. In fact, a very large proportion of the Macao shopkeepers have removed their establishments to Hong-kong; the former place being now useless for the purpose of trade since the English left it. The bazaar or market is also a most excellent one. Here we find all the natural productions of China, which are brought regularly from the main land; such as the fruits and vegetables indigenous to the country; fowls, ducks, teal, quails, and pheasants; meat of all kinds; and in fact every luxury which the natives or foreigners can possibly require. Besides these, English potatoes, green peas, and several other kinds of foreign vegetables, are plentiful at almost all seasons of the year.

The only other Chinese towns on the island of any note besides the new one just noticed are on the south side, and used to be called Little Hong-kong and Chuckchew: their names have been changed lately by the governor, Sir J. Davis, into *Stanley* and *Aberdeen.* They are merely fishing-towns; but the government always keeps up a military station at the latter, which renders it of some importance.

Hong-kong is one of the largest islands near the mouth of the Canton river. It is about eight miles from east to west, and the widest part of it is not more than six miles; but it is very irregular, some parts being only three miles in breadth, and the land jutting out here and there, forming a succession of headlands and bays. Imagine, then, an island considerably longer than it is broad, perfectly mountainous, and sloping in a rugged manner to the water's edge, having here

Chap. I.] EFFECTS OF RAINS. 5

and there deep ravines almost at equal distances along the coast, which extend from the tops of the mountains down to the sea, deepening and widening in their course. There are immense blocks of granite in these ravines, which have either been bared by the rapid currents of water in its descent during the rains, or which have tumbled into them from the sides of the mountains at some former period of time. The water in these ravines is abundant and excellent; and hence the poetical name which the Chinese have given our island. *Hong-kong,* or more properly *Heang-Keang,* the *"Island of fragrant streams"* During the wet season | for it rains in torrents then | these little streams swell with the augmentation of fresh water, and rush down from the mountains with a velocity which sweeps every thing before them. In May, 1845, one of these storms of thunder and rain visited Victoria; and the effects produced by it were perfectly astonishing; houses were undermined, roads made at a great expense only a few months before were swept away ; drains were burst open; and many of the bridges and other public works rendered perfectly useless. " The Hong-kong Register "thus notices the storm to wh ich I allude: |" The damage was very great, both to the recently-formed roads and to many buildings in the course of erection; and had the violence of the rain continued an hour or two longer, many houses must have been undermined and destroyed. As it was, much individual inconvenience has been sustained. About 5 o'clock

the whole of Queen's Road, from the entrance to the large bazaar to the market-place, was completely flooded, to the depth of from two to four feet. All the streets leading upwards to the hill served as feeders to this lake. In Peel Street particularly, the torrent rushed along, bearing every thing before it, and the street still resembles a dried-up watercourse, covered with stones and wrecks of buildings. The passages from the Queen's Road to the sea were all full; the one leading through Chunam's Hong for hours presented the appearance of a rapid river, and many of the houses on each side were only saved from the flood by mud walls hastily raised. About 6 o'clock the rain moderated, but for some time after the road was quite impassable. A Coolie, attempting to ford the stream rushing down D'Aguilar Sti'eet, was borne off his feet, but saved himself by catching hold of the frame of a mat-shed. The drain lately formed could not carry off the water, which committed great devastation, flooding a new house in its vicinity to the depth of nearly three feet, and destroying some new walls. All the open drains in the upper streets have suffered, many are entirely destroyed, leaving scarcely a trace of the street. A stream from a distant watercourse flowed along the road above the bungalow, occupied by the attorney- general, and descending with great fury upon the roof of one of his out-offices, carried away a great part of it. In many places the Queen's Road has been covered with soil, sand, &c., to the depth of more

Chap. I.] THE HAPPY VALLEY. 7

than two feet, and nearly all the cross drains are choked up. The bridge at the Commissariat has been carried away, and that in the Wang-nai-chung has also disappeared. Several lives were lost by the fall of a house in which some Chinese resided; and it is said the stream at Pokfowlum burst upon a mat hut in which were a number of Coolies, employed upon the new road; three saved themselves in a tree, but many more are missing, and are supposed to have been carried out to sea."

There is very little flat ground on the Island capable of being brought under cultivation ; indeed the only tract of any extent is the " Wang-nai- chung," or, as the English call it, the " happy Valley," about two miles east from the town; and even that is not more than twenty or thirty acres in extent. There are several other small plots of ground near the bottom of the hills, and some few terraced patches amongst them, but the whole is of very trifling extent. In former times the Chinese used to cultivate crops of rice and vegetables in the Wang-nai-chung Valley, but the place proved to be very unhealthy; and the Government, supposing that the malaria might proceed from the water necessary to bring the crops to maturity, prohibited the natives from cultivating them, and set about draining the land. From this description it will be seen that our settlement on this Island is entirely dependent on the dominions of his Celestial Majesty for supplies, which he, of course, can cut off when he pleases. Shortly after the presentGovernor, Sir John Francis Davis, took the helm of affairs in China, he, with the advice of the Legislative Council of Hong-kong, passed a law for registering all the inhabitants of the island, English and Chinese, the latter of course being under the rule of Her Britannic Majesty's representative. The Chinese population, ever jealous of foreigners, fancied there was more in this than met the eye, and that it was done for the purpose of *squeezing* them, and they actually rebelled against the decree. A meeting of all the Compradores and other great men took place, and one of the results was, that the " supplies" were stopped. For several days every thing stood still, the Coolies would not work, the boats would not bring provisions, in fact, the Chinese were in a fair way of starving the " Legislative Council of Hong-kong " into making better laws ; and they succeeded at last in making them alter the celebrated Registration Act into one more agreeable to their feelings.

From the tops of the mountains the view is grand and imposing in the extreme; mountain is seen rising above mountain, rugged, barren, and wildlthe elevation of the highest being nearly two thousand feet; the sea as far as the eye can reach is studded with islands of the same character as Hong-kong; on one side our beautiful bay lies beneath us, crowded with shipping and boats, and on the other, the far extending waters of the China sea.

The climate of Hong-kong is far from being agreeable, and up to the present time has proved

Chap. I.] CLIMATE. BOTANY.

very unhealthy, both to Europeans and to the native Chinese. During the months of July and August I the hottest in the year|the maximum heat shown by my thermometer was 94 Fahr., and the minimum in the same time was 80. The difference between the heat of day and night is generally about 10 degrees. In winter the thermometer sometimes sinks as low as the freezing point, but this is a rare occurrence. Even in the midst of winter, when the sun shines, it is scarcely possible to walk out without the shelter of an umbrella, and if any one has the hardihood to attempt it, he invariably suffers for his folly. The air is so dry that one can scarcely breathe, and there is no shade to break the force of the almost vertical rays of the sun. At other times in winter, the wind blows cold and cutting from the north, and fires are necessary in the houses ; indeed, at all seasons the climate is liable to sudden changes of temperature.

The botany of the island possesses a considerable degree of interest, at least would have done so some years ago, when the plants indigenous to it were less known than they now are. By far the most beautiful plants met with on the low ground are the different species of *Lagerstrcemia.* There are two or three varieties, having red, white, and purple flowers, and in the summer months, when they are in bloom, they are quite the hawthorns of China, I surpassing in their gorgeous flowers even that beautiful family. I have generally metwith them in a wild state very near the sea shore. A little higher up we find the beautiful *Ixora coccinea* flowering in profusion in the clefts of the rocks, and its scarlet heads of bloom under the Hong-kong sun are of the most dazzling brightness. The ravines are crowded with ferns and creeping shrubs of different kinds, not however of much interest to the lover of ornamental flowering plants. Here, however, under the ever-dripping rocks, we find the beautiful *Chirita sinensis,* a plant with elegant foxglove lilac flowers, which I sent to the Horticultural Society soon after I arrived in China, and which is now to be found in many of the gardens of England.

It is a curious fact connected with the vegetation of Hong-kong, that all the most ornamental flowering plants are found high up on the mountains, from a thousand to two thousand feet above the level of the sea. In the northern parts of China, such as Chusan and the mountainous country near Ning-po, the same description of plants are indigenous to less elevated situations, and there, on the tops of the hills, we find little else than species of grass, wild roses and violets, thus showing how plants accommodate themselves to the climate, by choosing a higher or lower altitude as the climate in which they are placed may be hot or cold. All the beautiful plants indigenous to Hong-kong, with the exceptions already pointed out, grow and flourish high up amongst the hills. Several species of *Azalea,* a plant now so well known in England,

Chap. I.] BOTANY. 11

are found covering the sides of the hills at least fifteen hundred feet above the level of the sea, and they are not met with at all at a low elevation on the same hills. The *Polyspora axillaris* grows in the same situations, and another plant, perhaps the most beautiful of all, I I mean the *Enkianthus reticulatus.* This plant is very highly prized by the Chinese. It flowers in February and March, about the time of their new year, and they then bring the branches down from the hills in great quantities for the decoration of their houses. The flowers are unexpanded when they are gathered, but by being placed in water they very soon bloom in the houses, and remain for more than a fortnight as fresh and beautiful as if they had been taken up with their roots in the most careful manner. Even the more beautiful amongst the native Orchids are only found at a considerable elevation. The tops of the highest hills are covered in the summer and autumn months with the purple *Arundina sinensis,* and the yellow *Spathoglottis Fortuni.*

The trees on the island are few, and generally in a stunted condition. The fir *(Pinus sinensis)* is common here, as it is all along the coast of China; *Cun- ninghamia sinensis* is rare on Hong-kong, although frequently met with on the main land; the tallow- tree is also indigenous, but no use is made of its fruit. Many kinds of the fig tribe are common, and one, the *Ficus nitida,* a kind of banyan, sometimes forms a very ornamental tree. Several species of bamboo seem to grow very well, and in thesituations where they are found are strikingly ornamental.

The only trees to the cultivation of which the Chinese pay any attention are the fruit-bearing kinds; and in some places there are very fair orchards containing the Mango, Leechee, Longan, Wangpee, Orange, Citrons, and Pumelows.

Although there are many more species of shrubs and trees indigenous to Hong-kong, yet after all the island has a barren and desolate appearance. The nature of the soil will always be a great barrier in the way of any improvement in this state of things; but even this, to a certain extent at least, may be overcome by the liberality of the Government, or even by the energy and taste of private individuals, and Hong-kong or Victoria may become in a few years very different from what it now is. We have only to look at what has been done as an earnest of what may follow. Trees lately planted are already growing beautifully in the grounds of Messrs. Dents, the Honourable Major Caine, Messrs. Jardine, and Messrs. Matheson, and at Mr. Stewart's, a considerable way up the hill.

The island is not rich in indigenous animals. I have frequently seen wild goats feeding in the most inaccessible parts of the rocky crags; there are also deer and foxes, but these are extremely rare. The only animals of the feathered tribe one meets with are, two or three species of king-fishers, some small singing birds and a few wood-pigeons where there are any trees or bushes to shelter

Chap. I.] QUARRIES. 13

them. The main land is much better stocked with birds. From thence the natives bring to the market large quantities of pheasants, partridges, quail, ducks, teal, and sometimes woodcocks and snipes. These birds are seldom seen wild amongst the mountains of Hong-kong, and when they are, they have only accidentally strayed from the main land. Luckily for the poor Chinese, their waters are much more productive than the land, and an inconceivable variety of fish is daily brought to the markets, and forms, with rice, the staple article of their food.

There are numerous fine quarries of granite along the coast, from which the stone has been obtained for the new town of Victoria. Much of the granite in different parts of the island is in a state of decay, and some ingenious persons have fancied that to this may be ascribed the prevalence of that malignant disease called the " Hong-kong fever," which has baffled medical skill, and carried hundreds to the tomb.

The autumnal months, August, September, and October, are most unhealthy. In 1843, when I first visited the island, it was in a lamentable condition. A place called the " West Point," where some barracks stood, and which was to all appearance as healthy as any other, proved fatal to the greater part of a detachment of our troops quartered there. The mortality was such, that Lord Saltoun, then commander-in-chief, was obliged to remove the wretched remnant, and ordered the barracks to bepulled down. The " Wang-nai chung," that" *happy* Valley" already noticed, was another most unhealthy spot. One of my fellow-passengers, Mr. Dyer, and his partner, who came out with high hopes of succeeding in business under the new regulations, went to live in this place, where, in a few days, they were seized with fever, and in a few more they had both gone to " that undiscovered country from whose bourne no traveller returns." In other parts of the island, which were at that time considered more healthy, fever prevailed to a great extent. Among those who were carried off, and whose death caused the greatest regret, were Major Pot- tinger and the Honourable J. R. Morrison, Chinese interpreter, son of the celebrated Dr. Morrison. The former had been only out for a few days, and was on the point of returning home with despatches for the Government. Many other instances might be mentioned; but these are sufficient to show the deplorable condition of our new settlement at this time; and so malignant and fatal was this disease, that few who were seized ever recovered.

Before leaving China, I had occasion to visit this spot of ground|the grave of many a brave soldier. A fine road leading round the island, for the recreation and pleasure of the inhabitants, passed through the place where they had been buried. Many of their coffins were exposed to the vulgar gaze, and the bones of the poor fellows lay scattered about on the public highway. No one could find fault with the road having been made there; but if it was necessary to uncover the coffins, common decency required that they should be buried again.

Chap. I.] ITS CAUSES. 15

The only advice the doctors gave, was at once to leave the island and fly to Macao.

The south side of Hong-kong was at this time considered much more healthy than the north, where the new town of Victoria was being built. The prevailing opinion amongst the inhabitants then was that the town ought to have been placed on the south side, which had the advantage of being exposed to the refreshing breeze of the south-west monsoon, from which the north was in a great measure shut out by the range of mountains. This theory, however, was soon disproved, for latterly the troops stationed at Aberdeen, on the south side, have suffered more than those in Victoria.

My own observation has led me to the following conclusions: | Much of the sickness and mortality, doubtless, proceeded from the imperfect construction and dampness of the houses in which our people were obliged to live when the colony was first formed; and a great deal may be also attributed to exposure to the fierce and burning rays of the Hong-kong sun. All the travellers in the East, with whom I had any conversation on the subject, agreed, that there was a fierceness and oppressiveness in the sun's rays here, which they never experienced in any other part of the tropics, even under the line. I have no doubt that this is caused by the want of luxuriant vegetation, and the consequent reflection of the sun's rays. The bare and barren rocks and soil reflect every ray that strikes them; there are no trees or bushes to afford shade, or to decompose the carbonic acid, and render it fit for the respiration of man, and thus the air wants that peculiar softness which makes it so agreeable even in hot tropical climates.

If these are the principal causes of the mortality in our new colony, the remedy will of course be apparent to every one. Already a great improvement has taken place in the houses of the merchants, and in the barracks of the soldiers, and the results have been most satisfactory. But the colonists must not stop at this stage in their improvements. Let the Government and the inhabitants use every means in their power to clothe the hill-sides in and around the town with a healthy vegetation; let them plant trees and shrubs by the road-sides, in gardens, and in every place available for such purposes ; and then I have no doubt that Victoria will be quite as healthy as Mucao. No one can approve of the selection of Hong-kong as a British settlement; but that part of the business being irremediable, we must make the most of our bargain.

The native population in Victoria consist of shopkeepers, tradesmen, servants, boat-people, and Coolies, and altogether form a most motley group. Unfortunately there is no inducement for the respectable Chinese merchant to take up his quarters there, and until that takes place we shall always have the worst set of people in the country. The town swarms with thieves and robbers, who are only kept under by the strong armed police lately established. Previous to this, scarcely a dark

Chap. I.] MIXED CHARACTER OF FOREIGNERS. 17

night passed without some one having his house broken into by an armed band, and all that was valuable being carried off or destroyed. These audacious rascals did not except the Governor even, for one night Government House was robbed; and another time they actually stole the arms of the sentries. These armed bands, sometimes a hundred strong, disappeared, as they came, in a most marvellous manner, and no one seemed to know whence they came or whither they went. Such attacks are fortunately now of rare occurrence. In all my wanderings on the island, and also on the main land hereabouts, I found the inhabitants harmless and civil. I have visited their glens and their mountains, their villages and small towns, and from all the intercourse I have had with them, I am bound to give them this character. But perhaps the secret of all was, that I had nothing for them to take, for I was always most careful not to have anything valuable about me, and my clothes, after scrambling amongst the rocks and brushwood, were not very tempting even to a Chinaman.

Since the island of Hong-kong has been ceded to England, the foreign population in it has been much changed. In former days there were only a few mercantile establishments, all known to each other, and generally most upright and honourable men. Now people from all countries, from England to Sydney, flock to the Celestial country, and form a very motley group.

Viewed as a place of trade, I fear Hong-kong will be a failure. The great export and import trade of Southern China must necessarily be carried on at Canton, as heretofore, there being at present, at least, no inducement to bring that trade to Hong-kong. It will, nevertheless, be a place of great importance to many of the merchants, more particularly to those engaged in the opium trade; and will, in fact, be the head-quarters of all houses who have business on the coast, from the facilities of gaining early information regarding the state of the English and Indian markets, now that steam communication has been established between this country and the south of China. Moreover, with all its faults, its importance may yet be acknowledged in the event of another war. Our countrymen cannot have so entirely forgotten the kind of protection which used to be afforded them by the Portuguese at Macao, as to make them wish to be put in the same circumstances again; and it is of no little importance to know that their lives and property are safe under the British flag, which has

   . . . . " braved a thousand years The battle and the breeze."

3

SECTION 3

CHAP. II.

LEAVE HONG-KONG FOR AMOY OPIUM STATION AT NAMOA.|
LIBERTY THE ENGLISH ENJOY THERE. CHINESE POPULATION, AND
THEIR MODES OF LIVING. A NEW ADMIRAL

MAKES NEW LAWS.| CHERRY-BRANDY ALTERS HIS VIEWS.
THE ACCOUNT WHICH, AS IN DUTY BOUND, HE SENDS TO
PEKING. NATURAL TUNNEL THROUGH CHAPEL ISLAND.

AMOY. | REMARKS ON ITS TRADE. TRAVELS IN THE COUNTRY AMONGST
THE PEOPLE. THE WANT OF A TAIL.

THE HILLS. | ISLAND OF KOO-LUNG-SOO. EFFECTS OF
WAR STRANGE ROCKS. UNHEALTHY NATURE OF THE
ISLAND.|BOTANY AND BIRDS. VISIT TO ONE OF THE CHIEF
MANDARINS HIS HOUSE AND GROUNDS.

I Left the pleasant bay of Hong-kong on the 23d of August, and sailed for Amoy. As we came out of the harbour by the western entrance, and rounded the south side of the island, I had an excellent view of the little town of Chuckchew, and the military station established there. The town, or village, for it is but a small place, is pleasantly situated on the shores of a deep bay, and fully exposed to the refreshing breezes of the south-west monsoon, and is generally considered much more healthy than the town of Victoria, on the opposite side of the island.

It was now my lot to be seized with that dreadful fever, which I have already noticed as so prevalent in our new settlement at this time. I layin a very precarious state for several days, without the means of procuring medical aid; but the sea air probably did more for me than any thing else, and, under Providence, was the means of saving my life. After encountering a strong gale of wind which we rode out in a deep bay for three days, we at last reached the opium station at Namoa.

Namoa is the name of a small island about half way between Hong-kong and Amoy, and is well known as one of the stations where the contraband trade in opium is carried on between foreign vessels and the Chinese smugglers. At this time I was fresh from England, and full of all the notions which we form there of the sacredness of the Chinese empire. I then thought that, although I might perhaps get a view of the celestial country, no barbarian feet would be allowed to pollute the sacred soil. Great was my surprise and pleasure when I found the captains of vessels wandering about all over the island unmolested. They had made roads to a considerable extent, and had built a cottage as a sort of smoking lodge when they landed in the evenings for recreation. They had also erected stables, and had small Chinese ponies for riding all over the island; in fact, they seemed quite the lords of the soil, and were not subjected to the least annoyance from the natives.

Hundreds of Chinamen gather round this spot, where they have erected huts and a bazaar, or market, for supplying the shipping, and, what appears not a little strange to European eyes, when-

Chap. n.] LIBERTY THE ENGLISH ENJOY. 21

ever the ships move to any other anchorage in the vicinity, the whole of the inhabitants, houses, market, and all, move along with them, so easily do these individuals change about from one place to another. One of the captains informed me that it was in contemplation to leave that particular spot shortly, and that if I happened to visit it a day or two after this event, all the motley groups would be gone, and the place entirely deserted. Nor was this statement at all exaggerated, for on my return a few months afterwards, the change of station had taken place, and not a vestige of the little village remained: men, women, and children, with their huts, boats, and all that belonged to them, had followed the ships, and had again squatted opposite to them on the beach.

The different modes which these people have of obtaining a livelihood are really astonishing: with one of these I was particularly struck. There are boats of all kinds engaged in bringing off stock, such as ducks, fowls, and other things, to the ships, but one kind consisted only of five or six thick pieces of bamboo fastened together in the form of a raft, and with this the poor fellows paddled along with two oars, the water washing all over the raft, and frequently also over its contents. The fowls which some of these people brought off were in a most pitiable plight, and certainly could not exist long in such a state.

A few months after this time a complaint was made to Sir Henry Pottinger, then governor ofHong-kong, by the Chinese authorities regarding this state of affairs at Namoa. It set forth that the subjects of her Britannic Majesty had built houses, made roads, and in fact were making another Hong-kong at the island of Namoa, which, according to the treaty, they had no right to do. The old Chinese admiral, who had shut his eyes to all these irregular proceedings, had been removed, and another, remarkable for his *prowess and bravery* in the suppression of piracy on that coast! had been appointed to this station, and it was the latter with whom the complaint originated. Sir Henry Pottinger acknowledged the irregularity of the proceeding, but blamed the Chinese authorities for allowing it for such a length of time, and claimed a period of six months to give time for the sale or removal of any articles the English might have on shore. This was agreed to on the part of the Chinese.

And now comes the part of the business which so nicely illustrates the peculiar character of the Chinese. When I visited Namoa, in October, 1845, I made enquiry regarding the state of affairs on shore, and found that a little civility, and a few bottles of cherry brandy, had wonderfully softened the good old admiral, and that a communication had been received stating that some little show of compliance was actually necessary: they must pull down the house, for example, but the stables and horses might remain as before, and the captains might go on taking their accustomed exercise and

Chap. II.] ISLAND OF NAMOA. 23

recreation on the island, as they had been in the habit of doing. It was even hinted that no objection would be made to their putting up another cottage, if they chose to do so. In the mean time, a fine account had doubtless gone to Peking, showing how the barbarians had been driven from the island which they had dared to set foot upon ; perhaps a battle had been fought, and a few of our ships and their crews taken and destroyed, which would give a certain amount of dclat to the affair. This is the way things are managed in China ! Matters being in this state, I had no difficulty in prosecuting my botanical researches amongst the hills. These hills are of the same barren nature as those formerly noticed, and the natural production?, both in the animal and vegetable kingdoms, resemble those of Hong-kong.

The island of Namoa is about fifteen miles long, and of irregular breadth; in some places about five miles. The principal town is situated on the northern side, having a very fine bay, swarming with fishing-boats; indeed the whole of the coasts of this celebrated country are studded with small sailing boats belonging to fishermen, who seem to be a most industrious and hard-working race of men ; many of them in this island go perfectly naked, a practice which I have not observed so common in any other part of China.

Leaving Namoa, and sailing up the coast towards Amoy, the stranger is continually struck with the barren rocky nature of the coast, and in some partshas a view of hills of sand, the particles of which, when a hurricane blows, mix with the wind, and whiten the ropes of vessels and render it most unpleasant to be in the vicinity. Here and there he has a view of what appear to be rather fertile plains amongst the hills, cultivated with sweet potatoes, rice, and the other staple productions of the country. On the top of the highest hills along the coast, and as far as the eye can reach inland, pagodas are seen towering, which serve as excellent marks to the mariner as he sails along the shores. As we approach nearer to Amoy we passed Chapel Island, remarkable for having a large natural tunnel right through its centre, which has a most striking and curious appearance when vessels come in a line with it. In the afternoon we anchored in the harbour of Amoy between that island and Koo-lung-soo.

Amoy is a city of the third class, seven or eight miles in circumference, and contains about 300,000 inhabitants. It is one of the filthiest towns which I have ever seen, either in China or elsewhere; worse even than Shanghae, and that is bad enough. When I was there in the hot autumnal months, the streets, which are only a few feet wide, were thatched over with mats to protect the inhabitants from the sun. At every corner the itinerant cooks and bakers were pursuing their avocations, and disposing of their delicacies; and the odours which met me at every point were of the most disagreeable and suffocating nature. The suburbs

Chap. H.] TRADE OF AMOY. 25

are rather cleaner than the city; but as it is not customary to use carriages of any kind in this part of China, the roads are narrow.

It is from this place and the adjacent coast that the best and most enterprising Chinese sailors come. Many, or rather most of those who emigrate to Manila, Singapore, and other parts of the straits are natives of Amoy and the coast of Fokien, and hence this place has generally been the head-quarters of the foreign junk trade. During the war it was remarked by our officers, that the merchants here showed more knowledge of English customs than those at other places did, and all were acquainted with our settlement at Singapore, and spoke highly of it.

Since this port has been thrown open several foreign merchants have established themselves, and the trade, although small when compared with that of the more northern port of Shanghae, is still considerable. Indian cotton, cotton twist, long cloths of English and American manufacture, and opium seem to be the principal articles of import, if we except the straits produce, which is chiefly brought in their own junks. Since the arrival of the British Consul the opium ships have been removed from the harbour, and now lie just outside its limits, where the Chinese smugglers are allowed to visit them with impunity.

Unfortunately for the trade at Amoy, the exports of which we are most in need|I mean teas and silk | are not so easily brought to it as to thenorthern port of Shanghae. This, of course, will be much against Amoy; but nevertheless it may do a considerable portion of business in other ways. All sorts of coins are current here: dollars, rupees, English shillings and sixpences, Dutch coins, &c. &c., are all met with, and pass current by weight. Native gold, in bars, is sometimes brought in considerable quantities, to pay for the cotton and opium, and is, I believe, considered of a very pure quality.

During my stay here I was continually travelling in the interior, going sometimes a considerable distance up the rivers, and then landing, and prosecuting my botanical researches in the adjacent country. Frequently in these excursions I came unexpectedly upon small towns and villages, and generally walked into them without the least obstruction on the part of the natives; indeed, they seemed in most cases highly delighted to see me. When the day was hot I would sit down under the shade of a large banyan-tree, generally found growing near the houses, and then the whole village|men, women, and children, would gather around, gazing at me with curiosity not unmixed with fear, as if I were a being from another world. Then one would begin to examine my clothes, another would peep into my pockets, while several others were examining my specimens. The general opinion seemed to be that I was a medical man, and in a very short time I was surrounded with invalids of all

Chap. II.] TRAVELS IN THE COUNTRY. 27

classes and ages, begging assistance and advice. The number of persons who are diseased in a Chinese village is really astonishing. Many of them are nearly blind, and a much greater number, in this part of the country at least, were affected with cutaneous diseases of the most loathsome description, originating probably in their peculiar diet, and dirty habits.

I was one day travelling amongst the hills in the interior of the island in places where I suppose no Englishman had ever been before. The day was fine, and the whole of the agricultural labourers were at work in the fields. When they first saw me, they seemed much excited, and from their gestures and language I was almost inclined to think them hostile. From every hill and valley they cried " Wyloe-Fokei," or " Wyloe-san-pan-Fokei," that is, "Be off to your boat, friend;" but on former occasions I had always found that the best plan was to put a bold face on the matter and walk in amongst them, and then try to get them into good humour. In this instance the plan succeeded admirably: we were in a few minutes excellent friends; the boys were running in all directions gathering plants for my specimen-box, and the old men were offering me their bamboo- pipes to smoke. As I got a little nearer to the village, however, their suspicions seemed to return, and they evidently would have been better pleased, had I either remained where I was, or gone back again. This procedure did not suit my plans, andalthough they tried very hard to induce me to " wyloe " to my " san-pan," it was of no use. They then pointed to the heavens, which were very black at the time, and told me that it would soon be a thunder-storm, but even this did not succeed. As a last resource, when they found that I was not to be turned out of my way, some of the little ones were sent on before to apprize the villagers of my approach, and when I reached the village, every living thing, down even to the dogs and pigs, were out to have a peep at the " Fokei." I soon put them all, the dogs excepted , in the best possible humour, and at last they seemed in no hurry to get rid of me. One of the most respectable amongst them, seemingly the head man of the village, brought me some cakes and tea, which he politely offered me. I thanked him and began to eat. The hundreds who now surrounded me were perfectly delighted. " He eats and drinks like ourselves," said one; " Look," said two or three behind me who had been examining the back part of my head rather attentively, " look here, the stranger has no tail;" and then the whole crowd, womenand children included, had to come round me, to see if it was really a fact, that I had no tail. One of them, rather a dandy in his way, with a noble tail of his own, plaited with silk, now came forward, and taking off a kind of cloth, which the natives here wear

The Chinese house-dog has a great antipathy to foreigners, and will scarcely make friends with them.

Chap. H.] ISLAND OF KOO-LUNG-SOO. 29

as a turban, and allowing his tail to fall gracefully over his shoulders, said to me in the most triumphant manner, " *look, at that.*" I acknowledged it was very fine, and promised if he would allow me to cut it off, I would wear it for his sake. He seemed very much disgusted at the idea of such a loss, and the others had a good laugh at him.

The hills in this part of the country are more barren than any I ever recollect to have seen either before or since; consisting entirely of bare rocks and gravelly sand, as hard and as solid as stone, with scarcely a vestige of vegetation. In height they vary from five hundred to two thousand feet above the level of the sea. Further inland the ground is more level: it is also much more fertile, and yields good crops of rice, sweet potatoes and earthnut, besides a considerable quantity of ginger and sugar.

The island of Koo-lung-soo is situated opposite to the town of Amoy, and commands it. At the time of the war this island was taken by the English troops, and occupied until the spring of 1845, when the Chinese paid a part of the ransom money, and it was again placed in their hands. It is scarcely two miles long, and of irregular breadth, and seems to have been, before the war, the residence of some of the principal inhabitants in this part of the country. Most of the houses on the island are in ruins, but their remains show what they were, and prove the wealth of their former residents. I could not look upon the ruinedwalls, the pretty fish-ponds, all overgrown with weeds and filled up with rubbish, the remains of gardens ruinous as the houses, without wishing most sincerely that war, and all its attending calamities, might long be kept from my own peaceful, happy home, and soon be unnecessary in every part of the world. According to all accounts, the less respectable part of the natives had done more to make the houses of this island have a ruinous appearance than our troops during the war, by pulling down every thing that they could possibly carry away and dispose of.

Some immense blocks of stone (granite) are here supported naturally on the tops of the hills in the strangest manner, and are objects of great interest to the traveller. One, in particular, appears as if some giant arm had raised it to its present position, and left it there solely to astonish the beholder in after-ages, and leave him to wonder not only how it came there, but how it could remain in its present position; and, most assuredly, a very small quantity of gunpowder exploded below it would hurl it from the hill to the plain beneath. Another huge rock stands near the entrance of the harbour; this, however, seems to have been on the point of giving way, for it is now supported by a mass of stone-work on one side. The natives have a tradition concerning this rock, and say that as long as it stands, the town of Amoy will never fall before a foreign enemy. Unfortunately for the prophecy, Amoy, like the rest of the places attacked

CiiAp.II.] UNHEALTHINESS OF KOO-LUNG-SOO. 31

by the English, was taken, although the rock still stands as before.

The island, particularly on the north-eastern and eastern sides, is very unhealthy; fever and cholera prevail to a great extent during the south-west monsoon, and are most fatal. Our troops suffered far more from the climate, when they had possession of the place, than from the guns of the Chinese at the taking of Amoy. In the autumn of 1843, the sickness amongst the officers and men of the 18th Royal Irish was almost unprecedented: dismay was painted in every countenance, for every one had lost his comrade or his friend. It was dismal indeed. I have known many who were healthy and well one day, and on the morrow at sunset their remains were carried to their last resting-place. The little English burial-place was already nearly full, and the earth was red and fresh with recent interments, scarcely a day passing without two or three being added to the number of the dead. And yet, what was rather strange, a detachment of the 41st M.N.I, commanded by Captain Hall, were, officers and men, all perfectly healthy; they were, however, on a different part of the island.

I fear that the more we know of China the more will be dispelled the notions of its being a healthy country, which we had formed from the experience of those who lived in their shaded airy houses at Macao and Canton. During my rambles on Koo- lung-soo I stumbled on the tombstones of someEnglishmen, who, according to the inscriptions on them, had been interred upwards of one hundred and fifty years: their graves had been preserved during that long period by the Chinese, who seem to pay great respect to the tombs of the dead. Lately the stones had been replaced and the tombs repaired by one of our captains on the coast, who for this respectful and praiseworthy act had acquired amongst his comrades the name of *Old Mortality.*

In the midst of such rocky mountains and barren scenery, it will not be expected that I could have much success in my botanical researches. Besides, the flora has still much of the same tropical character as the Canton province. In the gardens there were several pretty shrubs, but the greater part of them were well known, such, for example, as the *Jasminum Sambac, Olea fragrans, China rose, Chrysanthemums,* and various other common species. The hedges and crevices of the rocks abound in a little creeper called *Pcederia foetida,* very pretty, but having a most disagreeable odour. There are, however, some very pretty roses on the island, producing small double flowers of great neatness and beauty, although destitute of perfume. These I sent home to the garden of the Horticultural Society at Chiswick.

Birds are very rare, and the species most meagre in number : indeed this may be expected, as there is no shelter for them. A small Mina with white wings is met with in large flocks; white-necked

Chap, H.] VISIT TO A MANDA1UX. 33

crows are common, as well as paddy-birds, Indian kites, and two or three varieties of kingfishers. During my stay here I was much assisted by Captain Hall of the 41st N. I., who was fond of botany, and well acquainted with the localities of all the plants in the neighbourhood.

One day I went in company with this gentleman and the Rev. Mr. Abele, an American missionary, to pay our respects to one of the principal mandarins, and to see his houses and gardens. His residence is in the suburbs of the town, on the side of a rocky hill, close to the beach. When we entered the outer court, we were received by a number of officers of inferior rank, and conducted to a kind of office, where, after politely desiring us to sit down, they offered us their pipes to smoke, and snuff-boxes, or rather phials of glass and stone, containing something which was like Scotch snuff, and rather agreeable. There were two couches or beds in the room, on one of which I observed a small lamp burning and an opium pipe lying by its side, by which I conjectured we had disturbed an opium-smoker in the midst of his enjoyment. Tea was immediately set before us, as is the custom in this country; but it was very indifferent, and, as Mr. Abele informed us that we should get much better when we were introduced to the principal Mandarin, we only tasted it in compliment to our good friends.

In a few minutes the Mandarin himself came

to conduct us into a more splendid apartment. It was a large airy room, one side fitted up with finely carved cases, in the centre of which stood a time-piece and some beautiful jars filled with flowers. I here had an opportunity of seeing the great veneration with which the Chinese regard anything that is old. One of these pieces of porcelain, he informed us, had been in his family for five hundred years, and had the peculiar property of preserving flowers or fruits from decay for a lengthened period. He seemed to prize it much on account of its age, and handled it with great veneration. The other side of the room was elevated a little, and fitted up for the " sing-song," or theatricals, of which the Chinese, from the highest to the lowest, are passionately fond. Tea was soon brought in, in a tea-pot, in the European fashion, and not in the manner usual amongst the Chinese; for the custom with them is first to put the tea into the cup, and then to pour the water over it, the visitor drinking the beverage and leaving the leaves in the bottom of the cup|an admirable mode for such persons as the Aberdeen gentleman, who, some years since, when coffee was not so common as it is now, complained that " his landlady did not give him the thick as well as the thin." Sugar is never used by the Chinese with their tea.

The Mandarin, after making various inquiries about us|what our names were ? what our occu-

Chap. H.] CHINESE GARDEN. 35

pations? how long we had been from home? and more particularly how old we were?|and after minutely inspecting our clothes, the coloured waistcoats apparently gratifying him very much, asked us to walk out and see the grounds around the mansion. The house stands near the base of the hill, and the garden lies behind it: the whole is really pretty; the large banyan-trees overhanging the walks, and the huge and rugged rocks forming caves and shades from the sun. A very fine spring issues from the hill-side, from beneath a rock. This water the proprietor praised very much, and we all drank heartily of it to please him: really such a spring, in a place like this, is invaluable. A telescope was brought to us, which he evidently considered a great curiosity. He placed it upon a large stone table, carefully adjusting it to the desired view, and then asked us to look through it; but we were not accustomed to use the instrument in that way, and took it up in our hands in the usual manner. He seemed surprised that we could see through it this way. After showing us all the curiosities in the garden, he took us back into the house, where tea was again set before us, with the addition of six or seven kinds of cake, which, however good they may be considered by the Chinese, I must confess I did not like. I have since tasted excellent buns and short cakes in Chusan and Shanghae. After some further conversation, we withdrew, the Mandarin inviting us to renew our|visit as often as we pleased. It was now dark, and we were lighted to the river with torches, followed, as usual, by some hundreds of the Chinese, who were all respectful and civil. Indeed, we were always honoured with a body-guard of this description wherever we went.

4

SECTION 4

Having travelled all over the country adjacent to Amoy, and completed my researches, at the end of September I sailed again towards the Formosa Channel, on my way to our most northern stations of Chusan, Ningpo and Shanghae. The Monsoon, however, had now changed from southwest to north-east, and we experienced very stormy weather, with strong northerly currents, which, of course, were directly against us. The vessel was at last obliged to put into the Bay of Chinchew from stress of weather, and having sprung her bowsprit in the gale, it was impossible for her to proceed. At one time the sea was running so high, and the vessel plunging so much, that the whole of her decks were frequently under water. Some idea may be formed of the storm when I mention that a large fish weighing at least thirty pounds was thrownout of the sea upon the skylight on the poop, the frame of which was dashed to pieces, and the fish fell through, and landed upon the cabin table. In a day or two our cargo was got out and put into another vessel, in which I also embarked, and we again proceeded on our voyage. This attempt was even more disastrous than the last, for after being out for several days, and having got nearly through the Formosa Channel, we met one of those dreadful gales so well known to the navigators of these seas. Our newest and strongest sails were split to pieces, the bulwarks washed away, and in spite of the best seamanship, and every exertion, we were driven back far below the bay from which we started about a week before. I shall long remember one of these fearful nights. The poor Lascar crew were huddled together under the long boat, to shelter themselves from the wind: the sea was running very high, and washing our decks fore and aft, as if we had been a narrow plank tossing on the waves. I had gone below, and the Captain had come down for a second, to look at the barometer, when we felt a sea strike the vessel with terrible force, and heard a crash which sounded as if her sides had been driven in; at the same moment the glass of the skylight came down about our ears, and the sea forced its way into the cabin. I certainly thought the little schooner had gone to pieces; but Captain Landers rushed on deck to ascertain the damage which had been done, and to try to repair it. The night was very dark ; but he

Chap. III.] DRIVEN BACK TO CHIMOO. 39

soon found that our weather bulwarks had been stove in, and the long-boat carried over to leeward from its place in mid-ships, where it was fixed. Luckily the lee bulwarks held it fast, otherwise the boat and the whole of our crew would have been swept together into the angry foaming ocean, where no mortal arm could have rendered them any assistance. Two glazed plant-cases filled with plants from Amoy, which were on the deck, were dashed to pieces, and their contents, of course, completely destroyed. In the long voyage from England to China, even in rounding the celebrated " Cape of Storms," I never experienced such weather as I met with on the east coast of China, at the commencement of the north-east monsoon. After being three days in the storm, having only as much sail on the vessel as to steady her, the gale moderated a little, and we were able to hoist more sail, and make for the land, which proved to be a place called Chimoo, which was far below the point which we started from a week before.

Chimoo Bay is about fifty miles north of Amoy. It has been an opium station for foreign ships for some years; and here, even during the war, that trade was carried on in spite of the mandarins. The natives of the different towns on the shores of this bay are an independent and lawless race. An anecdote was related to me by one of -the captains, which gives a fair idea how things are managed in this part of the country.

Some of the opium merchants came on boardone of the ships in the bay, and requested the loan of some guns, for each of which they offered to deposit a large piece of Sycee silver, which was, of course, much more than its value; and promised to return them in a day or two. When asked what they intended to do with them, they replied, that the mandarins and officers of government were expected shortly to levy the taxes, and that the people were determined not to pay. They said they only wanted four or five guns for the purpose: these were granted them ; and in a day or two, when they returned them, inquiry was made if they had been successful. " Oh yes," they said: " they had driven the mandarins over the hills." It certainly had been no very difficult matter to effect this object.

The inhabitants in the towns and villages around the bay are frequently at war with each other; in this they resemble the borderers of our own country in ancient feudal times, when " might was right." As in those days, too, a sort of black mail is levied, and treaties of peace are concluded, one of the parties paying a stipulated sum to the other. This, however, I am sorry to say, is not the worst trait in their character: they are the greatest thieves and robbers in existence; as I myself found to my cost.

One day I had sent my Chinese servant on shore with orders to gather all the plants he could find in a certain direction, which I pointed out to him before he left the ship; but he returned to me the next morning with only a few useless

Chap. III.] CHARACTER OF THE NATIVES. 41

things, which he had evidently gathered very near the landing-place on the shore. I felt much annoyed at this, and scolded him pretty sharply for his conduct; but he excused himself by saying, that he durst not go in the direction to which I had pointed, as he would have been beaten and robbed by the Chinchew men. This I did not believe at the time, and imagined that it was laziness on his part, for, like most of the Chinese, who receive a specified sum per month for their services, he was rather remarkable for this propensity; I therefore determined to set out myself on the day following, and give him the treat of a long walk for his misconduct. The following morning was fine, and I jumped into a China boat which I had hired for the purpose, and reached the shore, after being completely drenched by the breakers, which roll high along the shores of this bay, and render the landing, particularly in small boats, rather dangerous. When I got on shore, and proceeded to walk in the direction I intended, the boatman and others came round me, and attempted to dissuade me from going, by intimating that I was sure to be attacked by the Chinchew men, and robbed or murdered. I also saw signs of warfare in the shape of matchlocks and long bamboo poles, in the hands of the Chinamen, who, as my servant informed me, were obliged to carry them in self-defence. I began to wish, then, that I had brought off from the ship a few of the crew for protection I indeed Captain Woodrow kindly offered to send some with mewhen I set out: however, it was now too late; and I determined to put a bold face on the matter and proceed. I set out towards the hills, on one of which stands the Chimoo pagoda, which I was anxious to visit on my route, as I expected to get a good view of the country from its summit.

Many acres of ground here, all along the shore, are used for evaporating sea water and forming salt, which is a great article of trade in China. As the traveller proceeds inland, the ground, capable of cultivation, is covered with crops of sweet potato and earth-nut, which form the staple productions of this part of the country in the autumnal months. Between the different fields, one often stumbles upon the graves of the natives, sometimes finely ornamented with those half-circular erections, so common in the south of China, and at other times without any ornament whatever ; this of course depending upon the wealth of the relatives. The hills are like those near Amoy, rocky and barren, having here and there a few wild plants growing on the sides of the ravines; some of which, however, are very beautiful. The pagoda, already mentioned, stands on the top of the highest hill, and affords an excellent landmark to the vessels on the coast.

On my way towards the hills, I was frequently surrounded by hundreds of the Chinese, and was evidently considered a great *natural curiosity.* The country, although barren, teems with inhabitants; indeed, I almost thought the very stones

Chap. III.] JOURNEY TO THE HILLS. 43

were changing into Chinamen, so rapidly did the crowd accumulate at times. The sight was droll enough: I here were I and my servant on one side of some ravine, with our specimen boxes and other implements, gathering samples of every thing we could find; there, on the top of the other, stood three or four hundred of the Chinese, of both sexes, and all ages, looking down upon us with wonder painted in every countenance. And then, their features, their manners and costume, were all so striking to a stranger, that I believe our surprise and curiosity were mutual. They were generally civil, but I ran a risk at last of getting into trouble, on account of a silk neckcloth which I had on, and to which some of them took a great fancy, telling me that it would look so well round their heads|for in this part of China they wear a handkerchief like a turban. I was much amused with the various plans they employed to get it from me: one brought a handful of chillies, which he held out in one hand, and with the other pointed to the neckcloth, intimating that he would close the bargain in that way; another did the same with a few earth-nuts, and some brought me a few weeds; all, however, taking care to offer nothing of value. I began blundering Chinese to them as well as I could, upon which two of the men ran off to the village as fast as they could, desiring me to wait until they returned. I could not divine the reason of this; but in order to please them, I complied with their wishes. They soon returned, bringing with thema bottle of sam-shew, or Chinese spirits; which they supposed I had asked for, and which they now tendered for the neckcloth, evidently considering that this offer must be irresistible. The crowd, however, was now becoming rather too great, and I walked on towards the hills, and began to ascend them|a plan which I always adopted when I wanted to get away from the Chinese, as they are generally too lazy to follow far, where much exertion is required. The manoeuvre answered my purpose, for I was soon left to my own meditations. When I reached the highest hill on which the pagoda stands, and looked down on the level plain over which I had passed, I was at no loss to comprehend from whence the numbers came by whom I had been surrounded, as large villages or towns now met my eye in all directions which had not been visible when I was on the plain.

On reaching the pagoda, I was astonished to find it in a most dilapidated condition, almost ruinous, although the main part of it, which had been strongly built, was nearly entire. A few stone josses or gods|a dome, with a double wall, containing a winding staircase leading to the different balconies through which the wind howled in a most dismal' manner, are all that I can particularise about the pagoda. I went over the whole of it, and obtained an excellent view of the surrounding country for many miles on all sides. As far as the eye can reach, it has the

Chap. III.] CIIIMOO PAGODA. 45

same barren and rocky character. No one noticed or molested me in any way.

After enjoying the view of the country from the top of the hills, I again descended to the low ground by a different way from that by which I had come; but no sooner did I reach the plain, than I was again surrounded by the natives. It was getting late in the afternoon, and my servant, I believe, felt rather tired, as I had intended he should when we started in the morning. He now began to scheme a little, to save himself from walking any farther than he could possibly help; and as I sometimes traversed rather wide circular routes in search of plants, he generally took the nearest way in the direction in which he knew we had ultimately to go. A few of the natives now began to follow me rather closely, and from their manner I suspected that their intentions were not good; but as they pretended to take me to some place where I should see some good plants and flowers, I allowed them to accompany me, and tried to keep them, all in good humour. We arrived at last in sight of a large mansion, standing in a retired part of the country, and I was proceeding with perfect confidence towards it, when the Chinamen began to press more closely round me; and upon feeling a hand in my pocket, I turned quickly round, and saw the thief running off with *a* letter which he had abstracted. As soon as he saw he was discovered, he threw it on the ground, and made off; but when I put my hand into my pocket, I found that I had lost several things of more value. This incident stopped my progress, and made me look about for my servant, whom I saw at some distance attacked by about eight or ten of the fellows. They had surrounded him, presenting their knives, and threatening to stab him if he offered the least resistance, at the same time endeavouring to rob and strip him of every thing of the slightest value, and my poor plants collected with so much care were flying about in all directions. I felt that we were in a dangerous situation, and instantly leaving my pickpockets, set off to his assistance as fast as I could. When the Chinamen saw me coming, they all took to their heels and left him, making off towards their companions, who were looking on from a distance. My servant was pale with fright when I reached him, and very much excited; nor did he fail to remind me of all he had said the day before. I felt there was no denying we were in dangerous company, and that the only thing to be done was to get out of it as soon as we could. Accordingly I made straight for the village where we had left the boat, and my servant took good care to follow close at my heels. As we approached the landing- place the boatman came to meet us in high spirits, saying he had expected us long ago, and was fearful that the Chinchew men had either robbed or murdered us. It was now ebb tide, and there was about half a mile of bare sand to cross, with the

Chap. III.] MY SEKVANT's OPINION OF MATTERS. 47

surf breaking furiously beyond it. The boatman at first said it was impossible to go to the ship before morning, and the people of the village promised me good chow-chow (food), and quarters for the night. I thanked them for all their kind offers, but told them that I should be much better pleased to go on board of the *Ka pan* with three masts, as I was to sail to Chusan early next day. Upon this, a sign was made to some other boatmen hard by, and immediately all were in motion. A boat was carried by a number of men across the sands to the water. I jumped upon the back of a stout Chinaman, who scampered like a race-horse across the wet sands, and deposited me in the boat ; and they rowed us through the rolling surf in a masterly manner. I reached the ship, all safe and sound, although completely drenched with wet, but with my opinion of the Chinese considerably lowered by the adventures of the day.

Amongst the plants which were nearly destroyed in the fight between my servant and the natives were several fine roots of *Campanula grandiflora,* which grows wild amongst these hills, and a new species of Abelia *(Abelia rupestris).* Both have ultimately arrived safe in England, and are now in the garden of the Horticultural Society at Chiswick.

The bay which bears the name of *Chimheic* has also a station for merchants' vessels, a few miles further north than that of Chimoo. I mention this place to show the great change which has taken place in the Chinese since the late war. Thecaptains of the ships here, as at Namoa, have now horses to take exercise in the morning and evening.

A little incident occurred about this time, which speaks for itself. It was necessary, from some cause or other, to remove the officers' stable, and build it on another part of the shore. The men employed for this purpose, when taking away the stones from the one place to the other, were stopped by some natives of the lower order, who took the stones and appropriated them to their own use. In going past the site of the old stable a few days afterwards, our people were surprised to see the stones all brought back; doubtless through the interference of some superior officer amongst the Chinese. This incident shows, I think, that the mandarins are anxious to preserve peace with the English, although some people, who pretend to secret sources of information, assert that in the interior they are preparing for another war.

The country, both with regard to vegetation and general features, is the same as at Chimoo : I was, however, much struck with the formation of one part of the main-land near the entrance to the bay. Part of the hill was rocky, but other parts were formed by immense banks of sea-sand, which appear to have been driven up from the bottom of the ocean by some terrific storm, or convulsion of nature. Sea shells, stony shingle, large fragments of rock, as well as sand, contribute their share in swelling the mighty mass, and all

Chap. III.] THE BAY OF CHINCHEW. 49

formed a great contrast with the appearance of every thing around it.

The natives bear the same character as those all along the coast in this provincelthat of thieves and pirates; but they are the best and most enterprising sailors in China, and you meet them in every port you go to. Their trade will be much injured by the admission of English vessels into the northern ports.

I must here notice the great kindness and assistance which I have always received from the captains of vessels at these opium stations, who were always ready to lend me a helping hand, and forward my views by every means in their power.

5

SECTION 5

CHAP. IV.

J,AND AT CHUSAN. I DESCRIPTION OF THE ISLAND. I TOWN OF
TINGIIAE. I AGRICULTURE. I STAPLE PRODUCTIONS. HEMP
PLANTS. PALM, OF WHICH ROPES ARE MADE. TREFOIL
CULTIVATED FOR MANURE. I OIL PLANT. FLORA. 1111.1.S
COVERED WITH AZALEAS, ETC. THE TALLOW TREE.
GREEN-TEA SHRUB. BAMBOOS AND OTHER TREES. FRUITS.
YANG MAI AND KUM-QUAT. INHABITANTS AND SHOPS IN
TINGHAE. I ENGLISH NAMES ON SHOP DOORS. A NEW LANGUAGE
MODE OF CLASSING FOREIGNERS. I DISEASES OF
THE EYE COMMON. SALT-MAKING. I METHOD OF PREPARING THE VEG-
ETABLE TALLOW. MODE OF HATCHING EGGS
BY ARTIFICIAL HEAT.

Our little vessel being sufficiently repaired, we were able to proceed on our voyage.
This time we were more fortunate, and reached the Chusan group of islands in ten
days from Chimoo. When we neared the islands, I was delighted with the change in
the aspect of the country; and as we anchored off Keto Point, waiting for the tide,
Captain Landers kindly allowed me to have the ship's boat and crew to go on shore.

The first glance at the vegetation convinced me that this must be the field of my future operations, and I had then no doubt that my mission would end most successfully. Here the hills were no longer barren, but either cultivated, or clothed with beautiful green grass, trees, and brushwood. I returned to

Ckap. IV.] DESCRIPTION OF THE ISLAND. 51

the vessel in high spirits, and in a few hours afterwards we were at anchor in the fine Bay of Chusan.

Chusan is a large and beautiful island, twenty miles in length, and ten or twelve in breadth at the broadest part. In approaching it, the view of the numerous other islands which stud the sea in all directions is striking and picturesque; noble mountains towering above the other land, and fertile valleys sloping gradually to the ocean. The island itself is a succession of hills, valleys, and glens, presenting an appearance not unlike the scenery in the Highlands of Scotland. At the head of every valley there are mountain passes, over which the inhabitants cross when they wish to visit the interior of the island. The valleys are rich and beautiful, surrounded by mountains, which in many parts are covered with trees, and in others under cultivation: these, in their turn, again open and expose other valleys no less fertile, rich in vegetation, and watered by the clear streams from the mountains. Thus the traveller can visit the whole of the island, his way winding through valleys and over mountain passes, until his prospect is at last arrested by the sea, of which he has had frequent glimpses during the journey. Did our island of Hong-kong possess the natural advantages and beauties of Chusan, what a splendid place it might have been made by our enterprising English merchants in a very few years!

The principal town is Tinghae, well known as the place twice taken by the English troops duringthe last war. It is but small, compared with any of the other five ports where foreigners are now trading: the walls are not more than three miles in circumference, and the suburbs not very extensive ; it contains about 26,000 inhabitants. When I was there, the island was in the hands of the English, being retained by them until 1846, under the treaty of Nanking, and Tinghae was of course 'the head quarters of the troops: we had also military stations at Sing-kong and Singkie-mun, the western and eastern parts of the island. Major- General Sir James Schoedde, the officer in command, to whom I had letters from Lord Stanley, very kindly procured me quarters in a house within the walls, and I immediately commenced operations. I was fortunate in becoming acquainted with Dr. Maxwell, of the 2d Madras native infantry, who was stationed there. This gentleman, an ardent lover of botanical pursuits, had been most indefatigable in his researches, and was consequently able to give me much valuable information. He had also made drawings of all the more striking plants which he had met with on the island, and I was thus at once put in possession of information which it would have taken me some months to acquire in any other way.

During two years from this date (Nov. 1843), I had frequent opportunities of visiting Chusan, at all seasons of the year, and was consequently enabled to gain a perfect knowledge of the soil, productions, and flora of the island. The soil of the hills is a rich gravelly loam; in the valleys it is more stiff,

Chap. IV.] PALM, OF WHICH HOPES ARE MADE. 53

from having less vegetable matter mixed with it, and from being almost continually under water. The rocks of granite, however, of the same kind as those noticed on the barren southern hills, exist here also; and, although they are generally covered with soil and vegetation, they have doubtless been at some former times as bleak and barren as their southern neighbours.

All the valleys and hill-sides are under cultivation ; paddy is the principal crop on the low grounds, and sweet potatoes on the hills. In the spring and early summer months, crops of wheat, barley, beans, peas, and maize are grown on the hilly and rising grounds, the low paddy land being too wet for such crops. Cotton is also grown on the island, but the quantity is inconsiderable, it is only for the home use of the small farmers on whose land it grows. There is a plant called *Urtica nivea,* both wild and cultivated, which grows about three or four feet in height, and produces a strong fibre in the bark, which is prepared by the natives, and sold for the purpose of making ropes and cables. The same species is said to yield a very fine fibre, which is used in the manufacture of grass cloth. Another strong fibre is obtained from the bracts of a palm-tree cultivated on the hill-sides of Chusan, as well as in similar situations all over the province of Chekiang. These articles answer the purposes to which they are applied, extremely well; but the rope made from the Manila hemp is of much greater strength and durability. From

the bracts of this same palm, the natives of the north make what they call a *So-e,* or garment of leaves, and a hat of the same material, which they put on during rainy weather; and, although they look comical enough in the dress, still it is an excellent protection from wind and rain. In the south of China, the *So-e* is made from the leaves of the bamboo and other broad-leaved grasses.

After the last crop of rice has been gathered in, the ground is immediately ploughed up and prepared to receive certain hardy green crops, such as clover, the oil plant, and other varieties of the cabbage tribe. The trefoil, or clover, is sown on ridges, to keep it above the level of the water, which often covers the valleys during the winter months. When I first went to Chusan, and saw this plant cultivated so extensively in the fields, I was at a loss to know the use to which it was applied, for the Chinese have few cattle to feed, and these are easily supplied from the road-sides and uncultivated parts of the hills. On inquiry I was informed that this crop was cultivated almost exclusively for manure. The large fresh leaves of the trefoil are also picked and used as a vegetable by the natives.

The oil plant, *Brassica chinensis,* is in seed and ready to be taken from the ground in the beginning of May. This plant is extensively grown in this part of China, both in the province of Che- kiang and also in Kiangsoo, and there is a great demand for the oil which is pressed from its seeds. For the information of readers not acquainted

Chap. IV.] PLOUGH AND WATER-WHEEL. 55

with botany, I may state that this plant is a species of cabbage, producing flower stems three or four feet high, with yellow flowers, and long pods of seed like all the cabbage tribe. In April, when the fields are in bloom, the whole country seems tinged with gold, and the fragrance which fills the air, particularly after an April shower, is delightful.

The small ox-plough, and the celebrated water- wheel which is here worked by hand, are the two principal implements in husbandry; the plough seems a rude thing, but it answers the purpose remarkably well, and is probably better for the Chinese in their present state, with their oxen and buffaloes, than our more improved implement. An immense quantity of water is raised with great ease by the water-wheel, and is made to flow into the different rice flats with great rapidity. I have often stood for a considerable time looking on and admiring the simplicity and utility of this contrivance.

The flora of Chusan, and all over the main land in this part of the province of Chekiang, is very different from that of the south. Almost all the species of a tropical character have entirely disappeared, and in their places we find others related to those found in temperate climates in other parts of the world. I here met, for the first time, the beautiful *Glytine sinensis* wild on the hills, where it climbs among the hedges and on trees, and its flowering branches hang in graceful festoons by the sides of the narrow roads which lead over the mountains. The *Ficus nitida,* so common around all the houses and temples in the south, is here unknown ; and many of those beautiful flowering genera, which are only found on the tops of the mountains in the south, have here chosen less exalted situations. I allude more particularly to the *Azaleas* which abound on the hill-sides of this island. Most people have seen and admired the beautiful azaleas which are brought to the Chiswick fetes, and which, as individual specimens, surpass in most instances those which grow and bloom on their native hills : but few can form any idea of the gorgeous and striking beauty of these azalea-clad mountains, where, on every side, as far as our vision extends, the eye rests on masses of flowers of dazzling brightness and surpassing beauty. Nor is it the azalea alone which claims our admiration ; clematises, wild roses, honeysuckles, the Glycine, noticed above, and a hundred others, mingle their flowers with them, and make us confess that China is indeed the " central flowery land." There are several species of myrtaceous and erica- ceous plants, which are also common on the hills, but no species of heath has ever been found, and I believe the genus does not exist in this part of the country.

The tallow tree *(Stillingia sebifera)* is abundant in the valleys of Chusan, and large quantities of tallow and oil are yearly extracted from its seeds: tallow mills are erected in several parts of the island for this purpose. The *Laurus Camphora,* or camphor

Chap. IV.] THE TALLOW TREE. 57

tree, is also abundant, but no camphor is extracted or exported from the island. The green tea shrub *(Thea viridis)* is cultivated every where; but, if we except a small quantity which is annually sent over to the main land|to Ningpo and the adjacent towns, | the whole of the produce is used by the inhabitants themselves. Every small farmer and cottager has a few plants on his premises, which he rears with considerable care, but seems to have no wish to enter on its cultivation on a larger scale. Indeed, it is questionable if it would answer, as the soil is scarcely rich enough; and, although the shrub grows pretty well, it is far from being so luxuriant as it is in the larger tea districts on the main land. The forests of different varieties of bamboo are very striking, and give a kind of tropical character to the Chusan scenery. I do not know any thing more beautiful than the yellow bamboo with its clean and straight stem, and graceful top and branches waving in the breeze: it always reminded me of our young larch forests at home. The fir tree, found in the south, is also common in this part of China: it seems to be an exception to a general rule, being met with all over the country, and in every degree of latitude. Here the *Cunninghamia sinensis,* another of the pine tribe, is also found in abundance: it is more rare in the south. Besides these, there are several species of cypress and juniper, which are always found growing around the tombs of the wealthy, which are scattered over the valley and hill-sides.

In fruits, Chusan is meagre indeed. All the peaches, grapes, pears, plums, oranges, &c., which are brought to the markets of Tinghae in the summer season, are from the main land. There are, however, two fruits cultivated on the island, which are of considerable excellence; the one is called *Yang- mat:* it is a scarlet fruit, not unlike an arbutus or strawberry, but having a stone like a plum in the centre; the other is the *Kum-quat,* a small species of Citrus, about the size of an oval gooseberry, with a sweet rind and sharp acid pulp. This fruit is well known in a preserved state by those who have any intercourse with Canton, and a small quantity is generally sent home as presents every year. Preserved in sugar, according to the Chinese method, it is excellent. Groves of the kum-quat are common on all the hill-sides of Chusan. The bush grows from three to six feet high; and, when covered with its orange-coloured fruit, is a very pretty object.

The islands of the Chusan Archipelago having every variety of elevation and soil, and a large proportion of the hills and ravines being in a state of nature, I found them not only rich in plants, but had also the satisfaction of meeting with several novelties of great interest.

The natives of Chusan are a quiet and inoffen- sive race, and were always civil and obliging to me.

This description will scarcely agree with those writers who inform us that such is the persevering industry of the Chinese, that every inch of ground in China is under cultivation! " Facts," however, "are stubborn things."

Chap. IV.] CHARACTER OF THE NATIVES. 59

Like the vegetation of their hills, they are very different from their countrymen of the south, and the change, I am happy to say, is for the better and not for the worse. Doubtless there are thieves and bad characters amongst them ; but these are comparatively few, and are kept in better check by the government, the result of which is, that unprotected property is in a great measure safe, and cases of theft are almost unknown. The people may be divided into three classes:lthe countrymen or agricultural farmers and labourers, the shopkeepers in the towns, and the mandarins or officers of government. The trade of Tinghae and the other towns seems to consist chiefly in articles of food and clothing, and owing to the number of British soldiers who were there from the time of our taking possession of the island until it was again handed over to the Chinese, this trade was of course in a flourishing condition. Fruits and vegetables were brought in great quantities from the main land, fish were plentiful ; good sheep were sold at about three dollars each, and the Chinese even got so far over their religious prejudices as to keep the market well supplied with bullocks, which were sold at prices varying from eight to twelve dollars. It was astonishing how quickly they got accustomed to our habits, and were able to supply all our wants. Bread baked in the English mode was soon exposed for sale in the shops, and evenready-made clothes were to be had in any quantity. The tailors flocked from all quarters: a large proportion of the shops near the beach were occupied by them, and they doubtless reaped a rich harvest, although they made and sold every article of dress on the most reasonable terms. Then there were curiosity shops without number, containing josses or gods carved in bamboo or stone, incense burners, old bronzes, animals of strange forms which only exist in the brains of the Chinese, and countless specimens of porcelain and pictures. Silk shops, too, were not wanting, and here were to be had beautiful pieces of manufactured silk, much cheaper and better than could be purchased in Canton. The embroidery in these shops was of the most elaborate and beautiful description, which must be seen before it can be appreciated; this the Chinese were making into articles, such as scarfs and aprons, for English ladies.

A mode of baking and cooking in use here is ingenious. A large rice-pan is filled with water, with a fire below it:upon this is placed a kind of sieve, made of bamboo, and filled with bread or other articles to be cooked; several of these sieves, one above another, have all their contents cooked at the same time, the steam rising through the lower to the upper ones. The sides of course fit nicely, and prevent the steam from escaping, and there is a close cover which fits on to the uppermost one. Our common brick oven is also in use here.

The shopkeepers in Tinghae supposed an English name indispensable to the respectability of their shops and the success of their trade, and it was quite amusing to walk up the streets and read the different names which they had adopted under the

Chap. IV.] ENGLISH NAMES ON SHOP DOORS. 61

advice and instruction of the soldiers and sailors to whom they had applied on the subject. There were " Stultz, tailor, from London;" " Buckmaster, tailor to the army and navy;" "Dominie Dobbs, the grocer;" " Squire Sam, porcelain merchant;" and the number of tradesmen "to Her Majesty" was very great, among whom one was " Tailor to Her Most Gracious Majesty Queen Victoria and His Royal Highness Prince Albert, by appointment," and below the name was a single word, which I could not make out for some few seconds,| *Uniformsofalldescriptions.* Certificates from their customers were also in great request, and many of these were most laughable performances. The poor Chinese were never quite at their ease about these certificates, as they were so often hoaxed by the donors, and consequently were continually showing them to other customers and asking " *what thing that paper talkie ; can do, eh?"* The answer was probably in this strain|"Oh, yes, *Fokei,* this can do, only a little alteration, more better." Poor Fokei runs and brings a pen, the little alteration is made, and it is needless to add that the thing is ten times more ridiculous than it was before.

Almost all the natives who come in contact with the English understand a little of the language; and as they have also a smattering of Portuguese, Malay, and Bengalese, they soon mix them up all together, and draw out of the whole a new tongue, which the most accomplished linguist would have verygreat difficulty in analysing. And, what is most amusing, they fancy all the time that this is capital English.

The way in which the Chinese classed the foreigners on the island was somewhat droll. There were three degrees of rank which they generally bestowed upon them,| Mandarins, or, as they pronounced it, *Mandalees, Sien-sangs,* and *A-says.* In the first class they included all persons of rank holding government situations, as well as the officers of the army and navy; the higher being styled " Bulla Bulla Mandalees," and the lower " Chotta Chotta Mandalees," corruptions of Hindostan words, signifying very large and very small. The merchants were honoured with the title of *Sien-Sang,* and the common soldiers, sailors, and the rest of the lower orders, were all classed under the head of *A-says.* The word Mandarin is not Chinese, but has always been used by the Portuguese at Macao, as well as by the English, to denote a Chinese government officer ; Sien-sang is a Chinese term, and signifies master or teacher, being generally used by the people as a title of respect, in the same way as we commonly use our word Sir: but *A-say* is quite a new appellation. " I say," or " Ay Say," is a very common expression amongst our soldiers and sailors ; and when the northern towns were taken by us during the war, the Chinese continually heard our men shouting it out to each other, and naturally concluded that this was the name of the class to which the lower orders belonged. It was quite

Chap. IV.] CUTANEOUS DISEASES AND BLINDNESS. 63

common to hear them asking each other whether such a one was a Mandarin, a Sien-sang, or an A-say.

Cutaneous diseases are less common amongst the natives here than amongst those in the south of China, probably owing to the more healthy nature of the climate. They are, however, dreadfully affected with diseases of the eye and ultimate blindness. This is, doubtless, caused in a great measure by the operations of the native barber, who, whenever he shaves the heads of his customers, also tickles their eyes and probes their ears, and the result is that they become both blind and deaf. The lashes of the eye, probably also from this cause, frequently grow inwards, and the hairs rubbing on the eyeball soon causes inflammation. Many of the poor natives were cured by my friend Dr. Maxwell, who, in the kindest and most philanthropic manner, set apart a portion of every day for the purpose. They flocked to him from all parts of the island, submitting cheerfully and without a murmur to operations of a most painful nature. Many most remarkable cures resulted from his skill, and his fame spread not only all over the island, but also to the main land|to Chinhae and Ningpo,|from whence numbers came and begged to be admitted on his list of patients. One day, when I was out with the Doctor on a botanising expedition, as we were passing a small cottage at the foot of the hills, a man and his wife rushed out, and begged us to enter their humble dwelling. We did so, chairswere set for us, tea was brought, and the worthy pair thanked the doctor in the most feeling and grateful manner for his former kindness to them. The man had been nearly blind and unable to work for his family, when, hearing of the wonderful English doctor, he came over to Chusan, and soon received his sight.

Many of the inhabitants of Chusan and the neighbouring islands gain their living by making salt on the shores. Large heaps of clay are scraped together in winter on the flats close by the sea; and when the weather becomes warm in summer, these heaps are spread out, and regularly watered with sea water several times a day, which quickly evaporates, and leaves a highly saline mixture. When by this means the soil is completely saturated, the next operation is to make a filter. This the natives do by forming a round basin of clay and mud; in the bottom of this they put a quantity of straw or grass, and some charcoal or ashes on the top; they then surround the whole with another layer of mud, and place a quantity of the saline earth in the centre. Water is then regularly poured over this earth, and the particles of salt are carried down through the filter in a liquid state. A pipe made of bamboo, which had been placed below, leads the liquid into a well dug at the side, into which it comes clear, pure, and highly saline. This mixture is now carried off to pans, where it is boiled, until the whole of the water is evaporated. I cannot say whether the Chinese have any means

Chap. IV.] VEGETABLE TALLOW. 65

of purifying the salt. In Chimoo Bay, the natives evaporate sea water with the aid of the sun alone, and do not saturate the soil as they do in Chusan ; but there the sea water is perfectly clear. Amongst the Chusan group of islands the water is yellow and muddy, being rendered so by the large rivers which are pouring in their waters from the main land, and more particularly by the Yang-tse- kiang.

For the following account of the Chinese method of extracting the tallow from the seeds of the *Stillingia sebifera* I am indebted to Dr. Rawes, of the Madras army, who was some time resident in the island of Chusan : |

" The seeds are picked at the commencement of the cold weather, in November and December, when all the leaves have fallen from the trees, | this I saw at Singkong when out shooting in the Sah-hoo valley, close by our quarters through the village. The seeds are in the first place taken to the building where the process of making the tallow is carried on, and picked and separated from the stalks. They are then put into a wooden cylinder, open at the top, but with a perforated bottom. This is placed over an iron vessel (about the same diameter or rather larger than the wooden cylinder, and about six or eight inches deep) containing water, by which means the seeds are well steamed, for the purpose of softening the tallow and causing it more readily to separate. The furnace I saw had four or five iron vessels in a row, was about

three feet high, four or five feet broad, and eight or ten feet long. The fire was placed at one end and fed with the husk of the rice, dry grass, and such like cheap materials which make a great flame, and the flue was of course carried directly under the whole of the iron vessels.

" When the seeds have steamed ten minutes or a quarter of an hour, they are thrown into a large stone mortar, and are gently beaten by two men with stone mallets for the purpose of detaching the tallow from the other parts of the seed. They are then thrown upon a sieve, heated over the fire, and sifted, by which process the tallow is separated, or nearly so, although they generally undergo the process of steaming &c. a second time that nothing may be lost. The other part of the seed is ground and pressed for oil.

" The tallow now resembles coarse linseed meal, but with more white spots in it, and derives its brown colour from the thin covering over the seed (between it and the tallow) which is separated by the pounding and sifting. In this state it is put between circles of twisted straw, five or six of which are laid upon each other, and thus forming a hollow cylinder for its reception. When this straw cylinder (we may call it so) has been filled, it is carried away and placed in the press, which is a very rude and simple contrivance, but which, like every thing Chinese, answers the purpose remarkably well. The press consists of longitudinal beams of considerable thickness, placed about a foot and

Chap. IV.] VEGETABLE TALLOW. 67

a half, or two feet, asunder, with a thick plank at the bottom, forming a kind of trough, and the whole is bound together with iron. The tallow is pressed out by means of wedges driven in very tightly with stone mallets, and passes through a hole in the bottom of the press into a tub, which is sunk there to receive it. It is now freed from all impurities, and is a semifluid of a beautiful white colour, but soon gets solid, and in cold weather is very brittle. The inside of the tubs which collect the tallow are sprinkled or dusted over, with a fine red earth, well dried, which prevents the tallow from adhering to their sides. It is thus easily removed in a solid state from the tubs, and in this condition the cakes are exposed for sale in the market. As the candles made from this vegetable tallow have a tendency to get soft and to melt in hot weather, they are commonly dipped in wax of various colours, as red, green, and yellow. Those which are intended for religious purposes are generally very large, and finely ornamented with golden characters.

" The cake, or refuse, which remains after the tallow has been pressed out of it, is used for fuel, or to manure the land, and so is the refuse from the other part of the seeds from which oil is extracted."

One of the greatest Lions in Chusan is an old Chinaman, who every spring hatches thousands of ducks' eggs by artificial heat. His establishment is situated in the valley on the north side of thecity of Tinghae, and is much resorted to by the officers of the troops and strangers who visit the island. The first question put to a sight-seer who comes here is, whether he has seen the hatching process, and if he has not, he is always recommended to pay a visit to the old Chinaman and his ducks.

When I set out upon this excursion for the first time, it was a beautiful morning in the end of May, just such a morning as we have in the same month in England, but perhaps a little warmer. The mist and vapour were rolling lazily along the sides of the hills which surround the plain on which the city of Tinghae is built; the Chinese, who are generally early risers, were already proceeding to their daily labours, and although the greater part of the labouring population are very poor, yet they seem contented and happy. Walking through the city, and out at the north gate, I passed through some rice fields, the first crop of which had been just planted, and a five minutes' walk brought me to the poor man's cottage. He received me with Chinese politeness; asked me to sit down, and offered me tea and his pipe, two things always at hand in a Chinese house, and perfectly indispensable. Having civilly declined his offer, I asked permission to examine his hatching house, to which he immediately led the way.

The Chinese cottages generally are wretched buildings of mud and stone, with damp earthen floors, scarcely fit for cattle to sleep in, and remind

Chap. IV.] HATCHING-HOUSE DESCRIBED. 69

one of what Scottish cottages were a few years ago, but which now, happily, are among the things that were. My new friend's cottage was no exception to the general rule: bad fitting, loose, creaking doors, paper windows, dirty and torn ; ducks, geese, fowls, dogs, and pigs in the house and at the doors, and apparently having equal rights with their masters. Then there were children, grand-children, and, for aught that I know, great-grand-children, all together, forming a most motley group, which, with their shaved heads, long tails, and strange costume, would have made a capital subject for the pencil of Cruikshank.

The hatching-house was built at the side of the cottage, and was a kind of long shed, with mud walls, and thickly thatched with straw. Along the ends and down one side of the building are a number of round straw baskets, well plastered with mud, to prevent them from taking fire. In the bottom of each basket there is a tile placed, or rather the tile forms the bottom of the basket; upon this the fire acts, I a small fireplace being below each basket. Upon the top of the basket there is a straw cover, which fits closely, and which is kept shut whilst the process is going on. In the centre of the shed are a number of large shelves placed one above another, upon which the eggs are laid at a certain stage of the process.

When the eggs are brought, they are put into the baskets, the fire is lighted below them, and an uniform heat kept up, ranging, as nearly as Icould ascertain by some observations which I made with a thermometer, from 95 to 102, but the Chinamen regulate the heat by their own feelings, and therefore it will of course vary considerably. In four or five days after the eggs have been subject to this temperature, they are taken carefully out, one by one, to a door, in which a number of holes have been bored nearly the size of the eggs ; they are then held against these holes, and the Chinamen look through them, and are able to tell whether they are good or not. If good, they are taken back, and replaced in their former quarters ; if bad, they are of course excluded. In nine or ten days after this, that is, about fourteen days from the commencement, the eggs are taken from the baskets, and spread out on the shelves. Here no fire-heat is applied, but they are covered over with cotton, and a kind of blanket, under which they remain about fourteen days more, when the young ducks burst their shells, and the shed teems with life. These shelves are large, and capable of holding many thousands of eggs; and when the hatching takes place, the sight is not a little curious. The natives who rear the young ducks in the surrounding country know exactly the day when they will be ready for removal, and in two days after the shell is burst, the whole of the little creatures are sold, and conveyed to their new quarters.

SECTION 6

I Visited Ning-po for the first time in the autumn of 1843. It is a large town, situated on the main land, nearly west from the Chusan group of islands, on the east coast of China, and contains about 380,000 inhabitants. It stands about twelve miles from the sea, at the junction of two fine streams, which by their union form a noble river capable of being navigated by the larger vessels and junks. One of these branches runs from the west, and the other from the south, meeting at Ning-po; and over the latter the Chinese have constructed a bridge of boats for the traific with the suburbs on the opposite shore. This bridge is a most simple and ingenious contrivance, consisting of a number of large boats moored at equal distances across the river, forming the basis on which the upper woodwork rests, and enabling the whole to rise and fall to a certain extent with the tide. By this means there is sufficient room under the bridge to allow fishing and passage boats to pass through at all times of the tide, providing it is not running too strong. At spring tides the water rushes through these spaces between the boats with great velocity, and sometimes it is next to impossible to get through.

The city itself is strongly fortified with high walls and ramparts about five miles round, and the space inside the walls is almost entirely filled with houses, in most parts densely crowded together. There are two or three very fine streets; finer, indeed, and wider than those of any other Chinese town which I have visited. A good view of the city and the surrounding country, as far as the eye can reach, is obtained from the top of a pagoda about one hundred and thirty feet high, having a staircase inside by which the top can be reached. (See following page.) This pagoda is named " *Tien-foong-tah"* or the " Temple of the Heavenly Winds;" it is evidently very old, and, like many others of the same kind, is in a state of decay. Whenever I visited this place, the Priests (Budhists) were always in attendance with their offerings of cake and tea, for which a small gratuity was expected.

When I first landed at Ning-po, the British consul, Mr. Thom, had not arrived, and I was quite at a loss where to go, or to whom to apply for

Chap. V.]

CITY AND PAGODA.

quarters. Leaving my boat and servant on the river, I strolled away into the city to reconnoitre,

Temple of the heavenly Winds.

thinking that something might turn up which I could use for my advantage. I was soon surrounded by crowds of the natives, and amongst them some blackguard boys, who had been corrupted to a great extent by the troops during the war, but who luckily understood a little of the English language, and were able to be of essential service to me. They informed me that there was

one " *Hong-mou-jin"* | (red-haired man)la term which they apply to all western nationslalready in the city, and immediately led the way to his quarters. When we arrived at the house, I was surprised to find a former acquaintance. He was an American Medical Missionary, and was dressed *h la Chinoise,* tail and all complete, but truth compels me to state that his dress was rather a ludicrous one. Afterwards, when my knowledge of the Chinese costume was more complete, I have often laughed when I thought of the figure the doctor must have appeared in the eyes of the Chinese. The large flowing gown which he wore was almost too fine for a mandarin, while the hat was one commonly worn by servants and coolies. The English reader, if he wishes to understand the strange sort of appearance the doctor presented, must imagine a London judge clothed in his fine black flowing gown, and wearing the hat of a dustman. I recollect one evening after dark going out into one of the main streets, accompanied by the doctor, to see an offering which was there presented to the Gods, and I soon found that he in his Chinese dress was a greater object of attention than I was in my English one. How the Chinese laughed and enjoyed the joke! I had obtained a room in the same house with my friend, who was visited daily by great numbers of the Chinese, and who, although not a very good Chinaman, was most zealous in the cause of medical missions.

As the winter approached the weather became

Chap. V.] CHINESE CLOTHING. 75

extremely cold, and in December and January the ice on the ponds and canals was of considerable thickness. The most attractive shops in the city now, were the different clothing establishments, where all articles of wearing apparel were lined with skins of various kinds, many of them of the most costly description. The very poorest Chinese has always a warm jacket or cloak lined with sheep skin, or padded with cotton, for the winter; and they cannot imagine how the Europeans can exist with the thin clothing they generally go about in. When the weather was cold, I used always to wear a stout warm great coat above my other dress, and yet the Chinese were continually feeling the thickness of my clothes, and telling me that surely I must feel cold. Their mode of keeping themselves comfortable in winter differs entirely from ours; they rarely or never think of using fires in their rooms for this purpose, but as the cold increases, they just put on another jacket or two, until they feel that the warmth of their bodies is not carried off faster than it is generated. As the raw damp cold of morning gives way to the genial rays of noon, the upper coats are one by one thrown off, until evening, when they are again put on. In the spring months, the upper garments are cast off by degrees, and when the summer arrives, the Chinese are found clad in thin dresses of cotton, or in the grass cloth manufactured in the country. In the northern towns the ladies sometimes use a small brass-stove, like a little oval basket, havingthe lid grated to allow the charcoal to burn and the heat to escape; this they place upon their tables or on the floor, for the purpose of warming the hands and feet. Nurses also carry these little stoves in their hands under the feet of the children. Such, however, is the thickness and warmth of their dresses, that it is only in the coldest weather they require them. Little children in winter are so covered up, that they look like bundles of clothes, nearly as broad as they are long, and when the padding is removed in warm weather, it is difficult to imagine that you see before you the same individuals.

I never felt so cold in England as I did during this winter in the north of China, and yet, as may be seen from the chapter on temperature, the thermometer did not indicate a very low degree. The house in which I lived was so open, that the wind rushed in at every crevice; the windows were large, not glazed, as with us, but papered, and in many places perfectly open. During the day I got on very well, as I was always out und moving about from morning until dark. But the long evenings, with the wind whistling through the windows, and blowing upon my candle, were dreary and cold enough.

To vary the monotony of the scene, as well as to warm myself, I used frequently to take a stroll down the main street. The Chinese, as a nation, are great gamblers; even the poorest of them cannot resist the temptation, and in this street after night-

Chap.v.] DESCRIPTION OF SHOPS. 77

fall, there used to be numerous stalls of oranges, sweetmeats, and trifling curiosities, at each of which there were dice of some kind, and a " wheel of fortune," surrounded by the Chinese in great numbers, trying their luck with a few copper cash, and evincing, by their looks and language, the most intense interest in the stopping of the wheel, or the throwing of the dice.

Besides the shops already noticed for the sale of clothes and skins, there are many others worthy of our attention. There are a number of excellent silk shops and warehouses a little off the main street, which, like our old established houses at home, have but little external show to attract notice. Here, too, are large quantities of that beautiful northern embroidery which is so much admired by all who have had an opportunity of seeing it. It is entirely different from that commonly procured at Canton, and much more elaborate and expensive. A considerable demand for articles of dress which would be fashionable in England, has induced the Chinese to get them made, and they are now exposed for sale in all the towns in the north frequented by the English. Ladies' aprons, scarfs, shawls, work-bags, and many other articles made up in the English style, and beautifully embroidered, are the things most in demand.

The Chinese estimate their celebrated jade stone very highly, and here there are numerous shops, both for cutting it and exposing it for sale, carved into all those curious and fantastic forms for which

this people are so well known. The process of cotton printing in its most simple and original form may be seen in most of the streets here, as well as in other towns in China. Rope-making is carried on extensively in the suburbs near the river, and some strong cables and ropes for junks are made from the bracts of the palm, formerly noticed, and from the bark of the urticaceous plant, commonly called hemp by the English in the north of China. There are, of course, the usual quantity of curiosity shops, containing bamboo ornaments carved into all possible forms; specimens of ancient porcelain, which are said to " preserve flowers and fruit from decay for an unusual time," lacquered ware, and other ornaments brought by the junks from Japan, many beautifully carved rhinoceros' horns, bronzes, and other articles to which the Chinese attach great importance, purchasing them at exorbitant rates, apparently far beyond their value. But what struck me as being most unique, was a peculiar kind of furniture, made and sold in a street, generally called " Furniture Street" by foreigners who visit Ning-po. There were beds, chairs, tables, washing-stands, cabinets, and presses, all peculiarly Chinese in their form, and beautifully inlaid with different kinds of wood and ivory, representing the people and customs of the country, and presenting, in fact, a series of pictures of China and the Chinese. Every one who saw these things admired them, and, what was rather strange, they seem peculiar to Ning-po, and are not met with at

Chap. V.] BANKING ESTABLISHMENTS. 79

any of the other five ports, not even in Shanghae. As all this beautiful work is expensive, it is, of course, only used in the houses of the wealthy.

There are some large banking establishments in Ning-po, having connection with all the other towns in the north, and it is here, therefore, that the value of money is regulated, the " stocks" rising and falling exactly as they do in England. There can be little doubt that it is a place of great wealth. There are a large number of retired merchants in the city and suburbs, who have made their fortunes in early life, and who now seek to enjoy themselves amid the luxuries and retirement of Ning-po. But these circumstances, unfortunately, do not fit it for a place of active foreign trade; and hence, although it is large, rich, and populous, our merchants find the northern port of Shanghae of far greater importance as regards the sale of European and American manufactures, and the purchase of tea and silk,|the staple productions of the country. And yet, judging from appearances, one would think that a considerable foreign trade might be carried on at Ning-po, as it is in itself a large town, is in the midst of a populous country, and has excellent water communication with all parts of the empire. Time, and the perseverance of our merchants, will soon show whether this supposition is a correct one.

Many of the temples in this town have been much admired by foreigners, but I must confess that, to me, the very best of them had a childish and tin- selly appearance, which I could not admire. Theone called the Fokien Temple is best and most showy. The Confucian Temple was formerly a large and celebrated place, but it was nearly destroyed during the war, and up to the time when I left China, no attempt had been made to rebuild it, or put it in a state of repair : the Chinese seemed to consider that the touch of the *barbarian* had polluted the sacred edifice. The Budhists' temples are crowded with painted wooden images of their gods. The " three precious Budhas," the " past, present, and future," are generally enormously large, being often thirty or forty feet in height. To these, and to the numerous small images, the poor deluded natives bow the knee, burn incense, and engage in other exercises of devotion. The traveller meets with these temples or joss-houses, as they are commonly called, in all the streets, at the gates of the city, and even on the ramparts, and cannot but admire the devotional spirit of the inhabitants, although he may wish that it was directed to a higher and purer object. I have often looked on when these simple people,|the women more particularly,| seemed actually, like Jacob of old, "wrestling with God in prayer," and using various means to ascertain whether the mind of the Deity had softened towards them, and granted their requests. Two small pieces of wood, flat on one side and rounded on the other, are generally used to accomplish this end; these are thrown up in the air, and if they fall on the desired side, it was well; if not, some more incense was burned, and again andChap. v.] Mandarins' Gardens. 81 again they prostrated themselves before the altar, and seemed engaged in earnest prayer. Many of their religious ceremonies have a great resemblance to those of the Roman Catholic church, and I remember being much struck on a Sunday afternoon, when passing out at one of the city gates, by hearing the sounds of prayer and praise, not unlike those of the Christian churches of other lands. I immediately walked into the place from whence the sounds came, and found, to my disappointment, that it was one of the numerous temples with which the city abounds, and that the sounds of praise which fell upon my ears were only addressed to the gods of the heathen. But many of these temples are in a most ruinous state, and are evidently not so well supported now as they have been at some former time. In fact, the town of Ning-po itself, with all its riches, and all its advantages, has been in a decaying state for years, and is one example, amongst many others, of the truth of what I formerly stated concerning the general state of this country.

My first business, when I reached Ning-po, was to make inquiries regarding the gardens of the Mandarins, which I had heard something of from the officers who were there when the city was taken by the English troops, during the war. I had the same difficulties to encounter as I had at Amoy, owing to the jealousy of the Chinese. Ultimately, however, these too were overcome, and I obtained access to several Mandarins' gardens and nurseries,

out of which several new plants were procured, which proved very valuable additions to my collections. Here, as at other places, I made many inquiries after the supposed yellow camellia, and offered ten dollars to any Chinaman who would bring me one. Any thing can be had in China for dollars ! and it was not long before two plants were brought to me, one of which was said to be light yellow, and the other as deep a colour as the double yellow rose. Both had flower-buds upon them, but neither were in bloom. I felt quite certain that the Chinaman was deceiving me, and it seemed foolish to pay such a sum for plants which I should in all probability have to throw away afterwards ; and yet I could not make up my mind to lose the chance, slight as it was, of possessing the *yellow camellia*. And the rogue did his business so well. He had a written label stuck in each pot, and *apparently* the writing and labels had been there for some years. I fancied I was as cunning as he was, and requested him to leave the plants and return on the following morning, when he should have an answer. In the mean time I asked a respectable Chinese merchant to read the writing upon the labels. All was correct ; the writing agreed with what the man had told me; namely, that Otic of the plants produced light yellow blooms, and the other deep yellow. " Did you ever see a camellia with yellow flowers ? " I inquired of my friend the merchant. " No," said he, in his broken English. " *My never have seen he, my thinkie no have got"* On the following morningChap, v.] Mandarins' Gardens. 83

the owner of the plant presented himself, and asked me if I had made up my mind upon the subject. I told him that I would take the plants to Hongkong, where I was going at the time; that they would soon flower there; and that, if they proved *yellow,* he should have his money. This, however, he would not consent to; and at last we compromised the matter, I agreeing to pay half the money down, and the other half when the plants flowered, providing they were " true." On these conditions I got the camellias, and took them with me to Hong-kong. It is almost needless to say that when they flowered there was nothing yellow about them but the stamens, for they were both semi-double worthless kinds.

The gardens of the Mandarins in the city of Ning-po are very pretty and unique; they contain a choice selection of the ornamental trees and shrubs of China, and generally a considerable number of dwarf trees. Many of the latter are really curious, and afford another example of the patience and ingenuity of this people. Some of the specimens are only a few inches high, and yet seem hoary with age. Not only are they trained to represent old trees in miniature, but some are made to resemble the fashionable pagodas of the country, and others different kinds of animals, amongst which the deer seems to be the favourite. Junipers are generally chosen for the latter purpose, as they can be more readily bent into the desired form ; the eyes and tongue are added afterwards, and therepresentation altogether is really good. One of the Mandarins of Ning-po, anxious, I suppose, to confer some mark of especial favour upon me, presented me with one of these animals, I plants, I should say; I but as it was of no real use to me, and as my collections of other things were large, I was obliged to decline his present, which he evidently considered of great value, and no doubt wondered at my want of taste.

Another example will show the passion which exists amongst the Chinese for things of this kind. When I was travelling on the hills of Hong-kong, a few days after my first arrival in China, I met with a most curious dwarf *Lycopodium,* which I dug up and carried down to Messrs. Dent's garden, where my other plants were at the time. " Hai-yah," said the old compradore, when he saw it, and was quite in raptures of delight. All the other coolies and servants gathered round the basket to admire this curious little plant. I had not seen them evince so much gratification since I showed them the " old man Cactus " *(Cereus senilis),* which I took out from England, and presented to a Chinese nurseryman at Canton. On asking them why they prized the Lycopodium so much, they replied, in Canton English, " *Oh, he too muchia handsome; he grow only a leete and a leete every year; and suppose he be one hundred year oula. he only so high"* holding up their hands an inch or two higher than the plant. This little plant is really very pretty, and often naturally takes the very form of a dwarf tree in

Chap. V.] DWARFED TREES. 85

miniature, which is doubtless the reason of its being such a favourite with the Chinese.

The dwarfed trees of the Chinese and Japanese have been noticed by every author who has written upon these countries, and all have attempted to give some description of the method by which the effect is produced. The process is in reality a very simple one, and is based upon one of the commonest principles of vegetable physiology. We all know that any thing which retards in any way the free circulation of the sap, also prevents to a certain extent the formation of wood and leaves. This may be done by grafting, by confining the roots, withholding water, bending the branches, or in a hundred other ways which all proceed upon the same principle. This principle is perfectly understood by the Chinese, and they make nature subservient to this particular whim of theirs. We are told that the first part of the process is to select the very smallest seeds from the smallest plants, which is not at all unlikely, but I cannot speak to the fact from my own observation. I have, however, often seen Chinese gardeners selecting suckers and plants for this purpose from the other plants, which were growing in their garden. Stunted varieties were generally chosen, particularly if they had the side branches opposite or regular, for much depends upon this ; a one-sided dwarf tree is of no value in the eyes of the Chinese. The main stem was then in most cases twisted in a *zigzag* form, which process checked the flow of the sap, and at thesame time encouraged the production of side branches at those parts of the stem where they were most desired. When these suckers had formed roots in the open ground, or kind of nursery where they were planted, they were looked over and the best taken up for potting. The same principles, which I have already noticed, were still kept in view, the pots used being narrow and shallow, so that they held but a small quantity of soil compared with the wants of the plants, and no more water being given than what was barely sufficient to keep them alive. Whilst the branches were forming, they were tied down and twisted in various ways; the points of the leaders and strong growing ones were generally nipped out, and every means was taken to discourage the production of young shoots which were possessed of any degree of vigour. Nature generally struggles against this treatment for a while, until her powers seem in a great measure exhausted, when she quietly yields to the power of art. The Chinese gardener, however, must be ever on the watch; for should the roots of his plants get through the pots into the ground, or happen to be liberally supplied with moisture, or should the young shoots be allowed to grow in their natural position for a short time, the vigour of the plant which has so long been lost will be restored, and the fairest specimen of Chinese dwarfing destroyed. Sometimes, as in the case of peach and plum trees, which are often dwarfed, the plants are thrown into a flowering state, and then,

Chap. V.] GARDENS OF THE MANDARINS. 87

as they flower freely year after year, they have little inclination to make vigorous growth. The plants generally used in dwarfing are pines, junipers, cypresses, bamboos, peach and plum trees, and a species of small-leaved elm.

Amongst the Mandarins' gardens, in the city of Ning-po, there is one in particular which is generally visited by all strangers, and is much admired. It is situated near the lake in the centre of the city. The old man to whom it belongs has long retired from trade with an independent fortune, and he now enjoys his declining years in the peaceful pursuits of gardening, and is passionately fond of flowers. Both his house and garden are unique in their way, but they are most difficult to describe, and must be seen to be appreciated. In this part of the country the building of artificial rockwork is so well understood, that the resemblance to nature is perfect, and it forms a principal feature in every garden. This old gentleman has the different parts of his house joined together by rude- looking caverns, and what at first sight appears to be a subterraneous passage, leading from room to room, through which the visitor passes to the garden which lies behind the house. The small courts, of which a glimpse is caught in passing through, are fitted up with this rockwork; dwarf trees are planted here and there in various places, and creepers hang down naturally and gracefully until their ends touch the little ponds of water which are always placed in front of the rockwork.

These small places being passed, we are again led through passages like those already noticed, when the garden, with its dwarf trees, vases, rockwork, ornamental windows, and beautiful flowering shrubs, is suddenly opened to the view.

It must be understood, however, that all which I have now described is very limited in extent, but the most is made of it by windings and glimpses through rockwork, and arches in the walls, as well as by hiding the boundary with a mass of shrubs and trees.

Here old Dr. Chang[I believe that was his name]was spending the evening of his days in peaceful retirement. When I called upon him he was extremely polite, and, after making a great many very low bows, requested me to take the seat of honour by his side. The servants were then ordered to bring tea, a beverage which is offered to every stranger, and which was of the very finest description. Messengers were sent round to all the old man's particular friends, who each hurried to see the foreigner. One by one they dropt in, until the room was nearly full. The servants, who seemed to think themselves quite as good as their masters, mixed with the company, and made their remarks upon me with the greatest freedom. Every thing about me was examined and criticised most minutely, particularly my watch, which they seemed to admire very much. I was frequently requested, as a great favour, to allow them to see the works, and to hold it to their ears, in order that they

Chap. V.] VIEW FROM THE NORTHERN HILLS. 89

might hear the sound which it made. The old mandarin now led me round his house, and showed me all the curiosities which it contained, and of which he was a great collector. Old bronzes, carved woods, specimens of porcelain, and other articles of that kind, were arranged with great taste in several of the rooms. From the house we proceeded to the garden, but as it was winter, and the trees leafless, I could form but little idea of the rarity or beauty of the plants which it contained. I took my leave, after drinking some more tea, promising to visit the old man again whenever I returned to Ning-po.

I visited also at this time several other Mandarins who had gardens, and from all of them I received the greatest civility. Some small articles which I brought out with me as presents were of the greatest use, not only in procuring me a civil reception, but also in enabling me to get plants or cuttings of rare species which were only found in the gardens of the rich, and which, of course, were not for sale.

The level plain on which the city of Ning-po is built is at least thirty miles across, surrounded on all sides by a circle of hills, but opening on the east to the sea, where the town of Chinhae stands, and forms, as it were, the sea-port town of Ning-po. The view from the hills is very fine—the broad extensive plain forming, as it were, a vast amphitheatre, traversed by beautiful winding rivers and by canals in all directions; thus enabling the natives to convey the produce of their country and its merchandise to Ning-po, and from thence to Hang-chow-foo, and any other part of the world. Rice is the staple production of the low land in this part of the country during the summer months, and the oil plant is cultivated extensively on the same land in winter and spring, being in seed and ready to harvest by the time for sowing the first crop of rice. Large quantities of the trefoil which I have noticed before are also grown here, and for the same purposes; indeed, the agricultural productions, both of the low lands and on the sides of the hills, are really the same as those formerly described on the island of Chusan.

The native flora of the hills to the north of Ning-po is nearly the same as that found on Chusan and the neighbouring islands, but more extensive. It is a curious fact, that I always found the main land of China more productive in species of animals and plants than the neighbouring islands, although these islands were large, and only separated from the main land by a narrow extent of sea. I met here, for the first time in a wild state, the beautiful yellow *Azalea sinensis.* These hills are somewhat more barren than most of the others in this part of the country, and there are few trees on them of any size. They are very different from those which I have yet to describe, a few miles to the south of Ning-po.

The graves of the dead are scattered all over the plain, and give the stranger a good idea of the

Chap. V.] EXPOSURE OF THE DEAD. 91

immense population of the country. In travelling from Ning-po to the hills, I could not account for the vast number of tombs which I met with on my way ; but when I reached the summit of the hills, and looked down upon the wide-spreading plain, covered with towns and villages in all directions, densely peopled with human beings, it was easily accounted for. Here, as at Chusan and Shanghae, the traveller is continually coming upon coffins placed on the surface of the ground, and in many instances decaying, and exposing the skeleton remains of the dead. I was much struck by frequently meeting with large numbers of coffins piled one above another, in heaps of from thirty to forty, chiefly those of young children. I was told that they are buried periodically, but from their appearance many of them must have remained in the same place for years, and their tenants must long ago have mouldered into dust.

7

SECTION 7

CHAP. VI.

nEMAHKS ON THE CHINESE LANGUAGE. | ICE-HOUSES NEAR NING-PO
DESCRIBED. | THEIR SIMPLICITY AND UTILITY. |
NOVEL MODES OF FISHING. FISHING CORMORANTS MET WITH.
| THEIR ACTIONS DESCRIBED. TWO PAIR PURCHASED.
ACCOUNT OF THEIR FOOD AND HABITS.

In sailing up the river towards *Ning-po,* I observed a great number of thatched houses, and desired my Chinese servant to go to the boatman and inquire what they were. He went immediately to the man at the helm, and, after a conversation of at least ten minutes' duration, came back hanging his head, and slunk away without reporting the result of his inquiries. " Well," said I, " what is the use of all these houses which we now see on the shore ? " With all the gravity in the world, he replied that the boatman said they were places built to keep Chinese soldiers in during the cold winter months. " Nonsense," said I, " they cannot fill all these places with soldiers." " Well," said he, " *he have talkie my so fashion.* " Aa I could not conceive this to be true, I went to the man myself, and with the little knowledge of the language which I then possessed, soon found out that the buildings in question were ice-houses, for which commodity, he informed me,

Chap. VI.] ICE-HOUSES. 93

there was a great demand during the summer months. This shows that the Chinese language differs so much in different provinces, that a native of Canton and another in the north, cannot understand each other: and indeed this is so much the case, that my Macao servant was almost entirely useless to me in the north, in so far as the language was concerned. In this instance the Chinese word " *Ping* "| or I should rather say sound | means both soldier and ice, and it immediately struck my servant, who I suppose had never seen ice in his life, that the buildings in question were soldiers' houses instead of ice-houses; rather cold barracks, I should think.

I was much struck with the simplicity of the construction of these ice-houses, and my only doubt about them was whether or not the ice would keep well in them throughout the hot summer months. The results of my investigation I sent in the following letter to Professor Lindley, who published it in the " Gardener's Chronicle " for 1845 : |

" A short time before I left England, you published in the ' Gardener's Chronicle ' a number of letters and plans for the construction of icehouses, but, as far as I can remember, nothing at all resembling the Chinese one which I shall now describe to you. On the right bank of the Ning-po river, above the town and fort of Chinhae, and in various other parts of the north of China, I have met with these ice-houses. When I inspected them for the first time last winter (1843), their construction and situation differed so much from what I had been accustomed to see at home, | differing, too, in things which I used to consider as indispensable to an ice-house, | that I had great doubts regarding their efficiency; but at the present time, which is now the end of August, 1844, many of these houses are yet full of ice, and seem to answer the end most admirably. You are probably aware, from my former descriptions of the country, that the town of Ning-po stands in the midst of a level plain from twenty to thirty miles across. These ice-houses are built on the sides of the river in the centre of the plain, completely exposed to the sun | a sun, too, very different in its effects

from what we experience in England, | clear, fierce, and burning, which would try the efficiency

Chap. VI.] ICE-HOUSES. 95

of our best English ice-houses as well as it does the constitution of an Englishman in China.

" The bottom of these ice-houses is nearly on a level with the surrounding fields, and is generally about twenty yards long, by fourteen broad. The walls, which are built of mud and stone, are very thick, twelve feet in height, and are, in fact, a kind of embankment rather than walls, having a door on one side level with the floor, for the removal of the ice, and a kind of sloping terrace on the other, by which the ice can be thrown into the house. On the top of the walls or embankment a tall span roof is raised, constructed of bamboo, thickly thatched with straw, and in appearance exactly like an English haystack. And this is the simple structure which keeps ice so well during the summer months, and under the burning sun of China !

" The Chinaman, with his characteristic ingenuity, manages also to fill his ice-houses in a most simple way, and at a very trifling expense. Around the house he has a small flat level field connected with the river. This field he takes care to flood in winter before the cold weather comes on. The water then freezes and furnishes the necessary supply of ice at the very door. Again in spring these same fields are ploughed up and planted with rice, and the water which drains from the bottom of the ice-house helps to nourish the young crop. Of course here, as in England, when the house is filled the ice is carefully covered up with a thick coating of straw. Thus the Chinaman,with little expense in building his ice-house, and an economical mode of filling it, manages to secure an abundant supply for preserving his fish during the hot summer months.

" It now, I think, becomes a question whether we could not build ice-houses at less expense and more efficient, upon the Chinese plan, than upon the old under-ground system common in England. The accompanying sketch will enable you to form an idea of the appearance which these ice-houses present to the traveller, in going up the Ning-po river. *Ning-po, August,* 1844."

Since this letter was published I have had frequent opportunities of testing the qualities of the Chinese ice-house, both at Ning-po and also at Chusan and Shanghae, and I have found that it answers the purpose admirably. The winter of 1844- 1845 was unusually mild in this part of China, little or no ice was formed on the ponds and canals, and of course the ice-houses could not be filled; but many of them contained large quantities which had been laid up the year before, and by this means the market was supplied with ice which had been in store at least a year and a half, and would probably have kept some time longer.

This ice is of great importance to the Chinese, who depend so much for their food upon the fish which is caught in their waters. They are enabled by this means to keep their fish during the hottest weather for a considerable time, and transmit them in this way to different parts of the country.

Chap. VI.] CHINESE FISHERMEN. 97

Immense quantities of fish are daily caught in the river above the town. Their mode of catching them is ingenious and amusing. One day I was going up a considerable distance in a boat, and set out a little before low water, that I might have the full benefit of the flow of the tide, and get as far up as possible before it turned. On the side of the river, a few miles above Ning-po, I observed some hundreds of small boats anchored, each containing two or three men; and the tide turning just as I passed, the whole fleet was instantly in motion, rowing and sculling up the river with the greatest rapidity. As soon as the men reached a favourable part of the stream they cast out their nets and began to make a loud noise, splashing with their oars and sculls, with the intention, I suppose, of driving the fish into the nets. After remaining in this spot for about a quarter of an hour, all the boats set off again, farther up, for the next station, when the crew commenced again in the same noisy manner, and so on, for a long way up the river, as long as the tide was flowing; they then returned with the ebb, loaded with fishes for the next morning's market.

There is another mode of catching fish, which I have frequently seen in the northern provinces, even more curious than that which I have just noticed. Every one acquainted with Chinese history knows that fish abound in all the rivers and lakes of the north; indeed, every little pond swarms with them. I was greatly surprised when I first saw the fish-catcher following his profession in these places. He is literally amphibious. He is to be seen perfectly naked, half walking, half swimming; nowhe raises his arms and hands above his head, and, bringing them down, strikes a sharp blow upon the water, making a loud and splashing noise. His feet are not idle: they warn him that a fish is at hand, and they are now feeling for him amongst the mud at the bottom of the pond. The next moment the fisherman has disappeared: he is now under water, and he remains so long that you think something has happened to him. There is, however, no cause of fear; a few seconds more and he appears, rubbing his face and eyes with one hand, and in the other triumphantly holding up the poor little fish which he has just captured. It is immediately placed safely in his basket, and the work goes on as before. The surface of the water is struck and splashed, as I have just described, in order to frighten the fish, which are swimming amongst the feet of the Chinamen. Being frightened, they dive immediately to the bottom amongst the mud, where they are felt by the feet, and are soon taken by these expert divers.

But the most singular of all the methods of catching fish in China is that of training and employing a large species of cormorant for this purpose, generally called the fishing cormorant. These are certainly wonderful birds. I have frequently met with them on the canals and lakes in the interior, and, had I not seen with my own eyes their

Chap. VI.] THEIR ACTIONS DESCRIBED. 99

extraordinary docility, I should have had great difficulty in bringing my mind to believe what authors have said about them. The first time I saw them was on a canal a few miles from Ning-po. I was then on my way to a celebrated temple in that quarter, where I intended to remain for some time in order to make collections of objects of natural history in the neighbourhood. When the birds came in sight I immediately made my boatmen take in our sail, and we remained stationary for some time to observe their proceedings. There were two small boats, containing one man and about ten or twelve birds in each. The birds were standing perched on the sides of the little boat, and apparently had just arrived at the fishing ground, and were about to commence operations. They were now ordered out of the boats by their masters; and so well trained were they, that they went on the water immediately, scattered themselves over the canal, and began to look for fish. They have a beautiful sea-green eye, and, quick as lightning, they see and dive upon the finny tribe, which, once caught in the sharp-notched bill of the bird, never by any possibility can escape. The cormorant now rises to the surface with the fish in his bill, and the moment he is seen by the Chinaman he is called back to the boat. As docile as a dog, he swims after his master, and allows himself to be pulled into the San-pan, where he disgorges his prey, and again resumes his labours. And, what is more wonderful still, if one of the cormorants gets hold of a fish of large size, so large that he would have some difficulty in taking it to the boat, some of the others, seeing his dilemma, hasten to his assistance, and with their efforts united capture the animal and haul him off to the boat. Sometimes a bird seemed to get lazy or playful, and swam about without attending to his business; and then the Chinaman, with a long bamboo, which he also used for propelling the boat, struck the water near where the bird was, without, however, hurting him, calling out to him at the same time in an angry tone. Immediately, like the truant school-boy who neglects his lessons and is found out, the cormorant gives up his play and resumes his labours. A small string is put round the neck of the bird, to prevent him from swallowing the fish which he catches; and great care is taken that this string is placed and fastened so that it will not slip farther down upon his neck and choke him, which otherwise it would be very apt to do.

Since I first saw these birds on the Ning-po canal I have had opportunities of inspecting them and their operations in many other parts of China, more particularly in the country between the towns of Hang-chow-foo and Shanghae. I also saw great numbers of them on the river Min, near Foo-chow- foo. I was most anxious to get some living specimens, that I might take them home to England. Having great difficulty in inducing the Chinese to part with them, or, indeed, to speak at all on the subject, when I met them in the country, owing to

Chap. VI.] THEIR FOOD AND HABITS. 101

our place of meeting being generally in those parts of the interior where the English arc never seen, I applied to Her Majesty's Consul at Shanghac (Captain Balfour), who very kindly sent one of the Chinese connected with the Consulate into the country, and procured two pairs for me. The difficulty now was to provide food for them on the voyage from Shanghae to Hong-kong. We procured a large quantity of live eels, this being a principal part of their food, and put them into a jar of mud and fresh water. These they ate in a most voracious manner, swallowing them whole, and in many instances vomiting them afterwards. If one bird was unlucky enough to vomit his eel, he was fortunate indeed if he caught it again, for another, as voracious as himself, would instantly seize it, and swallow it in a moment. Often they would fight stoutly for the fish, and then it either became the property of one, or, as often happened, their sharp bills divided the prey, and each ran off and devoured the half which fell to his share. During the passage down we encountered a heavy gale at sea, and as the vessel was one of those small clipper schooners, she pitched and rolled very much, shipping seas from bow to stern, which set every thing on her decks swimming. I put my head out of the cabin- door when the gale was at its height, and the first thing I saw was the cormorants devouring the eels, which were floating all over the decks. I then knew that the jar must have been turned over or smashed to pieces, and that of course all the eelswhich escaped the bills of the cormorants were now swimming in the ocean. After this I was obliged to feed them upon any thing on board which I could find; but when I arrived at Hong-kong they were not in very good condition : two of them died soon after ; and as there was no hope of taking the others home alive, I was obliged to kill them and preserve their skins.

The Chinaman from whom I bought these birds has a large establishment for fishing and breeding the birds about thirty or forty miles from Shanghae, and between that town and Chnpoo. They sell at a high price even amongst the Chinese themselvesl I believe from six to eight dollars per pair, that is, from 30s. to 40s. As I was anxious to learn something of their food and habits, Mr. Medhurst, jun., interpreter to the British Consulate at Shanghae, kindly undertook to put some questions to the man who brought them, and sent me the following notes connected with this subject: I

" The fish-catching birds eat small fish, yellow eels, and pulse-jelly. At five P.m. every day each bird will eat six taels (eight ounces) of eels or fish, and a catty of pulse-jelly. They lay eggs after three years, and in the fourth or fifth month. Hens are used to incubate the eggs. When about to lay their faces turn red, and then a good hen must be prepared. The date must be clearly written upon the shells of the eggs laid, and they will hatch in twenty-five days. When hatched, take the young and put them upon cotton, spread upon some warm

Chap. VI.] TDEIR FOOD AND IIABITS. 103

water, and feed them with eels' blood for five days. After five days they can be fed with eels' flesh chopped fine, and great care must be taken in watching them.

"When fishing, a straw tie must be put upon their necks, to prevent them from swallowing the fish when they catch them. In the eighth or ninth month of the year they will daily descend into the water at ten o'clock in the morning, and catch fish until five in the afternoon, when they will come on shore. They will continue to go on in this way until the third month, after which time they cannot fish until the eighth month comes round again. The male is easily known from the female, in being generally a larger bird, and in having a darker and more glossy feather, but more particularly in the size of the head, the head of the male being large and that of the female small."

Such are the habits of this extraordinary bird. As the months named in the note just quoted refer to the Chinese calendar, it follows that these birds do not fish in the summer months, but commence in autumn, about October, and end about May| periods agreeing nearly with the eighth and third months of the Chinese year.

8

SECTION 8

CHAP. VII.

8 IIAHGHAE VISITED AT THE END OF 1843 MY LODGINGS.I
PREJUDICES AND SUPERSTITIONS OF TOE INHABITANTS. THE
CITY DESCRIBED. SHOPS AND MERCHANDISE FOOD. AN
IMPORTANT STATION FOR FOREIGN TRADE THE EXPORTS OF
THE COUNTRY ; TEAS AND SILK EASILY BROUGHT TO IT. THE
ADJACENT COUNTRY DESCRIBED. I ITS CANALS.IAGRICULTURE TOMBS
OF THE DEAD. TREES AND SHRUBS.

GARDENS AND NURSERIES. DIFFICULTY OF ACCESS TO THEM.

I CUNNING AND DECEIT OF THE CHINESE. I A CHINESE DINNER. I THE-
ATRICALS.

Shanghae is the most northerly of the five ports at which foreigners are now
permitted to trade with the Chinese. Its population is estimated at 210,00.0. It is
situated about a hundred miles, in a north-west direction, from the island of Chusan.
The city stands on the bank of a fine river, about twelve miles from the point where it
joins the celebrated Yang-tse-Kiang, or "Child of the Ocean." The Shanghae river, as
it is generally called by foreigners, is as wide at Shanghae as the Thames at London
Bridge. Its main channel is deep, and easily navigated when known, but the river

abounds in long mud-banks, dangerous to large foreign vessels unless they happen to go up with a fair wind, and manage to get a good pilot on board at the entrance of the river.

Chap. VII.] MY LODGINGS. 105

I visited this place for the first time at the end of 1843, as soon as the port was opened by Her Majesty's Consul, Captain Balfour, and took upjay quarters in a kind of bank or government shroff establishment, in company with two or three gentlemen who were here for purposes of trade. As none of us carried a cooking establishment with us, our meals were necessarily of the roughest description, neither exactly Chinese nor English, but something between the two. Our bed-rooms were miserably cold: often, in the mornings, we would find ourselves drenched in bed with the rain; and if snow fell, it was blown through the windows and formed " *wreaths* " on the floor. Nevertheless, the excitement produced on our minds by every thing around us kept us in excellent health and in good spirits, and we made light of many things which in other circumstances we might have considered as hardships. Whenever we moved out of the house hundreds of people crowded the streets, and followed in our wake, as anxious to catch a glimpse of us as the crowds in London are to see the Queen. Every door and window was crammed with men, women, and children, who gazed upon us with a kind of stupid wonder, as if we had been inhabitants of the moon, and not the ordinary sons of earth. The children more particularly looked upon us with a kind of fear and dread, doubtless implanted in their young minds by their parents, who had less or more of the same feelings themselves. The name we bore|*Kwei-tsz,* or devil's child|

was also calculated to produce erroneous impressions, particularly on the minds of the young, and make them regard us with superstitious horror. In these times it was quite common for us to hear such expressions as the following: " The devil's children are coming," or " Come and see a devil's child;" and not unfrequently " Kwei-tsz " was called out to us in derision. Several complaints were made of this conduct to the British Consul by parties who believed it to be very bad policy at the first commencement of the trade to submit to any marks of contempt, however slight; and strong remonstrances were promptly made by him to the Taoutae, or head Mandarin, of Shanghae. This policy was the very best which could have been pursued with the Chinese authorities; and the consequence was, that in a very short time the offensive appellation was rarely heard in the streets of Shanghae ; and if some little urchin, remembering the lesson so early taught him, came out with it unawares, he was immediately rebuked by the respectable part of the bystanders.

The following incident shows the kind of superstitious dread in which we were held by the inhabitants. A friend and myself were asked to a dinner given on board one of the vessels in the river, and as the cabin was much more comfortable than our cheerless, fireless rooms on shore, we remained until nearly eleven o'clock. Not only are the gates of a Chinese town closed after dark, but all communication even with the streets in the suburbs is cut off

Cuap. VII.] SUPERSTITIONS OF THE CHINESE. 107

by numerous gates and doors, which are fastened up about ten or eleven o'clock at night. This has doubtless been a very ancient custom, to prevent any sudden surprise by an enemy, or by the unruly populace themselves, and is still kept up in more peaceful times. When, therefore, we landed, we found all the gates in the suburbs closed and locked; and we had to pass through one at least before we could reach our quarters. Not a sound was heard; every house was closed; and all that dense multitude which thronged the street by day had sunk into repose. "How shall we get through?" said my friend. " Shake the gate," said I; " perhaps the noise Avill bring some one ; or perchance, as it seems pretty old, it may give way." We took hold of the gate and gave it a good shake, calling out at the same time for some one to come and open it. The watchman's light was now seen coming towards us, and my friend again called out to him to make haste. At last two men with their lanterns came up, in that dreamy state which I have already noticed as a characteristic feature in the Chinese race, and muffled up with skins, as the night was very cold. They could not see distinctly who were on the other side of the door; and, as we mumbled a word or two of Chinese, they were put completely off their guard, and supposed we were benighted Chinamen. The bolts were drawn, the door opened, and behold, two of the dreaded " red-haired race" stood before them. I shall never forget their astonishment when they got their eyes upon us afterthe gate was opened; and whether they actually believed us to be beings of another world, or supposed we had another army at our back to take the city a second time, it is impossible to say, but quick as lightning they both turned their backs and fled, leaving us to shut the gates or admit an army, if we chose. We walked quietly home, and neither saw nor heard any thing more of the bold guardians of the night.

The city of Shanghae is surrounded with high walls and ramparts built upon the same plan as all other Chinese fortifications of this kind. The circumference of the walls is about three and a half miles, and the greater part of the inside is densely studded with houses ; the suburbs, particularly all along the side of the river, are very extensive. Although the gates of the city are closed soon after dark, the people are allowed to pass through afterwards on the payment of a few " cash." When the gate is opened to one, a whole crowd are ready to rush through along with him, the first only paying the " cash." Such is the custom, so that if a poor man comes to the gate he has only to wait until one richer than himself arrives, when, the fee being paid, they pass through together. Joss-houses are met with in all directions, both in the city and suburbs; at certain parts on the ramparts, also, these temples are built and crowded with idols, where the natives come to burn incense, bow the knee, and engage in the other ceremonies of heathen idol worship. Fortune-tellers and jugglers are also in great request,

Chap. VII.] ITS SHOPS AND MERCHANDISE. 109

and reap a rich harvest by working upon the credulity of their countrymen. You meet these characters in all the streets and public squares in Shanghae, and, what is very strange, the *sing-song* or theatricals, of which the Chinese are particularly fond, are frequently exhibited in the temples. This is much opposed to our ideas of religion and propriety; but, somehow or other, the customs of our Celestial friends are in many instances directly opposed to ours.

The streets are generally very narrow, and in the day-time are crowded with people actively engaged in business. The merchandise, which is the most striking to a stranger walking through the streets, it is the silk and embroidery, such as I formerly noticed at Ning-po, cotton and cotton goods, porcelain, ready-made clothes of all kinds beautifully lined with skins and fur, bamboo pipes six feet long and nicely arranged in the shops, pictures, bronzes, and numerous curiosity shops for the sale of carved bamboo ornaments, old pieces of porcelain, and things of that kind, to which the Chinese attach great value. But articles of food form of course the most extensive trade of all; and it is sometimes a difficult matter to get through the streets for the immense quantities of fist, pork, fruit, and vegetables which crowd the stands in front of the shops. Besides the more common kinds of vegetables, the shepherds' purse, and a kind of trefoil or clover, are extensively used amongst the natives here ; and really these things,

when properly cooked, more particularly the latter, are not bad. Dining-rooms, tea-houses, and bakers' shops, are met with at every step, from the poor man who carries his kitchen or bakehouse upon his back, and beats upon a piece of bamboo to apprise the neighbourhood of his presence, and whose whole establishment is not worth a dollar, to the most extensive tavern or tea-garden crowded with hundreds of customers. For a few cash (1000 or 1200=one dollar) a Chinese can dine in a sumptuous manner upon his rice, fish, vegetables, and tea; and I fully believe, that in no country in the world is there less real misery and want than in China. The very beggars seem a kind of jolly crew, and are kindly treated by the inhabitants.

Shanghae is by far the most important station for foreign trade on the coast of China, and is consequently attracting a large share of public attention. No other town with which I am acquainted possesses such advantages: it is the great gate |the principal entrance, in fact|to the Chinese empire. In going up the river towards the town, a forest of masts meets the eye, and shows at once that it is a place of vast native trade. Junks come here from all parts of the coast, not only from the southern provinces, but also from Shantung and Peechelee: there are also a considerable number annually from Singapore and the Malay Islands. The convenience of inland transit is also unrivalled in any part of the world. The country, being as

Chap. VH.] TRADE OF SIIANGIIAE. Ill

it were the valley of the Yang-tse-kiang, is one vast plain, intersected by many beautiful rivers, and these again joined and crossed by canals, many of them nearly natural, and others stupendous works of art. Owing to the level nature of the country, the tide ebbs and flows a great distance inland, thus assisting the natives in the transmission of their exports to Shanghae, or their imports to the most distant parts of the country. The port of Shanghae swarms with boats of all sizes, employed in this inland traffic; and the traveller continually meets them, and gets a glimpse of their sails over the land, at every step of his progress in the interior. Since the port has been opened these boats bring down large quantities of tea and silk to supply the wants of our merchants who have established themselves here, and return loaded with the manufactures of Europe and America, which they have taken in exchange. Our plain cotton goods are most in demand amongst the Chinese, because they can dye them in their own peculiar style, and fit them for the tastes of the people. From what we know of the geographical nature of the country, there can be no doubt that all the green teas, and perhaps the greatest portion of the black, can be brought to Shanghae at less expense than they can be taken to Canton, or any of the other southern towns, except, perhaps, Ning-po; and as the tea-men incur less risk in taking their money home from the North, owing to the peaceable nature of the inhabitants, this will be anothervery great inducement to bring their teas to Shanghae. I am aware that people generally suppose the black-tea districts to be nearer the port of Foo-chow-foo than either Ning-po or Shanghae; but it must be recollected that very few of the black teas now imported to England are from the Bohee hills, as these teas are considered coarser, and much inferior in quality to other kinds, which are from a very different country, much farther to the north, and on the northern side of the great mountain range. The large silk districts of Northern China are close at hand ; and there can be no doubt that a large proportion of that commodity in a raw state will be disposed of at Shanghae. Taking, therefore, all these facts into consideration|the proximity of Shanghae to the large towns of Hangchow, Soo-chow, and the ancient capital of Nanking; the large native trade, 'the convenience of inland transit by means of rivers and canals ; the fact that teas and silks can be brought here more readily than to Canton; and, lastly, viewing this place as an immense mart for our cotton manufactures, which we already know it to be,| there can be no doubt that in a few years it will not only rival Canton, but become a place of far greater importance. And, when I add that the climate is healthy, the natives peaceable, and foreign residents respected, and allowed to walk and ride all over the country to any distance not exceeding a day's journey, it will be acknowledged that, as a

Chap. VII.] CANALS OF CHINA. 113

place to live at, it has many advantages over its southern rival.

I have already sai 1 that this part of China is a complete net-work of rivers and canals. These were often most annoying to me in my travels over the country, when I happened to get *off* the Emperor's highway, a circumstance of no rare occurrence. I have often been obliged to press a boat into my service much against the will of the owners, more particularly when I visited this region for the first time, because I was then unacquainted with the localities, and the Chinese always seemed to fear I might take, or rob, their boats if I succeeded in getting into them, such were the opinions formed of foreigners at that time.

One day, in particular, I had been a considerable distance inland to the westward of Shanghae, and on my return, by some means or other, I got off the; beaten track, and in pursuing my way, as I supposed in the proper direction, I was " brought up" by a large and deep canal. About two miles from where I stood, I saw a bridge, and, as it was nearly dark, I made for it as fast as I could. Unluckily, however, just as I thought my difficulties were over, being within gun-shot of the bridge, I was again stopped by another canal, which crossed the former one at right angles. I was now completely brought to a stand-still, but in a few minutes I perceived a boat approaching, and a man tracking it on the same side as that on which we were. As soon as it came near, we called out to the men on board to

pull the boat towards us, and allow us to get across to the other side. They seemed much frightened, and after making the man who was tracking the boat come on board, they pulled her into the middle of the canal, and then sculled away with all their might. They would soon have passed far beyond our reach, and left us to feel our way in the dark, or plunge through the deep muddy canal. Necessity, they say, has no law. " Call out to them," said I to my servant, " that if they do not immediately stop I will fire into the boat and kill the whole of them," and at the same moment I fired one of my barrels a little way ahead. This was quite sufficient. They immediately came towards us, and put us quickly over to the other side. I paid them for their trouble, and desired them to be more civil to the next traveller they might meet in the same circumstances. They went *off* in high spirits, and we heard them laughing and joking about the adventure long after they had passed out of our sight.

As an agricultural country, the plain of Shanghae is by far the richest which I have seen in China, and is perhaps unequalled by any district of like extent in the world. It is one vast beautiful garden. The hills nearest to Shanghae are distant about thirty miles. These have an isolated appearance in the extensive plain, and are not more than two or three hundred feet high. From their summit, on a clear day, I looked round in all directions, and was only able to see some few hills, apparently having the

Cn.vp.VI!.] THE SOIL AND ITS PRODUCTIONS. 115

same isolated character, far away on the horizon, to the south; these, I have since ascertained, are near the Tartar city of Chapoo. All the rest of the country was a vast level plain, without a mountain or a hill to break the monotony of the view. The soil is a rich deep loam, and produces heavy crops of wheat, barley, rice, and cotton, besides an immense quantity of green vegetable crops, such as cabbages, turnips, yams, carrots, egg-plants, cucumbers, and other articles of that kind which are grown in the vicinity of the city. The land, although level, is generally much higher than the valleys amongst the hills, or the plain round Ning- po; and, consequently, it is well adapted for the cultivation of cotton, which is, in fact, the staple production of the district. Indeed this is the great Nanking cotton country, from which large quantities of that article are generally sent in junks to the north and south of China, as well as to the neighbouring islands. Both the white kind, and that called the " yellow cotton," from which the yellow Nanking cloth is made, are produced in the district. The soil of this district is not only remarkably fertile, but agriculture seems more advanced, and bears a greater resemblance to what it is at home, than in any part of China which I have seen. One here meets with a farmyard containing stacks regularly built up and thatched in the same form and manner as we find them in England ; the land, too, is ridged and furrowed in the same way; and were it not for plantations of bamboo, and the long tailsand general costume of the natives, a man might almost imagine himself on the banks of the Thames. A very considerable portion of the land in the vicinity of the town is occupied by the tombs of the dead. In all directions large conical-shaped mounds meet the eye, overgrown with long grass, and in some instances planted with shrubs and flowers. The traveller here, as well as at Ning-po and Chusan, constantly meets with coffins placed on the surface of the ground out in the fields, carefully thatched over with straw or mats to preserve them from the weather. Sometimes, though rarely, when the relatives are less careful than they generally are, I met with coffins broken or crumbling to pieces with age, exposing the remains of the dead. I was most struck with the coffins of children, which I met with every where; these are raised from the ground on a few wooden posts, and carefully thatched over to protect them from the weatherlreminding the stranger that some parent, with feelings as tender and acute as his own, has been bereaved of a loved one, whom he, perhaps, expected should cheer and support him in his declining years, and whose remains he now carefully watches. Those in the higher ranks of life have generally a family burial-place at a little distance from the town, planted with cypress and pine trees, with a temple and altar built to hold the josses or idols, and where the various religious ceremonies

It *is* stated in Davis's " Chinese," that the dead are all buried on the sides of the barren hills.

Chap. VII.] TREES AND SHHUBS. 117

are performed. A man with his family is stationed there to protect the place, and to burn candles and incense on certain high days. Others, again, are interred in what may be called public cemeteries, several of which I met with in the vicinity of Shanghae. These are large buildings, each containing a certain number of spacious halls or rooms, and having the coffins placed in rows around the sides.

A flat and highly cultivated country, such as I have just described, cannot be expected to be rich in indigenous plants. There are, however, many beautiful clumps of the bamboo growing round all the villages and small farm-houses, which give a kind of tropical character to the scenery, but it is the *only* type of the tropics met with in this district, at least as regards trees. I have already mentioned the clumps of cypress and pine trees planted in the cemeteries of the rich, which are seen studded all over the country, and form one of its most striking features. Among these, I met for the first time with the beautiful *Cryptomeria japo- nica,* a species of pine not unlike the *Araucarias* of Norfolk Island and Brazil. When growing luxuriantly, it is highly ornamental, rising from the ground as straight as a larch, and sending out numerous side branches almost horizontally from the main stem, which again droop towards the ground in a graceful and " *weeping* " manner. The wood of the tree has a kind of twisted grain, and possesses great strength and durability. It ishighly valued by the Chinese, and from its beauty and straightness is often used by the mandarins and priests for those long poles which are generally seen in front of their houses and temples. It is also well known and highly prized by the natives of Japan. My first seeds and plants of this beautiful fir were sent from Shanghae, in the autumn of 1843, and fortunately reached the garden of the Horticultural Society, at Chiswick, in excellent order. It is to be hoped that it will prove hardy, and if so, it will form a striking feature in the woods of England.

The only tree which I met with of very large size in this district is the *Salisburia adiantifolia,* commonly called the Maiden-hair tree, from the resemblance its leaves bear to a fern of that name. This is one of the plants which the Chinese are fond of dwarfing, and it is, consequently, often seen in that state in their gardens. Its fruit is sold in the markets in all Chinese towns by the name of " *Pa-Kwo"* and is not unlike dried almonds, only whiter, fuller, and more round. The natives seem very fond of it, although it is rarely eaten by Europeans. The weeping-willow, apparently the same species as we possess in England, is also common on the sides of all the rivers and canals, as well as in the gardens of the Chinese; and there is also a species of elm, but it never attains any great size, and can therefore be of little value.

Although there is a paucity in the number of

This has proved itself perfectly hardy.

Chap. VII.] GARDENS AND NURSERIES. 119

plants which are really indigenous to this district, yet Shanghae is rich in species which have been brought from other parts of the empire, and are here exposed in gardens for sale: but there are here no mandarin gardens similar to those at Ning-po, this being essentially a mercantile city, and all the residents engaged in active business. The difference between the two towns, in this respect, is indeed very striking. To make up, however, for the deficiency of private collections, I found a number of nursery gardens containing excellent assortments of plants for sale, many of which were new to me, and are unknown in Europe ; and, being at the same time very ornamental, were consequently of great value. At first I had great difficulty in finding out these gardens. The Chinese, from motives which it would be difficult to define|perhaps jealousy or fear,|were unwilling to give me the slightest information about any of these places outside of the town. They told me there were numbers of flower shops in the city, but denied having any knowledge of nurseries or gardens in the country.

" If you want flowers," said they, " there they are in the shops; why do you not buy them? Shanghae men do this, and you should do the same."

" But then shops do not contain the things which I want," said I.

" Then give us the names of the things you want, and we will get them for you."

" But how can I give you the names ? I do not understand your language; you would, of course, send to your nurseries for them if I could only furnish you with their names ? "

"Yes."

" Oh, then, you have nursery gardens in the country ? "

" Yes: but they are a very long way off."

Of course I knew enough of the Chinese by this time to doubt every word they told me, unless I had good reasons for believing them to be speaking the truth, which I had not in this case. I also saw at a glance, from the state of the plants, that they had not only been grown in the country, but I knew from their condition that they could have come but a very short distance, for they had been dug out of the ground with a portion of the soil adhering to the roots. For some few days, however, all my efforts were completely baffled, until a lucky circumstance enabled me to get the better of my Chinese friends. My servant and myself were returning home from the country, after an unsuccessful day's search, when, as we neared the north gate of the city, I shot a bird, which was new to me; being at that time engaged in making a collection of the skins of Chinese birds. I was of course immediately surrounded by all the boys in the neighbourhood, who were quite in raptures at my gun, as it was so different from their own clumsy matchlock. " Now," said I to the juvenile crowd around me, " who can show me the way to

CHINESE NURSERY. 121

the nearest flower-garden, where I can purchase some flowers." " Lyloe, lyloe," said half a dozen of them at once, and I found, to my surprise and pleasure, that I was almost close to the gate of a very good nursery belonging to an individual who had a flower-shop in the city, and with whom I had had the conversation related above. It was now getting too dark to see the plants well, but I marked the spot, and returned on the following day. This time, however, I was not successful, for, as I approached, a boy, who was on the watch, scampered away to the gardener's house and gave notice of my appearance ; and long before I reached the gate it was closed and barricaded, and no persuasion nor entreaty could remove their fears, or induce them to allow me to enter. The next day, and the next again, the very same thing took place, although I took different roads, in the hopes of finding the young sentinel off his guard. I was now obliged to have recourse to other means to gain my end. Her Majesty's consul, Captain Bal- four, had from the first taken great interest in the success of my pursuits, and kindly offered me every assistance in his power, should I find any difficulties in my way. I therefore related the circumstance to him, and requested him to allow one of the Chinese officers attached to the consulate to accompany me to the garden, and explain that my object was to purchase plants, and not to take any thing away against their will. From our

" Come, come."

experience of Chinese character, we were well aware that, if this were properly explained, the poor people, whose livelihood depended upon the propagation and sale of plants, would be very glad to allow me to make purchases at their garden. I therefore set out again on the following day, accompanied by an officer from the consulate. When we approached the garden, my young friend was at his post, as usual, and ran off immediately, and forthwith the gate was closed and barricaded as before. We walked quietly up to it, and knocked, but there was no answer; and the place seemed all at once to be deserted. The officer well knew that the family had hid themselves just inside the gate, and commenced talking to them, and laughing at their fears. In a few seconds we heard a movement amongst the bushes, and then the inmates, gaining courage, ventured to approach the gate to reconnoitre. At last, being apparently satisfied, the bolts were withdrawn, and we were admitted within the sacred precincts of the garden, when I soon found several very valuable plants. The ice was now broken, and, with the assistance of the Chinese officer, I got the names and localities of several other gardens, which I soon found out: and, although it was the winter season, and vegetation in a state of repose, I was able in a few weeks to get together a collection of plants, which, when they flowered, proved not only quite new, but highly ornamental. A few months wrought a great change upon these diffident and timid

Chap. VII.] CHINESE NURSERY. 123

people, and, at length, they not only received me with pleasure, but begged me to bring my friends and acquaintances to see their flowers. I frequently did so, and as we always treated them with kindness and consideration, a favourable impression was made upon their minds, which, I have no doubt, will long continue. When I was leaving Shanghae for the last time on my return to England, I went to remove a collection of plants which 1 had in one of these gardens : as I was doing so, the proprietor said to me, " the next time you come to Shanghae I shall have left this garden, and gone to one which I have taken in the next district, where I shall be glad to see you, and supply you with the plants you want."

" Thanks, my good friend," said I, " but as my labours in the ' central flowery land ' are ended, I shall now return again to my own country, ' Ta- Eng-co ,' a land in the far distant west, and you shall never sec me again ; fare you well."

He then kindly wished me fair winds, smooth seas, and a happy meeting with my friends at home.

I merely mention this circumstance to show what a change took place in the feelings of these poor people in the course of two years, and which I regard as an earnest of what may be done with the northern Chinese, who differ widely from their haughty and insolent countrymen in the south.

Great England, or Great Britain, the name which our country is known by in the north of China.

Another example may be given to show the cunning and deceit of many of the Chinese here as elsewhere. A flower painter in Chusan had informed me that several very valuable varieties of the *Moutan,* or Tree Poeony, were to be found in gardens near Shanghae. Those varieties of this flower, which are yearly brought from the northern provinces to Canton, and which are now common in Europe, have blossoms, which are either rose- coloured or white: but it was always asserted, although not believed, that in some part of China purple, blue, and yellow varieties were produced, although these were never brought to Canton for sale. It was for these that I made the most particular inquiries, and this painter not only affirmed he had seen them, but also offered, for a small sum, to make me drawings from memory of all the different kinds. I employed him at once, and when he had finished the drawings, I took them with me to Shanghae. A nurseryman, who had a flower- shop in the town, to whom I showed these drawings, promised at once to procure living plants for me, but said they would be very expensive, as he would have to send to Soo-chow, a distance of nearly one hundred miles, for they were not to be procured in the vicinity of Shanghae, and a man would be absent at least eight days. I was, of course, glad to get them upon any terms, and gave the man the price he asked, which, after all, was not much out of the way, if they were to be brought a hundred miles. At the specified time

Chap. VII] CHRYSANTHEMUMS. 125

the Moutans arrived, and proved most valuable kinds, which, in England, would have brought a very high sum. Amongst them there were *lilacs* and *purples; some* nearly *black;* and one which the Chinese called " *the yellow,"* which, however, was only white with a slight tinge of yellow near the centre of the petals. Altogether the collection was a valuable one, and I was highly satisfied with my bargain. Great was my surprise when I afterwards found that these plants were brought a distance not more than six miles from the walls of Shanghae, and that the celebrated town of Soo-chow was, in fact, supplied with " Moutans " from the very same place.

It was the winter season when I paid my first visit to Shanghae, and of course few plants were then in bloom except the Chrysanthemum, the varieties of which are as numerous here as in the south of China; and as the Chinese gardeners understand their cultivation well, they were, at this particular season, objects of great interest. My collections were chiefly deciduous plants, which it was impossible to determine or describe at the time, being chosen partly on account of the families they belonged to, and partly from the characters given them by the Chinese. Every one acquainted with practical botany can form a very fair idea of the value of plants even in this condition, and I was not disappointed in the expectations I had formed regarding this collection, many of the specimens afterwards proving plants of great beauty and value.

Whilst at Shanghae, I, with some other Europeans, had an invitation to go to the house of a mandarin, to see a theatrical performance or " Singsong," and to dine with him in Chinese style afterwards. Sedan chairs were sent to take us to his house, where we were introduced to a number of his friends, and, as the invariable custom is, tea was immediately handed round. Shortly afterwards a servant came with a tray full of wet, warm towels, not unlike those generally used in kitchens at home, and presented one to each of us. At first, we could not conjecture what these were for; but, on looking at our Chinese friends, we observed them rubbing their faces and hands with them, and, although not very agreeable to us, we immediately did the same. I afterwards found that this was a common custom amongst the Chinese, and I have often been much refreshed by it after a warm walk. In hot countries like China this plan is much better, and more conducive to health, than either washing or bathing in cold water.

While this was going on in the house, the players were getting every thing ready in the large room where the performance was to take place. In a little while one of them entered the room where we were, carrying in his hand several fine long ivory cards, on which were written a number of the most popular plays of the day, any one of which the players were ready to perform at the command of our host and his friends. We were most politely consulted on the subject, which, as we did not know a single character of the language, and had

Chap. VH.] PRIVATE THEATRICALS. 127

the greatest difficulty in understanding what was said to us, was not of much use. Having at last fixed upon a particular piece for the evening's entertainment, we were all led into the theatre. The room was large and nearly square, having a platform at the upper end for the actors and band, and one of the sides being only separated from an open lane by a railing, so that the public might also have a view of the play. The centre of the room was completely filled with guests, and from the roof hung a number of lanterns in the Chinese style. As it was early in the afternoon when the play commenced, the lanterns were not lighted and the piece went on in daylight, the Chinese actors not excluding it as we do in our theatres in England.

The play began with some pantomime-like feats, such as we see in English theatres at Christinas. This was succeeded by something which appeared to be very pathetic, judging from the language and gestures of the performers. A.11 was gone through in a kind of opera style, the actors singing their parts with false voices. The feats of tumbling which were now and then performed were extremely dexterous and clever, and attracted our notice more than any thing else, probably because they were best understood.

The dresses of the actors were superb, and must have cost a large sum of money. There were no females amongst them, as it is not customary for them to act; but their places were supplied by men or boys, chosen from amongst those who are most" lady-looking," and so well were their appearance and dresses arranged, that it would have required a practised eye to have detected the difference.

The voices of the actors were not musical, at least to English ears, but the whole was in unison with the noisy gong, and the wind instruments, like bagpipes, which are in common use amongst the Chinese. In fact, noise seemed to be the thing which produced the greatest effect, and we certainly had enough of it.

I was struck by the various figures made by the actors on the stage, intended, no doubt, to represent something like those scenes or pictures which are so much studied in our theatres at home. A quadrant seems to be a great favourite, and was constantly made by them in the different acts. They have no scenery to assist the delusion, only a simple screen, which is sometimes used to represent a room out of which some actor is to make his appearance. Fencing is much practised, and is, perhaps, the most curious part of these exhibitions. Each individual has two swords, which he swings about his head in the wildest manner, at the same time throwing his feet and legs about in a most fantastic way, as if they had as much to do in the business as the hands and arms. The exhibition or play lasted for three hours, and then we left the theatre and retired into another room. While we were there the servants were busily employed in rearranging the theatre, which was now to be converted into a dining-room.

Chap. VII.] A CHINESE DINNER. 129

When all was ready we were led in with great ceremony, and placed in the principal seats of honour. We had now an opportunity of seeing the extent to which the Chinese carry their ceremony and politeness amongst themselves when they are about to be seated at table. Our host and his friends were nearly a quarter of an hour before the whole of them were seated. Each one was pressing the most honourable seat upon his neighbour, who, in his turn, could not think of occupying such a distinguished place at the board. However, after a great deal of bowing and flattery, all was apparently arranged satisfactorily, and dinner com- menced.

The tables were now covered with a profusion of small dishes, which contained all the finest fruits and vegetables of the season, besides many of the most expensive kinds of soups, such as the celebrated bird's-nest and others, many of which were excellent even to the palate of an Englishman. The servants were continually employed in removing the centre dishes and replacing them by others of a different kind, until at last every one seemed perfectly satisfied. Still, however, the ceremony of bringing in new dishes went on, and these were merely looked at and removed. Our maiden efforts with the chopsticks must have been a source of great amusement to our Chinese friends, but they were polite enough not to laugh at us, and did every thing in their power to assist us. The play was resumed again as soon as the dinner com-

menced, and continued as briskly as ever. The " lady actors" at intervals came down from the platform and supplied the guests with different kinds of wines. During the entertainment, a piece of money was handed to each of the guests, which they were desired to leave as a present for the actors at the conclusion of the piece. When this was given them, the whole of the *corps dramatique* came round, and each made a most polite bow of acknowledgment and withdrew. Still, however, the dinner ceremonial went on ; hundreds of fresh dishes were brought in, and as many in their turn removed. The Chinese guests were sometimes smoking, sometimes eating, just as it seemed good to them, and uniformly praising every thing which made its appearance on the table.

We had now been three or four hours at table, and although the whole affair had been very amusing, we had had enough of it, and were beginning to tire. " How long shall the dinner last?" said I to a linguist who was placed next me, and who had most politely explained every thing which had occurred during the entertainment. " Oh," said he, " it will last for three or four hours longer, but if you want to go away, you may do so now." We were very glad to find that Chinese etiquette permitted us to withdraw, and ordered our chairs, which were waiting in the court-yard to receive us. Our host and his friends lighted us out with lanterns, and we took our departure in the same style in which we came. So

Chap. VII.] A CHINESE DINNER. 131

ended my first Chinese dinner. Since then such things have been no rarity, either in the palaces of the rich or in the cottages of the poor, and they have been even more frequent in the temples with the priests.

9

SECTION 9

CHAP. VIII.

RETURN TO THE SOUTH OF !IIN.|THE CANTON BIVER DESCRIBED. FORTS AT THE BOCCA TIGRIS. PRODUCTIONS OF

THE COUNTRY. THE " SIGHING" WILLOW. CULTIVATION

OF THE NELUMBIUM. BOATS ON THE RIVER. THE BARBER'S

BOAT. SPLENDOUR OF THE FLOWER BOATS. APPEARANCE OF THE RIVER AT FESTIVALS. I ORDER WHICH PREVAILS IN THIS FLOATING CITY. HOUSES BUILT OVER WATER.

CHINESE DEXTERITY IN SWIMMING AND DIVING. FA-TEE

GARDENS. |THEIR PLANTS. I OLD ACHING GETS A BAD NAME BECAUSE HIS SEEDS DO NOT GROW. I HE DOES NOT DESERVE

IT. ADVICE TO THE BUYERS OF SEEDS ENGLISH AND

AMERICAN PUBLIC GARDENS AT CANTON. CHINESE NEW YEAR.

I ATTACKED AND ROBBED BY THE CHINESE. I A SUBSEQUENT ATTACK MADE UPON SOME OFFICERS OF THE ENGLISH GOVERNMENT. THEIR LETTER TO HER MAJESTY'S CONSUL.

As the island of Chusan was my head-quarters in the north of China, I now proceeded thither with my collections from Shanghae, preparatory to sailing forHongkong and the southern ports of the country. The Chusan hills were now covered with snow, and the weather was piercingly cold. Large quantities of pheasants and water-fowl were daily brought to the markets by the Chinese, who found the English good customers. A small species of deer was also brought from the main-land, and frequently alive. Four or five fine pheasants were often to be purchased for a dollar, and duck and teal were also remarkably cheap: I believe from two to four rupees were generally given for a deer.

The officers of the troops stationed at Chusan, who were fond of shooting, obtained excellent sport

Chap. Vin.] CANTON RIVER DESCRIBED. 133

by engaging Chinese boats and going across to the hills on the main-land, there being little game of any kind upon the island itself.

Having got all my things packed, I took a passage in a vessel bound for the South, and having a fair monsoon down the China Sea, we arrived at Hong-kong in a few days, without any thing occurring worthy of notice. The various collections which I had made in the North were now put up in glazed cases and shipped for England.

As the south of China had been ransacked by former botanists, I could not expect to find much which was new or worthy of being sent home, and I therefore arranged to proceed north again in March or April, in order to have a whole season before me. In the mean time, as I had a few weeks to spare in the south, I determined on a visit to Canton and Macao, which are both within a short distance from Hong-kong.

The Canton river is certainly one of the most imposing and striking objects which the traveller meets with in this celebrated country. The sea, near its mouth, is studded all over with numerous islands, of which a good view is obtained in going over from Hong-kong to Macao; and in sailing from either of these places to Canton, we pass a succession of them, most of which are mountainous, having huge masses of rock, and yellow gravelly clay, protruding here and there through the surface, and but thinly covered with vegetation of any kind.

Sometimes, however, in our progress, we obtainedviews of beautiful bays, with a few acres of level land near the shore, in the midst of which there are some pretty houses or huts, surrounded by a few trees and shrubs. In sailing amongst these islands one is apt to think that, in the retirement of such places, far removed from the vicious world, and the " busy hum of men," the inhabitants must, indeed, be happy and innocent, having their few wants abundantly supplied by the rice which grows luxuriantly around their dwellings, and by the never- failing supply of excellent fish, which are easily caught in the sea. But these dreams of happiness and innocence are soon dispelledlthese quiet villages abound with pirates, who frequently commit acts of the most cold-blooded cruelty, and render the passage between Hong-kong, Canton, and Macao, an alarming and dangerous affair. Lorchas, and other small vessels, with valuable cargoes on board, are frequently attacked, the crew and passengers murdered, and the vessels disabled or destroyed.

A few hours' sail, with a fair wind and tide, brought me in sight of the celebrated Bocca Tigris, the entrance to the Canton river. The forts destroyed during the war had been rebuilt on a more extensive scale; and, if manned with English soldiers, no hostile fleet in the world could pass them without being blown to pieces. I fancy, however, that the Chinese, although they have had a lesson in the art of war, which will make them more difficult to conquer in future, would still, with all their forts, afford but a feeble resistance against the

Chap. VIII.] PRODUCTIONS OF THE COUNTRY. 135

military and naval tactics of the English and other civilised nations of the West.

Inside the Bogue, the river widens very much, and presents the appearance of an inland sea. The view now becomes beautiful and highly picturesque, the flat cultivated land near the shores forming a striking contrast to the barren hills on the outside of the forts ; the mountains in the distance appear to encircle the extensive plain; and although, like the others, they are barren, yet they make a fine back-ground to the picture. A few miles further up the river, the shipping in Blenheim and Wham- poa reaches come into view, and the celebrated Whampoa pagoda, with several more of less note, besides numerous other towers and joss-houses, all remind the traveller that he is approaching the far- famed city of Canton, one of the richest and most important in the celestial empire. The noble river, with its numerous ramifications, forms many islands, on one of which the small town or village of Whampoa is built.

Large quantities of rice are grown, both on the islands formed by the river, and on the flats on the main-land. The tide is kept out by embankments,and the ground can be overflowed at will. These embankments are not allowed to lie idle, but are made to produce crops of plantains. When the land is too high to be flooded by the tide, the water-wheel is brought into play, and it is perfectly astonishing how much water can be raised by this simple contrivance in a very short space of time.

By late accounts from China (May, 1847), it appears, that these and other forts on the Canton river have been again taken by the English. The force employed consisted of Her Majesty's Brig Espiegle and three steamers, containing only about 900 men. 879 guns were spiked, and this small force was ready to take the provincial capital itself, had the demands of Her Majesty's Plenipotentiary not been complied with. Such is an example of what has been called " War" in China.

Sugar-cane is also grown rather extensively near Whampoa, and, in its raw state, is an article in great demand amongst the Chinese. It is manufactured into sugar-candy and brown sugar ; many kinds of the latter being particularly fine, though not much used by the foreigners residing in the country; who generally prefer the candy reduced to powder, in which state it is very fine and white. I did not see our loaf-sugar in any part of China, and I conceive that it is not made there.

A great number of the common fruit trees of the country grow all over the plains and near the side of the river. The mango, guava, wangpee *(Cookia punctata),* leechec, longan, oranges, and pumeloes, are the principal kinds. Besides these, there are the cypress, thuja, banyan and other kinds of fig-trees, and a species of pine, called by the Chinese the water pine, from its always growing by the sides of the rivers and canals. The bamboo, and a sort of weeping willow very much like our own, are also frequently met with. The name which the Chinese give to the latter is the " sighing" willow, coinciding rather curiously Avith our own term of " weeping;" and when taken in connection with the historical fact of the JewsChap, viii.] Bakber's Boat. 137

weeping by the streams of Babylon, and hanging their harps upon the willows, show that this is regarded as the emblem of sorrow, as universally as the dark and sombre pine and cypress are considered in all countries fit companions to the cemetery and churchyard.

On the sides of the river, both below and above the city, large quantities of the water lily, or lotus, are grown, which are enclosed by embankments in the same manner as the rice fields. This plant is cultivated both as an ornament, and for the root, which is brought in large quantities to the markets, and of which the Chinese are remarkably fond. In the summer and autumn months, when in flower, the lotus fields have a gay and striking appearance, but at other seasons the decayed leaves and flowers, and the stagnant and dirty water, are not at all ornamental to the houses which they surround.

One of the most striking sights on the Canton river, is the immense number of boats which are moored all along the shore, near the foreign factory. There are *hundreds of thousands* of all kinds and sizes, from the splendid flower-boat, as it is called, down to the small barber's boat, forming a large floating city, peopled by an immense number of human beings. In sailing up the river you may observe a very small boat, perhaps the smallest you ever saw, exposed on the water, being nothing more than a feAV planks fastened together. This is the barber's boat, who is going about, or rather swimming about, following his daily avocation of shaving the heads, and tickling the ears and eyes ofthe Chinamen. By the by, this same barber has much to answer for, for his practice has a most prejudicial effect upon the eyes and ears of his countrymen. He, however, works his little boat with great dexterity, and with his scull manages to propel himself with ease and swiftness through the floating city of boats, larger and more powerful than his own. Then you see boats of various sizes, such as those at Macao and Hong-kong, covered over, divided into three compartments, and kept remarkably clean and neat. These are hired by either natives or foreigners for the purpose of going off to the large junks or other vessels moored out in the river, or for short excursions to the island of Honan, the Fa-Tee Gardens, or such places. The centre division of the boat forms a very neat little room, having windows in the sides, ornamented with pictures and flowers of various kinds. The compartment at the bow is occupied by the rowers, and that at the stern is used for preparing the food of the family to whom the boat belongs.

The boats of the Hong merchants, and the large flower-boats are very splendid. They are arranged in compartments like the others, but are built in a more superb and costly manner. The reader must imagine a kind of wooden house raised upon the floor of the boat, having the entrance near the bows, space being left there for the boatmen to stand and row. This entrance being the front, is carved in a most superb style, forming a prelude to what may be seen within. Numerous lanterns hang from the roof of these splendid showy cabins;

Chap. VIII.] ORDER OF THE FLOATING CITY. 139

looking-glasses, pictures, and poetry, adorn their sides; and all the peculiarities of this singular people are exposed to our view in these their floating palaces.

Then there are the Chop boats, which are used by the merchants for conveying goods to the vessels at Whampoa; the passage-boats to Hong-kong, Macao, and various parts of the country; the Mandarin-boats, with their numerous oars, which have a strange appearance as they pass up and down the river (I have seen a single boat of this kind with forty oars on each side); and, lastly, the large unwieldy sea-going junks. There are various modifications of all these kinds of boats, each adapted for the particular purpose for which il; is designed. At festival times, the river has a singularly gay and striking appearance, particularly at night, when the lanterns are lighted, and numberless boats gaily decorated with them move up and down in front of the factory. The effect produced upon a stranger at these times by the wild and occasionally plaintive strains of Chinese music, the noisy gong, the close and sultry air, the strange people, Ifull of peculiarities and conceit,Iis such as he can never forget, and leaves upon his mind a mixed impression of pleasure, pity, admiration, and contempt. Throughout the whole of this immense floating city, the greatest regularity prevails; the large boats are arranged in rows, forming streets, through which the smaller craft pass and repass, like coaches and other vehicles in a large town.The families who live in this manner seem to have a great partiality for flowers, which they keep in pots, either upon the high stern of their boats, or in their little parlours. The Chinese arbor vitae, gardenias, cycas revoluta, cockscombs, and oranges, seem to be the greatest favourites with them. A joss-house I small indeed, in many cases, but yet a place of worshipIis indispensable to all these floating houses. Here the joss-stick and the oil are daily burned, and form the incense which these poor people offer to their imaginary deity.

The city and suburbs of Canton are supposed tc contain about a million of inhabitants. Upon the sides of the river, and the numerous canals in the suburbs of Canton, whole streets of wooden houses are built upon stakes which are driven firmly into the mud. These dwellings very much resemble the travelling shows which are often seen in the market towns of England; except, that posts supply the place of wheels, and that they are crowded together in hundreds, forming crooked and irregular streets. Thousands of the inhabitants live and enjoy health and happiness in such places, which would soon be graves for Europeans I such is the difference of constitution.

But what surprised me most was the old women and young children bathing in the river, which seemed as if it were their natural element, and they appeared quite as much at home there as the fishes themselves. The Chinese boat population are famous for their dexterity in and under the water.

Chap. VIII.] FA-TEE GARDENS. 141

Since the island of Hong-kong became an English settlement, officers of the government, sent to apprehend thieves in the bay, have frequently failed to do so owing to this circumstance. The Chinamen, whenever they found that there was any danger of being taken, jumped all together overboard, diving out of sight, and swimming under water until they were out of the reach of their pursuers, or until they found shelter in some of the numerous boats belonging to their own clan, which lay moored in the bay.

I lost no time in visiting the celebrated Fa-tee Gardens, near Canton, the " flowery land," as the name implies, from whence a great number of those fine plants were first procured which now decorate our gardens in England. They are situated two or three miles above the city, on the opposite side of the river, and are, in fact, Chinese nursery gardens, where plants are cultivated for sale.

Here, then, I beheld a specimen of the far-famed system of Chinese gardening, about which we have read so much in European authors: I will, therefore, describe them somewhat fully. The plants are principally kept in large pots arranged in rows along the sides of narrow paved walks, with the houses of the gardeners at the entrance through which the visitors pass to the gardens. There are about a dozen of these gardens, more or less extensive, according to the business or wealth of the proprietor ; but they are generally smaller than the smallest of our London nurseries. They have also stock-grounds, where the different plants are

planted out in the ground, and where the first process of dwarfing their celebrated trees is put in operation. These contain large collections of Camellias, Azaleas, oranges, roses, and various other well-known plants, which are purchased by the Chinese when in flower. The most striking plant in autumn or winter is the curious fingered citron, which the Chinese gather and place in their dwellings or on their altars. It is much admired both for its strange form, and also for its perfume. The mandarin orange is also much grown at Fa-tee, where the plants are kept in a dwarf state, and flower and fruit most profusely, producing large, flat, dark, red-skinned, fruit. The Chinese have a great variety of plants belonging to the orange tribe; and of one, which they call the *cum quat* I a small oval-fruited variety I they make a most excellent preserve. The *Murraya exotica, Aglaia odorata, Ixoras,* and *Lagerstrcemias* are very ornamental here in autumn.

But it is of course in spring that the Fa-tee gardens possess the greatest attractions. They are then gay with the tree pseony, azaleas, camellias, roses, and various other plants. The azaleas are splendid, and reminded me of the exhibitions in the gardens of the Horticultural Society at Chiswick, but the Fa- tee exhibitions were on a much larger scale. Every garden was one mass of bloom, and the different colours of red, white, and purple, blended together, had a most beautiful and imposing effect. The principal kinds grown were *Azalea indica, indica*

Chap. VIII.] CULTIVATION OF CHRYSANTHEMUMS. 143

alba, phcenicea, lateritia, variegata, and the yellow *Azalea sinensis.* I may mention in passing, that I found the latter plant wild on the Ning-po hills, so that there is no doubt of its being a genuine Chinese species. The air at this season around Fa-tee is perfumed with the sweet flowers of *Olea fragrans,* and the *Magnolia fuscata,* both of which are grown extensively in these gardens. Dwarf trees, as may be supposed, occupy a principal station; they are trained into the most grotesque and curious forms. The plants which stand next to dwarf trees in importance with the Chinese are certainly chrysanthemums, which they manage extremely well, perhaps better than they do any other plant. So high do these plants stand in the favour of the Chinese gardener, that he will cultivate them extensively, even against the wishes of his employer; and, in many instances, rather leave his situation than give up the growth of his favourite flower. I was told, that the late Mr. Beale used to say that he grew chrysanthemums in his garden for no other purpose than to please his gardener, not having any taste for this particular flower himself.

Tree pseonies are not natives of the south of China, but are brought down in large quantities every year, about the month of January, from the northern provinces. They flower soon after they arrive, and are rapidly bought up by the Chinese to ornament their houses ; after which they are thrown away, as they do not thrive well so far south as Canton or Macao, and will not flower asecond season. They are sold according to the number of flower-buds they may have upon them, many of them fetching rather high prices.

One of the old gardeners here speaks the English language very well, and carries on a considerable trade in seeds with the English and American residents ; but, unfortunately, he has got a bad name, owing to his seeds generally failing to grow when they are sent home. It is now currently reported that the old man boils them, in order that his trade may not be spoiled by some enterprising propagator in England or America. Such, however, is not the case; on the contrary, I am quite certain that he does every thing in his power to preserve them, but very likely some may be a year or two old before they are despatched to Europe. Besides, the long voyage round the Cape|during which the seeds have twice to cross the tropics I is very prejudicial to their germination. There is, however, no great loss in these seeds not growing, as there is nothing amongst them new, or of any value, for they are gathered from the plants common in the Fa-tee gardens, the greater part of which have been years ago introduced to our gardens at home. I would, therefore, strongly advise my friends in China not to spend their money upon such seeds.

Although the botanist can find little that is new to him in these gardens, yet they are well worthy of a visit; and in the spring months, when most of the plants are in bloom, they have a singularly gorgeous and imposing appearance, and really deserve. vrn.] New Year's Day. 145

the poetical name of " Fa-tee," or flowery land, which the Chinese have given them.

The garden which formerly belonged to the East India Company is still in existence. It is but a small plot of ground on the river side, not more than sixty paces each way, having broad chunamed walks round it, and a clump, with a few trees in the middle, and a few more between the walk and the wall all round. Since Mr. Reeves's time no one seems to have paid any attention to the plants here, and if there ever were any rare species, they are now all lost. A few Palms, Plantains, *Magnolia grandiflora, Clerodendron fragrans, Justicia Adha- toda, Ligustrum, Murray a exotica,* the Leechee, and two or three other well-known things, are all that it contains. In front of the American factory there is a very nice public garden, at least six times the size of the Company's, with fine broad walks for recreation, and containing numerous shrubs and trees indigenous to the country; nothing, it is true, of any rarity, but sufficient to make it look extremely well. A good garden and promenade are of much importance here; for it is likely to be some years before foreigners enjoy the same liberty at Canton of walking about the country as they do in the other parts of China.

At this period the Chinese were making great preparations for the celebration of New Year's Day, which then fell on the 18th of February. Flowers of all kinds were in great demand amongst the inhabitants, who employ them in the decoration of their houses and temples. In going up the river towards the Fa-tee Gardens, I met boats in great numbers loaded with branches of peach and plum trees in bloom, *Enkianthus quinqueflorus,* camellias, cockscombs, magnolias, and various other plants which flower at this season. The Enkianthus is brought down from the hills with the buds just expanding; and after being placed in water for a day or two, the flowers come out as healthy and fresh as if the branches had not been removed from the parent tree. This plant is a great favourite amongst the Chinese. The common jonquil too comes in for a very extensive share of patronage; and in the streets of Canton one meets with thousands of bulbs growing in small pans amongst water and a few white stones. In this case the Chinese exhibit their peculiar propensity for dwarf and monstrous growth, by planting the bulbs upside down, and making the plants and flowers assume curious twisted forms, which appear to be so agreeable to the eyes of a Chinaman. Large quantities of all these flowers are exposed for sale in many of the shops and in the corners of the streets in Canton, where they seem to be eagerly bought up by the Chinese, who consider them quite indispensable at this particular season. Not only are the houses and temples decorated with them, but the boats on the river also come in for a most extensive share. Indeed, these boats are only floating houses, for a very great part of the population of Canton lives upon the river. The flower-boats, as they are com-

Chap. YiH.) ADVENTURE AMONG THE CHINESE. 147

monly called, are particularly gay at new-year time with flowers of all hues, and gaudy flags streaming from each mast and stern. Crackers or fireworks, of which the Chinaman is so fond, are let off in large quantities for several days in all parts of the town, and form part of their religious ceremonies or offerings to their gods. Their shops are closed on New Year's Day, and for two or three days afterwards. The greater part of the natives wear their holiday clothes, and tramp about amongst their relations and friends to *chin-chin* them, and wish them a happy new year, as we do at home. Large parties are made at this season to go up to the gardens at Fa-tee; and on particular days you find there hundreds of these flower-boats crowded with young Chinese of the better classes, enjoying themselves as our own population do at Richmond or Hampton Court. Great numbers of well dressed ladies also go over to Fa-tee in the flower-boats, and walk about in the gardens; and this is the only season when they are visible at Canton.

After having been several months in the north of China, and, with one or two exceptions, always experiencing the greatest civility from the natives, 1 was beginning to form a high opinion of the Chinese as a nation, and inclined to trust the people about Canton in the same manner as I had done in the northern provinces. I very soon, however, found out my mistake, and in a most disagreeable manner. There were some hills behind the city, a few miles distant, which I had often wished to visit for thepurpose of examining their botanical productions. One morning I started off through the town, in the direction of these hills; and after walking between two and three miles, I reached the suburbs on the side of the town, opposite to that where the foreign factory stands. The sounds of " *Fankicei"* with which I was assailed in the early part of my walk, had now nearly ceased, and I began to imagine that I had got out from amongst the impertinent boys and low Chinese, whom one continually meets in the back streets of Canton. I was now on a good road, amongst fields and gardens, and had an excellent view of the surrounding country, and hills. How very strange, thought I, that the foreign residents in the factories never avail themselves of the opportunity of coming here, when they might enjoy the fresh air, and see the country, which would help to relieve the monotonous life they are compelled to lead.

As I was walking quietly along, I met a Chinese soldier on horseback, who by gestures and words did every thing in his power to induce me to retrace my steps. I knew nothing of the Canton dialect at this time, and as I thought he only wished to prevent me from taking a walk in the country, I paid no attention to him, but passed onwards. Soon afterwards, however, I began to suspect the ill intentions of several groups of ill-looking fellows who seemed to be eyeing me narrowly

Literally, "foreign devil."

Chap. VHi.] AMONG THE CHINESE. 149

as I proceeded. I now came to a little hill which seemed to be used as a cemetery: it was enclosed, but the door which led to it was wide open, and the place appeared to be quite public. In order to have a more extended view of the country, I walked in and began to ascend the hill. I had only proceeded about half way up, when a number of Chinamen who had followed me in, began to crowd round me, asking for " *comeshaws"* and becoming every moment more numerous and urgent. I tried what civility would do with them for a little while, but by the time I reached the top of the hill I clearly perceived that I was in a trap, out of which it would be a difficult matter to extricate myself.

Up to this time, however, no one had attempted to lay hands upon me. Taking a cursory view of the surrounding country, I began to devise in my mind the best mode of getting rid of my troublesome companions. There seemed no other way than putting a bold face on the matter, and retracing my steps to Canton. " You more better come down this way," said a fellow to me in broken English, pointing to a ravine on the opposite side of the hill. My suspicions, however, were now roused, and I saw at once the object of my adviser, which was to get me into some place out of sight, where I should doubtless have been robbed of every article I had about my person, and probably stripped into the bargain. " No, no," said I, " I have nothingto do down there," and began to retrace my steps down the hill. The Chinese now closed upon me, and seemed determined to obstruct my progress. Some laid hold of my arms ; one fellow seized my cap, and ran off with it, another did the same with my umbrella, several hands were in my pockets, and others were even attempting to get my coat off. I now saw that nothing short of getting every thing I possessed would satisfy them, as each one wanted something, and "their name Avas legion." Collecting all my strength, I threw myself upon those who were below me, and sent several of them rolling down the side of the hill. This, however, was nearly fatal to me, for, owing to the force which I exerted, and the uneven nature of the ground, I stumbled and fell; but fortunately I instantly recovered myself, and renewed the unequal struggle, my object being to reach the door of the cemetery by which I had entered. The Chinese on the hill now called out to their friends below to shut the door, and thus prevent me from reaching the open road. Seeing at once that if this were accomplished I should be an easy prey to them, I determined if possible to prevent it. Springing out of the grasp of those by whom I was surrounded, I made for the door, which I reached just as it was closed, but fortunately before it was fastened on the other side. The force with which I came against it burst it open, and threw the Chinamen on their backs who were busily fastening it. I was now in the open road, where some hun-

Presents.

Chap. Vm.] ATTACK OF THE CHINESE. 151

dreds of the Chinese were congregated together; some of them apparently respectable, but the greater part evidently nothing but thieves and robbers. The respectable part would not, or probably durst not, render me any assistance. Stones were now flying about me in all directions, and a brick struck me with great force on the back, and nearly brought me to the ground. I was stunned for a few seconds, and leaned against the wall to breathe and recover myself, thinking that I was now comparatively safe as I was out on the open road. I was soon undeceived, however, for the rascals again surrounded me, and relieved me of several articles which had escaped them before. As the whole neighbourhood was evidently a bad one, it would have been madness to have taken shelter in any of the houses, and I therefore had to struggle with the robbers for nearly a mile, sometimes fighting, and sometimes running, until I got out of their territory, and near the more populous parts of the town. The plight I was now in may easily be conceived, but taking everything into account, I came off better than might have been expected.

On my way home, having neither hat nor umbrella, I suffered greatly from exposure to the sun, which, in the south of China, is very powerful on a clear day, even in spring. I would have gladly gone into a shop and bought a Chinese hat, but the rascals had not left me even a copper cash for the purpose. Fortunately I had left my watch at home, otherwisethat would have been taken amongst the first things, as Chinese thieves are very partial to watches and know their value well.

The Honourable F. C. Drummond, with whom I was staying at the time, informed me afterwards that the place where I had been attacked was one of the worst in the suburbs of Canton, and that three gentlemen of his acquaintance, a year or two before, had come off even worse than I had done, the Chinese having taken away nearly all their clothes.

About two years after this attack upon me three gentlemen holding government appointments in China, Mr. Montgomery Martin, the Rev. V. Stanton, and Mr. Jackson, having incautiously strolled into the suburbs, were also attacked; and the letter which they addressed officially to Her Majesty's consul complaining of the treatment they had received, shows so clearly the state of things at Canton, that I give it entire: I

" About seven o'clock this morning, while walking for exercise along the north wall, on the outside of the city, we were attacked by several Chinese, who had been following us, and increasing in numbers, from the building known to foreigners as the Five-storied Pagoda. At first they commenced by throwing stones, which endangered our lives, and by some of which we were struck. This attack was aided and encouraged by a number of Chinese, who followed us along the top of the city wall, hurling large stones, which, if they had struck, would have killed those at whom they were aimed. Mr. Jack-

Chap. VIII.] UPON SOME BRITISH OFFICERS. 153

son was first attacked by men brandishing swords and daggers ; his arras were pinioned, and his gold chain snatched from his neck. The Rev. Mr. Stanton and Mr. Martin perceiving that Mr. Jackson was not following returned to aid him, and were themselves seized. One of the assailants thrust a dagger at Mr. Martin's breast, two endeavoured to throw him on the ground, and, whilst struggling with them, his pockets were rifled. The same course was pursued with Mr. Jackson and Mr. Stanton. The latter lost his watch; the former still retained his, but every thing else was taken. The assailants then left us; but the persons on the wall followed us for some time, hurling large stones and using menacing gestures and opprobrious language.

" Proceeding southward beneath the wall to reach to the river side, we were again followed and attacked by another party. Mr. Jackson received a violent blow on his chest, and a roof was torn up to furnish large sticks to the assailants. In this attack Mr. Jackson was deprived of his watch; our clothes were torn ; and at one time the people were disposed to strip us. No resistance was offered: it was hopeless to have attempted it, not only by reason of the numbers and weapons of the multitude, but also on account of the attack on us from the watch tower and along the walls.

" The outrage was entirely unprovoked. Our own official character, and the presence of a minister of religion, was a guarantee for peaceful conduct;and had his presence not restrained Mr. Jackson and Mr. Martin, bloodshed might probably have ensued. Reaching a more populous part of the suburbs, we rested a moment and then proceeded home; but not unfrequently hearing opprobrious epithets, mingled with cries of 'Kill them, kill them!'

" From no nation in Europe would British subjects suffer this treatment. There can be no excuse for tolerating a continuance of such conduct towards us in China; and we think there cannot be a doubt that the Chinese government have it in their power effectually to put a stop, not only to the personal insults which the English daily experience, but also to prohibit effectually the repetition of the injuries we have experienced. By the prohibition to enter the city of Canton, the lower classes of the Chinese are encouraged to regard ua as inferiors, and to treat us with marked contumely. No measures, that we are aware of, have ever been taken by the authorities to prevent the constant insults to which the British community are subjected ; and which, instead of diminishing by time, or being subdued by acts of kindness, seem to become more frequent and more virulent.

" Anxiously desirous to maintain peace and to promote amity, we make this representation, believing that, unless the Chinese authorities remedy the evils complained of, the most serious consequences must inevitably and ere long ensue."

10

SECTION 10

Having despatched my collections to England by three different vessels from Hong-kong, I sailed again, at the end of March 1844, for the northern provinces. During the summer of this year, and in that of 1845, I was able to visit several parts of the country, which were formerly sealed to Europeans, and which contained subjects of much interest.

About the beginning of May I set out upon an excursion with Mr. Thom, the British consul, and two other gentlemen, to visit the green tea district near Ningpo. We were informed that there was a large and celebrated temple, named *Tein-tung*, in the centre of the tea district, and above twenty miles distant, where we could lodge during our stay in this part of the country. Twelve or fourteen miles of our journey was performed by water, but the canal ending at the foot of the hills we were obliged to walk, or take chairs for the re-

Mountain Chair.

mainder of the way. The mountain travelling chair of China is a very simple contrivance. It consists merely of two long bamboo poles, with a board placed between them for a seat, and two other cross pieces, one for the back and the other for the feet; a large Chinese umbrella is held over the head to afford protection from the sun and rain.

Chap. IX.] TEMPLE OF TEIN-TUNG. 157

The Chinese are quite philosophers after their own fashion. On our way to the temple, when tired with sitting so long in our boat, we several times got out and walked along the path on the sides of the canal. A great number of passage- boats going in the same direction with ourselves, and crowded with passengers, kept very near us for a considerable portion of the way, in order to satisfy their curiosity. A Chinaman never walks when he can possibly find any other mode of conveyance, and these persons were consequently much surprised to see us apparently enjoying our walk.

" Is it not strange," said one, " that these people prefer walking when they have a boat as well as ourselves ? " A discussion now took place amongst them as to the reason of this apparently strange propensity, when one, more wise than his companions, settled the matter by the pithy observation, " It is *their nature* to do so;" which was apparently satisfactory to all parties.

It was nearly dark when we reached the temple, and as the rain had fallen in torrents during the greater part of the day, we were drenched to the skin, and in rather a pitiable condition. The priests seemed much surprised at our appearance, but at once evinced the greatest hospitality and kindness, and we soon found ourselves quite at home amongst them. They brought us fire to dry our clothes, got ready our dinner, and set apart a certain number of their best rooms for us to sleep in. We were evidently subjects of great curiosity to most of them who had never seen an Englishman before. Our clothes, features, mode of eating, and manners were all subjects of wonder to these simple people, who passed off many a good humoured joke at our expence.

Glad to get off our clothes, which were still damp, we retired early to rest. When we arose in the morning, the view which met our eyes far surpassed in beauty any scenery which I had ever witnessed before in China. The temple stands at the head of a fertile valley in the bosom of the hills. This valley is well watered by clear streams, which flow from the mountains, and produces most excellent crops of rice. The tea shrubs, with their dark green leaves, are seen dotted on the lower sides of all the more fertile hills. The temple itself is approached by a long avenue of Chinese pine trees. This avenue is at first straight, but near the temple it winds in a most picturesque manner round the edges of two artificial lakes, and then ends in a flight of stone steps, which lead up to the principal entrance. Behind, and on each side, the mountains rise, in irregular ridges, from one to two thousand feet above the level of the sea. These are not like the barren southern mountains, but are clothed nearly to their summits with a dense tropical looking mass of brushwood, shrubs, and trees. Some of the finest bamboos of China are grown in the ravines, and the sombre coloured pine attains to a large size on the sides of the hills. Here, too, I

Chap. IX.] HISTORY OF THE TEAIPLE. 159

observed some very beautiful specimens of the new fir (*Cryptomeria japonica),* and obtained some plants and seeds of it, which may now be seen growing in the Horticultural Gardens at Chiswick. After we had breakfasted, one of the head priests came and gave us a very pressing invitation to dine with him about mid-day; and in the meantime he accompanied us over the monastery, of which he gave the following history:|"Many hundred years ago a pious old man retired from the world, and came to dwell in these mountains, giving himself up entirely to the performance of religious duties. So earnest was he in his devotions that he neglected everything relating to his temporal wants, even to his daily food. Providence, however, would not suffer so good a man to starve. Some boys were sent in a miraculous manner, who daily supplied him with food. In the course of time the fame of the sage extended all over the adjacent country, and disciples flocked to him from all quarters. A small range of temples was built, and thus commenced the extensive buildings which now bear the name of " Tein-tung," or the " Temple of the Heavenly Boys;" *Tein* signifying heaven, and *tung* a boy. At last the old man died, but his disciples supplied his place. The fame of the temple spread far and wide, and votaries came from the most distant parts of the empire|one of the Chinese kings being amongst the number|to worship and leave their offerings at its altars. Larger temples were built in front of the original ones, and these|again in their turn gave way to those spacious buildings which form the principal part of the structure of the present day.

All the temples are crowded with idols, or images of their favourite gods, such as the " three precious Buddhas," " the Queen of Heaven"|represented as sitting on the celebrated lotus or nelumbium| " the God of War," and many other deified kings and great men of former days. Many of these images are from thirty to forty feet in height, and have a very striking appearance when seen arranged in these spacious and lofty halls. The priests themselves reside in a range of low buildings, erected at right angles with the different temples and courts which divide them. Each has a little temple in his own house' | a family altar crowded with small images, where he is often engaged in private devotion.

After inspecting the various temples and the belfry, which contains a noble bronze bell of large dimensions, our host conducted us back to his house, where the dinner was already on the table. The priests of the Buddhist religion are not allowed to eat animal food at any of their meals. Our dinner therefore consisted entirely of vegetables, served up in the usual Chinese style, in a number of small round basins, the contents of each|soups excepted |being cut up into small square bits, to be eaten with chopsticks. The Buddhist priests contrive to procure a number of vegetables of different kinds, which, by a peculiar mode of preparation, are

Chap. IX.] FIKST TRIAL WITH CHOPSTICKS. 161

rendered very palatable. In fact, so nearly do they resemble animal food in taste and in appearance, that at first we were deceived, imagining that the little bits we were able to get hold of with our chopsticks were really pieces of fowl or beef. Such, however, was not the case, as our good host was consistent on this day at least, and had nothing but vegetable productions at his table. Several other priests sat with us at table, and a large number of others of inferior rank with servants, crowded around the doors and windows outside. The whole assemblage must have been much surprised at the awkward way in which some of us handled our chopsticks, and, with all their politeness, I observed they could not refrain from laughing when, after repeated attempts, some little dainty morsel would still slip back again into the dish. I know few things more annoying, and yet laughable too, than attempting to eat with the Chinese chopsticks for the first time, more particularly if the operator has been wandering on the hills all the morning, and is ravenously hungry. The instruments should first of all be balanced between the thumb and forefinger of the right hand; the points are next to be brought carefully together, just leaving as much room as will allow the coveted morsel to go in between them; the little bit is then to be neatly seized; but alas! in the act of lifting the hand, one point of the chopstick too often slips past the other, and the object of all our hopes drops back again into the dish, or perhaps even into another

dish on the table. Again and again the same operation is tried, until the poor novice loses all patience, throws down the chopsticks in despair, and seizes a porcelain spoon, with which he is more successful. In cases like these the Chinese themselves are very obliging, although scarcely in a way agreeable to an Englishman's taste. Your Chinese friend, out of kindness and politeness, when he sees the dilemma in which you are, reaches across the table and seizes, with his own chopsticks, which have just come out of his mouth, the wished-for morsel, and with them lays it on the plate before you. In common politeness you must express your gratitude and swallow the offering.

During dinner our host informed us that there were about a hundred priests connected with the monastery, but that many were always absent on missions to various parts of the country. On questioning him as to the mode by which the establishment was supported, he informed us that a considerable portion of land in the vicinity belonged to the temple, and that large sums were yearly raised from the sale of bamboos, which are here very excellent, and of the branches of trees and brush wood, which are made up in bundles for firewood. A number of tea and rice farms also belong to the priests, which they themselves cultivate. Besides the sums raised by the sale of these productions, a considerable revenue must be derived from the contributions of the devotees who resort to the temple for religious purposes, as well as from the

Chap. IX.] USUAL DINNER COMPANY. 163

sums collected by those of the order who are out on begging excursions at stated seasons of the year. The priests are of course of all grades, some of them being merely the servants of the others, both in the house and in the fields. They seem a harmless and simple race, but are dreadfully ignorant and superstitious. The typhoon of the previous year, or rather the rain which had accompanied it, had occasioned a large slip of earth on one of the hill-sides near the temple, and completely buried ten or twelve acres of excellent paddy land. On our remarking this, the priests told us with great earnestness that every one said it was a bad omen for the temple; but one of them with true Chinese politeness remarked that he had no doubt any evil influence would now be counteracted, since the temple had been honoured with a visit from us.

After inspecting the tea farms and the mode of manufacturing it, Mr. Thom, Mr. Morrison, a son of the late Dr. Morrison, and Mr. Sinclair, returned to Ningpo, leaving me to prosecute my research in natural history in this part of the country. I was generally absent from the temple the whole day, returning at dark with the collections of plants and birds which I had been lucky enough to meet with in my peregrinations. The friends of the priests came from all quarters of the adjacent country to see the foreigner; and, as in the case of a wild animal, my feeding time seemed to be the most interesting moment to them. My dinner was placed on a round table in the centre of the room, and although rather curiously concocted, being half Chinese and half English, the exercise and fresh air of the mountains gave me a keen appetite. The difficulties of the chopsticks were soon got over, and I was able to manage them nearly as well as the Chinese themselves. The priests and their friends filled the chairs, which are always placed down the sides of a Chinese hall, each man with his pipe in his mouth, and his cup of tea by his side. With all deference to my host and his friends, I was obliged to request the smoking to be stopped, as it was disagreeable to me while at dinner; in other respects, I believe I was " polite " enough. I shall never forget how inexpressibly lonely I felt the first night after the departure of my friends. The Chinese one by one dropt off to their homes or to bed, and at last my host himself gave several unequivocal yawns, which reminded me that it was time to retire for the night. My bed-room was upstairs, and to get to it I had to pass through a small temple, such as I have already noticed, dedicated to *Tein-hoiv,* or the ': Queen of Heaven," and crowded with other idols. Incense was burning on the altar in front of the idols ; a solitary lamp shed a dim light over the objects in the room, and a kind of solemn stillness seemed to pervade the whole place. In the room below, and also in one in an adjoining house, I could hear the priests engaged in their devotional exercises, in that singing tone which is peculiar to them. Then the sounds of the gong fell upon my ears; and, at intervals, a single solemn toll of the

Chap. IX.] ATTENTIONS OF THE PRIESTS. 165

large bronze bell in the belfry; all which showed that the priests were engaged in public as well as private devotion. Amidst scenes of this kind, in a strange country, far from friends and home, impressions are apt to be made upon the mind, which remain vivid through life; and I feel convinced I shall never forget the strange mixture of feelings which filled my mind during the first night of my stay with the priests in the temple of Tein-tung. I have visited the place often since, passed through the same little temple, slept in the same bed, and heard the same solemn sounds throughout the silent watches of the night, and yet the first impressions remain in my mind distinct and single.

The priests, from the highest to the lowest, always showed me the most marked attention and kindness. As many of them as I wished cheerfully followed me in my excursions in the vicinity of the temple; one carrying my specimen paper, another my plants, and a third my birds, and so on. The gun seemed an object of great interest to them, being so different from their own clumsy matchlocks; and percussion caps were looked upon as most magical little objects. But they were great cowards, and always kept at a most respectful distance when I was shooting.

One evening a deputation, headed by the high priest, came and informed me that the wild boars had come down from the mountains at night, and were destroying the young shoots of the bamboo, which were then just coming through the ground,and were in the state in which they are highly prized as a vegetable for the table. " Well," said I, " what do you want me to do ?"

" Will you be good enough to lend us the gun ?" " Yes; there it stands in the corner of the
room."

" Oh, but you must load it for us."

" Very well, I will;" and I immediately loaded the gun with ball. " There, but take care and don't shoot yourselves." There was now a long pause; none had sufficient courage to take the gun, and a long consultation was held between them. At length the spokesman came forward, with great gravity, and told me they were afraid to fire it off, but that if I would go with them, and shoot the boar, I should have it to eat. This was certainly no great sacrifice on the part of the Buddhist priesthood, who do not, or at least should not, eat animal food. We now sallied forth in a body to fight the wild boars; but the night was so dark that we could see nothing in the bamboo ravines, and, perhaps, the noise made by about thirty priests and servants warned the animals to retire to the brushwood higher up the hills. Be that as it may, we could neither see nor hear any thing of them, and I confess I was rather glad, than otherwise, as I thought there was a considerable chance of my shooting, by mistake, a priest instead of a wild boar.

The priests have two modes of protecting their property from the ravages of these animals. Deep

Chap. IX.] NARROW ESCAPE. 167

pits are dug on the hill sides, and, as there are springs in almost all these places, the pits are scarcely finished before they are half full of water. The mouth of each pit is then covered over with a quantity of sticks, rubbish, and grass, to attract the animal, and no sooner does he begin to bore into it with his snout, than the whole gives way, and he is plunged, head foremost, into the pit, from which it is quite impossible for him to extricate himself, and he is either drowned or becomes an easy prey to the Chinese. These pits are most dangerous traps to persons unacquainted with the localities in which they are placed. I had several narrow escapes, and once in particular, when coming out of a dense mass of brushwood, I stept unawares on the treacherous mouth of one of them, and felt the ground under my feet actually giving way; but managing to throw my arms forward I caught hold of a small twig which was growing near, and by this means supported myself until I was able to scramble on to firmer ground. On turning back to examine the place, I found that the loose rubbish had sunk in, and a deep pit, half full of water, was exposed to my view. The pit was made narrow at the mouth and widening inside like a great China vase, being constructed in this manner to prevent the boar from scrambling out when once fairly in it. Had I fallen in, it would have been next to impossible to have extricated myself without assistance, and as the pits are generally dug in the most retired and wild part of the mountains, my chance would have been a bad one. The fate of my predecessor, Mr. Douglas, who perished in a pit of this kind on the Sandwich Islands, must still be fresh in the recollection of many of my readers, and his melancholy end naturally coining to my mind at the time made me doubly thankful for my escape.

The other method of protecting the young bamboos from the ravages of the wild boar is an ingenious one. A piece of bamboo wood, about eight or ten feet long, and rather thicker than a man's arm, is split up the middle to within a fourth of its length. This is made fast to a tree in the bamboo thicket, and at an angle of about forty-five degrees, the split part being left loose, a cord, also made of bamboo, is fastened to it by one end, and the other is led to some convenient place out of the thicket, where a man is stationed. When the boars come down in the dead of night to attack the young shoots, the man pulls the rope backwards and forwards, and clank, clank, clank goes the bamboo, producing a loud and hollow sound, which on a quiet evening may be heard at a great distance. The animals are frightened and make off to their dens on the hills. The first time I heard these things beating at night, all over the country, I imagined that some religious ceremony was going on, the hollow sounds of the bamboo being not unlike those produced by an instrument used in the Buddhist worship in all Chinese temples.

There are a large number of Buddhist temples

Chap. IX.] MOUNTAIN SCENERY. 169

scattered over all this part of the country. One, named *Ah-yu-wang,* which I also visited, is, like *Tein-tung,* of great extent, and seemingly well supported. They both own large tracts of land in the vicinity of the monasteries, and have numerous small temples in different parts of the district which are under their control. All the temples, both large and small, are built in the most romantic and beautiful situations amongst the hills, and the neighbouring woods are always preserved and encouraged. What would indicate the residence of a country gentleman in England, is in China the sign of a Buddhist temple, and this holds good over all the country. When the weary traveller, therefore, who has been exposed for hours to the fierce rays of an eastern sun, sees a large clean-looking house showing itself amongst trees on the distant hill-side, he may be almost certain that it is one of Buddha's temples, where the priests will treat him not only with courtesy, but with kindness.

Poo-to, or the Worshipping Island, as it is commonly called by foreigners, is one of the eastern islands in the Chusan Archipelago, and seems to be the capital or stronghold of Buddhism in this part of China. This island is not more than five or six miles in circumference, and, although hilly, its sides and small ravines are pretty well wooded, particularly in the vicinity of the numerous temples. As it is only a few hours' sail from Chusan, it had been visited at different times by a number of our officers during the war, all of whom spoke highly of its natural beauties and richness of vegetation. I was also informed that the resident priests were fond of collecting plants, particularly Orchidacese, and that their collections were much increased by the itinerant habits of the begging priests, who visit the most distant provinces of the empire, as well as by the donations of the lay devotees, who come to Poo-to at stated seasons of the year, to worship and leave their offerings in the temples. I therefore determined to visit the place in order to judge for myself, and accordingly set out in July, 1844, accompanied by my friend Dr. Maxwell, of the Madras army.

Leaving Chusan at night, with the tide in our favour, we reached the island at sun-rise on the following morning. We landed, and pursued our way over a hill and down on the other side by a road which led us into a beautiful and romantic glen. It is here that the principal group of temples is built, and when we first caught a glimpse of them, as we wended our way down the hill, they seemed like a town of considerable size. As we approached nearer, the view became highly interesting. In front there was a large artificial pond, filled with the broad green leaves and noble red and white flowers of the *Nelumbium speciosum,* | a plant in high favour with the Chinese. Every body who went to Poo-to admired these beautiful water-lilies. In order to reach the monastery we crossed a very ornamental bridge built over this pond, which, when viewed in a line with an old tower close by, has a pretty and striking appearance.

Chap. IX.] POO-TO-SAN | ITS TEMPLES AND IDOLS. 171

The temples or halls which contain the idols are extremely spacious, and resemble those which I have already described at *Tein-tung* and *Ah-yu- Wang*. These idols, many of which are thirty or forty feet in height, are generally made of wood or clay, and then richly gilt. There is one small temple, however, of a very unassuming appearance, where we met with some exquisite bronze statues, which would be considered of great value in England. These, of course, were much smaller than the others, but, viewed as works of art, they were by far the finest which I saw during my travels in China.

Having examined these temples, we pursued our way towards another assemblage of them, about two miles to the eastward and close on the seashore. We entered the courts through a kind of triumphal arch, which looks out upon the sea, and found that these temples were constructed upon the same plan as all the others. As we had determined to make this part of the island our home during our stay, we fixed upon the cleanest looking temple, and asked the High Priest to allow us, without farther delay, to put our beds and travelling baggage into it.

On the following day we inspected various parts of the island. Besides the large temples just noticed, there are about sixty or seventy smaller ones, built on all the hill sides, each of which contains three or four priests, who are all under the superior, or abbot, who resides near one of the large temples.Even on the top of the highest hill, probably 1500 or 1800 feet above the level of the sea, we found a temple of considerable size and in excellent repair. There are winding stone steps from the sea-beach all the way up to this temple, and a small resting- place about half way up the hill, where the weary devotee may rest and drink of the refreshing stream which flows down the sides of the mountain, and in the little temple close at hand, which is also crowded with idols, he can supplicate Buddha for strength to enable him to reach the end of his journey. We were surprised to find a Buddhist temple in such excellent order as the one on the summit of the hill proved to be in. It is a striking fact, that almost all these places are crumbling fast into ruins. There are a few exceptions, in cases where they happen to get a good name amongst the people from the supposed kindness of the gods; but the great mass are in a state of decay.

From the upper temple on Poo-to-san the view is strikingly grand. Rugged mountains are seen rising one above another and capped with clouds. Hundreds of islands, some fertile, others rocky and barren, lay scattered over the sea. When we looked in one direction amongst the islands, the water was yellow and muddy; but, to the eastward, the deep blue ocean had resumed its usual colour, and the line between the yellow waters and the blue was distinctly and curiously marked.

The wood on the island is preserved in the same manner as it is around all the other Buddhist

Chap. IX.] POO-TO-SAN | ITS TREES AND SHRUBS. 173

temples. The principal species of trees and shrubs met with are *Pinus sinensis, Cunningham lanceolata,* yews, cypresses, the camphor tree, tallow tree, oaks and bamboos. The *Camellia japonica* grows spontaneously in the woods, where we met with many specimens from twenty to thirty feet in height and with stems thick in proportion. The variety, however, was only the well-known single red. In other respects the flora of Poo-to is nearly the same as on the island of Chusan.

A few pet plants were cultivated by all the priests who were fortunate enough to have private residences at the little temples on the sides of the hills. We were much pleased with the interest these poor people took in their favourite flowers, but were disappointed in the number and variety of plants, which, from the reports of others, we expected to have found. Almost the only orchidaceous plant which they had proved to be the common and well-known *Cymbidium sinense. Daphne odorata,* two or three species of *Gardenia,* several varieties of Rose, the common Balsam, and the favourite *Nelumbium,* were nearly all the plants met twith in the gardens of the priests.

The island of Poo to is set apart entirely as a residence for the priests of the Buddhist religion. Few other persons are allowed to live there, and these are either servants or in some way connected with the priests. No women are permitted to reside on the island, it being against the principles of the Buddhists to allow their priests to marry. The

number of priests is estimated at 2000, but many of them are constantly absent on begging expeditions for the support of their religion. This establishment, like *Tein-tung,* has also a portion of land allotted to it for its support, and the remainder of the funds are made up by the subscriptions of the devotees. On certain high days, at different periods of the year, many thousands of both sexes, but particularly females, resort to these temples, clad in their best attire, to pay their vows and engage in the other exercises of heathen worship. Little stalls are then seen in the temples or at the doorways for the sale of incense, candles, paper made up in the form of the ingots of Sycee-silver, and other holy things which are considered acceptable offerings to the gods, and are either consumed in the temples or carried home to bring a blessing upon the houses and families of those who purchase them. The proBts of these sales, of course, go to the support of the establishment. When we consider that these poor deluded people sometimes travel a distance of several hundred miles to worship in the temples on Poo-to-san and other celebrated places, we cannot but admire their spirit of devotion. I was once staying in the temple of *Tein-tung* when it was visited for three days by devotees from all parts of the country. As they lined the roads on their way to the temple, clad in the graceful and flowing costume of the East, the mind was naturally led back to those days of scripture history when Jerusalem was in its glory, and the Jews, the chosen

Chap. IX.] RELIGIOUS CEREMONIES AT POO-TO. 175

people of God, came from afar to worship in its temple.

Although no Christian can look upon the priests and devotees of the Buddhist creed without an eye of pity, yet he must give them credit for their conduct, since he has every reason to believe them sincere, and I am inclined to believe that justice has not been done them in this respect. Mr. Gutzlaff, in describing his visit to Poo-to, is of a different opinion. He says, " We were present at the vespers of the priests, which they chanted in the Pali language, not unlike the Latin service of the Romish church. They held rosaries in their hands, which rested folded upon their breasts. One of them had a small bell, by the tinkling of which their service was regulated; and they occasionally beat the drum and large bell to rouse Buddha's attention to their prayers. The same words were a hundred times repeated. *None of the officiating persons shoiced any interest in the ceremony,* for some were looking around laughing and joking, while others muttered their prayers. The few people who were present, not to attend the worship, but to gaze at us, did not seem, in the least degree, to feel the solemnity of the service." What Mr. Gutzlaff says is doubtless true, but after residing for months in their temples, at different times, and in different parts of the country, I have no hesitation in saying that such conduct is very far from being general. In certain instances I have seen it myself, but this levity and apparent want of attention was exhibitedby the servants and lookers-on, who were taking no part in the ceremony, and not by the respectable portion of the priests. On the contrary, I have generally been struck with the solemnity with which their devotional exercises were conducted. I have often walked into Chinese temples when the priests were engaged in prayer, and, although there would have been some apology for them had their attention been diverted, they went on in the most solemn manner until the conclusion of the service, as if no foreigner were present. They then came politely up to me, examining my dress and every thing about me with the most earnest curiosity. Nor does this apply to priests only; the laity, and particularly the female sex, seem equally sincere when they engage in their public devotions. Whether they are what they appear to be, or how often they are in this pious frame of mind, are questions which I cannot answer. Before judging harshly of the Chinese let the reader consider what effect would be produced upon the members of a *Christian* church by the unexpected entrance of a small-footed Chinese lady, or a Mandarin, with the gold button and peacock feather mounted on his hat, and his long tail dangling over his shoulders. I am far from being an admirer of the Buddhist priesthood; they are generally an imbecile race, and shamefully ignorant of every thing but the simple forms of their religion, but nevertheless there are many traits in their character not unworthy of imitation.

Chap. IX.] RELIGIOUS SECTS OF THE CHINESE. 177

There are two other sects in China, namely, the followers of *Kong-foo-tze* or Confucius, and the sect of *Taou* or Reason. Although these three sects form the principal part of the population, it is well known that there are a great number of

Mohammedans in every part of the empire, who are not only tolerated, but admitted to offices under government in the same manner as the members of the three established sects. Jews also are found in several districts, but more particularly at a place called Kae-foong-foo, in the province of Honan.

The various religious ceremonies which the Chinese are continually performing prove at least that they are very superstitious. In all the southern towns every house has its temple or altar both inside and outside. The altar in the inside is generally placed at the end of the principal hall or shop, as the case may be, raised a few feet from the ground, and having some kind of representation of the family deity placed upon it. This is surrounded with gaudy tinsel paper, and on the first of the Chinese month or other high days candles and incense are burned on the table which is placed in front of it. The altar on the outside of the door resembles a little furnace, in which the same ceremonies are regularly performed. In the vicinity of small villages, and sometimes in the most retired situations, the stranger meets with little joss- houses or temples, gaudily decorated with paintings and tinsel paper, and stuck round about with

the remains of candles and sticks of incense. In almost all Chinese towns there are shops for the sale of idols of all kinds and sizes, varying in price from a few " cash " to a very large sum. Many of those exposed for sale are of great age, and have evidently changed hands several times. I am inclined to believe that the Chinese exchange those gods which do not please them for others of higher character, and which they suppose are more likely to grant an answer to their prayers, or bring prosperity to their homes or their villages.

The periodical offerings to the gods are very striking exhibitions to the stranger who looks upon them for the first time. When staying at Shanghae, in November, 1844, I witnessed a most curious spectacle in the house where I was residing. It was a family offering to the gods. Early in the morning the principal hall in the house was set in order, a large table was placed in the centre, and shortly afterwards covered with small dishes filled with the various articles commonly used as food by the Chinese. All these were of the very best description which could be procured. After a certain time had elapsed a number of candles were lighted, and columns of smoke and fragrant odours began to rise from the incense which was burning on the table. All the inmates of the house and their friends were clad in their best attire, and in turn came to *Ko-tou,* or bow lowly and repeatedly in front of the table and the alter. The scene, although it was an idolatrous one, seemed to me to

Chap. IX.] OFFERINGS TO THE GODS. 179

have something very impressive about it, and whilst I pitied the delusion of our host and his friends, I could not but admire their devotion. In a short time after this ceremony was completed a large quantity of tinsel paper, made up in the form and shape of the ingots of Sycee silver common in China, was heaped on the floor in front of the tables, the burning incense was then taken from the table and placed in the midst of it, and the whole consumed together. By and by, when the gods were supposed to have finished their repast, all the articles of food were removed from the tables, cut up, and consumed by people connected with the family.

On another occasion, when at Ning-po, having been out some distance in the country, it was night and dark before I reached the east gate of the city, near which I was lodged in the house of a Chinese merchant. The city gates were closed, but two or three loud knocks soon brought the warder, who instantly admitted me. I was now in the widest and finest street in the city, which seemed in a blaze of light and unusually lively for any part of a Chinese town after nightfall. The sounds of music fell upon my ear, the gong, the drum, and the more plaintive and pleasing tones of several wind instruments. I was soon near enough to observe what was going on, and saw, at a glance, that it was a public offering to the gods, but far grander and more striking than I had before witnessed. The table was spread in the open street, and every thing was on a large and expensive scale. Instead of small dishes, whole animals were sacrificed on the occasion. A pig was placed on one side of the table, and a sheep on the other, the former scraped clean, in the usual way, and the latter skinned ; the entrails of both were removed, and on each were placed some flowers, an onion, and a knife. The other parts of the table groaned with all the delicacies in common use amongst the respectable portion of the Chinese, such as fowls, ducks, numerous compound dishes, fruits, vegetables, and rice. Chairs were placed at one end of the table on which the gods were supposed to sit during the meal, and chopsticks were regularly laid at the sides of the different dishes. A blaze of light illuminated the whole place, and the smoke of the fragrant incense rose up into the air in wreaths. At intervals the band struck up their favourite plaintive national airs, and altogether the whole scene was one of the strangest and most curious which it has ever been my lot to witness.

There is another ceremony of a religious character which I frequently observed in the northern cities | I allude to processions in honour of the gods. I saw one of them at Shanghae, which must have been at least a mile in length. The gods, or josses, were dressed up in the finest silks, and carried about in splendid sedan chairs, preceded and succeeded by their numerous devotees, superbly dressed for the occasion, and bearing the

Chap. IX.] IN SHANGHAE AND NING-PO. 181

different badges of office. The dresses of the officials were exactly the same as of those who form the train of some of the high mandarins. Some had a broad fan, made of peacock feathers, which they wore on the sides of their hats, others were clad in glaring theatrical dresses, with low caps, and two long black feathers stuck in them, and hanging over their shoulders like two horns. Then there were the ill-looking executioners with long, conical, black hats on their heads, and whips in their hands for the punishment of the refractory. Bands of music, placed in different parts of the procession, played at intervals as it proceeded. Anxious to see the end of this curious exhibition, I followed the procession until it arrived at a temple in the suburbs, where it halted. The gods were taken out of the sedan-chairs, and replaced, with due honours, in the temple, from which they had been taken in the morning. Here their numerous votaries bent low before them, burned incense, and left their gifts upon the altar. Numerous groups of well-dressed ladies and their children were scattered over the ground in the vicinity of the temple, all bending their knees and seemingly engaged in earnest devotion. A large quantity of paper, in the form of the Sycee ingots, was heaped up on the grass as it was brought by the different devotees, and, when the ceremonies of the day were drawing to a close, the whole was burned in honour of, or as an offering to, the gods. The sight was interesting, but itwas one which no Christian could look upon without feelings of the deepest commiseration.

In the course of my travels in China I often met with Christian missionaries, both Protestant and Roman Catholic, who have been labouring amongst the Chinese for many years. Until very lately the efforts of the Protestants had been chiefly confined to Macao and Canton. Since the war, however, they have had an opportunity of extending their operations, and some are now settled at all the new ports which have been opened for foreign trade, as well as on our island of Hongkong, which will now become their head-quarters.

The medical missionaries also act in conjunction with the others, and are of great use in curing many of the diseases which prevail in the country, while, at the same time, the truths of the Christian faith are presented to the minds of their patients. Dr. Lockhart of the London Missionary Society, who has established himself in the town of Shang- hae, had his hospital daily crowded with patients, many of whom had come from very distant parts of the country. All were attended to in the most skilful and careful manner, "without money and without price." The Rev. Mr. Medhurst, who has laboured long and zealously as a Christian missionary in the East, was also at Shanghae. This gentleman is well known as an eminent Chinese scholar, and, besides preaching to the people in their own tongue, he has a printing establishment with Chinese type continually at work, for the

Chap. IX.] MEDICAL MISSIONARY SOCIETY. 183

dissemination of the truths of the Gospel. Several other gentlemen and their families had arrived at the same port previous to my departure, and were closely engaged in the study of the language. Ning-po and Amoy were also occupied by missionaries both from England and America, and I suppose, ere this time, some have also reached Foo-chow-foo on the River Min.

From my own experience of Chinese character, and from what I have seen of the working of the Medical Missionary Society, I am convinced that it must be a powerful auxiliary to the missionaries in the conversion of the Chinese. I regret, however, to say, that up to the present time little progress appears to have been made. One portion of the people, and a large one, is entirely indifferent to religion of any kind, and the rest are so bigoted and conceited, that it will be a most difficult task to convince them that any religion is better or purer than their own.

The Roman Catholic missionaries conduct their operations in a manner somewhat different from the Protestants. They do not restrict themselves to the out-ports of the empire, where foreigners are permitted to trade, but penetrate into the interior, and distribute themselves over all the country. One of their bishops, an Italian nobleman, resides in the province of Keang-soo, a few miles from Shanghae, where I have frequently met him. He dresses in the costume of the country, and speaks the language with the most perfect fluency. Inthe place where he lives he is surrounded by his converts; in fact it is a little Christian village, where he is perfectly safe, and I believe is seldom if ever annoyed in any way by the Chinese authorities. When new Roman Catholic missionaries arrive, they are met by some of their brethren or their converts at the port nearest their destination, and secretly conveyed into the interior; the Chinese dress is substituted for the European ; their heads are shaved, and in this state they are conducted to the scene of their future labours, where they commence the study of the language, if they have not learned it before, and in about two years are able to speak it sufficiently well to enable them to instruct the people. These poor men submit to many privations and dangers for the cause they have espoused, and although I do not approve of the doctrines which they teach, I must give them the highest praise for enthusiasm and devotion to their faith. European customs, habits, and luxuries are all abandoned from the moment they put their feet on the shores of China; parents, friends, and home, in many instances, are heard of no more; before them lies a heathen land of strangers, cold and unconcerned about the religion for which they themselves are sacrificing everything, and they know that their graves will be far away from the land of their birth and the home of their early years. They seem to have much of the spirit and enthusiasm of the first preachers of the Christian religion, when they were

Chap. IX.] ROMAN CATHOLIC MISSIONARIES. 185

sent out into the world by their Divine Master to " preach the Gospel to every creature," and " to obey God rather than man."

According to the accounts of these missionaries, the numbers of converts to their faith is very considerable ; but I fear they, as well as the Protestants, are often led away by false appearances and assertions. Many of the Chinese are unprincipled and deceitful enough to become Christians or in fact any thing else, in name, to accomplish the object they may have in view, and they would become Buddhists the very next day should any inducement be offered them to do so. Judging from appearances, the day must yet be very distant when the Chinese, as a nation, will be converted to the Christian faith. Could those individuals in our time, who predict the near approach of the Millennium, see the length and breadth of this vast country, with its three hundred millions of souls, they would surely pause and reflect before they published their absurd and foolish predictions.

11

SECTION 11

CHAP. X.

THE TEA-PLANT OF CHINA. I THE SPECIES FOUND IN THE GREEN AND BLACK TEA DISTRICTS. I BEST SITUATION FOR TEA PLANTATIONS. RE-MARKS ON THEIR MANAGEMENT. I SEASONS,
AND METHOD, OF GATHERING THE LEAVES. MANUFACTURE
OF TEA COTTAGES AMONGST THE TEA HILLS. FURNACES,
AND DRYING PANS. FIRST APPLICATION OF HEAT. I ROLLING
PROCESS. EXPOSURE OF THE LEAVES TO THE AIR. I SECOND
HEATING. LENGTH OF TIME REQUIRED TWO KINDS OF TEA.
DIFFERENCE IN THE MANUFACTURE OF EACH. SELECTING AND PACK-ING TEAS. APPEARANCE AND COLOUR OF
THE LEAF. I PECULIAR TASTE OF FOREIGNERS FOR DrED
TEAS. I GOOD SENSE OF THE CHINESE. MR. WARINGTON's
EXPERIMENTS.

There are few subjects connected with the vegetable kingdom which have attracted such a large share of public notice as the tea-plant of China. Its cultivation on the Chinese hills, the particular species or variety which produces the black and green teas of commerce, and the method of preparing the leaves, have always been objects of peculiar interest. The jealousy of the Chinese government, in former times, prevented foreigners from visiting any of the districts where tea is cultivated, and the information derived from the Chinese merchants, even scanty as it was, was not to be depended upon. And hence we find our English authors contradicting each other, some asserting

Chap. X.] TEA DISTRICTS VISITED. 187

that the black and green trees are produced by the same variety, and that the difference in colour is the result of a different mode of preparation, while others say that the black teas are produced from the plant called by botanists *Thea Bohea*, and the green from *Thea viridis*, both of which we have had for many years in our gardens in England.

During my travels in China since the last war, I have had frequent opportunities of inspecting some extensive tea districts in the black and green tea countries of Canton, Fokien, and Chekiang, and the result of these observations is now laid before the reader. It will prove that even those who have had the best means of judging have been deceived, and that the greater part of the black and green teas which are brought yearly from China to Europe and America are obtained from the same species or variety, namely, from the *Thea viridis*. Dried specimens of this plant were prepared in the districts I have named by myself, and are now in the herbarium of the Horticultural Society of London, so that there can be no longer any doubt upon the subject.

In various parts of the Canton province, where I had an opportunity of seeing tea cultivated, the species proved to be the *Thea Bohea*, or what is commonly called the black tea plant. In the green tea districts of the north I I allude more particularly to the province of Chekiang I never met with a single plant of this species, which is so common in the fields and gardens near Canton. All the plants in the green tea country near Ning-po, on the Islands of the Chusan Archipelago, and in every part of the province which I had an opportunity of visiting, proved, without exception, to be the *Thea viridis*. Two hundred miles further to the north-west, in the province of Kiang-nan, and only a short distance from the tea hills in that quarter, I also found in gardens this same species of tea.

Thus far my actual observation exactly verified the opinions I had formed on the subject before I left England, viz. that the black teas were prepared from the *Thea Bohea*, and the green from *Thea viridis*. When I left the north, on my way to the city of Foo-chow-foo, on the River Min, in the province of Fokien, I had no doubt that I should find the tea hills there covered with the other species, *Thea Bohea*, from which we generally suppose the black teas are made ; and this was the more likely to be the case as this species actually derives its specific name from the Bohee hills in this province. Great was my surprise to find all the plants on the tea hills near Foo-chow exactly the same as those in the green tea districts of the north. Here were then green tea plantations on the black tea hills, and not a single plant of the Thea Bohea to be seen. Moreover, at the time of my visit, the natives were busily employed in the *manufacture* of *black teas*. Although the specific differences of the tea-plants were well known to me, I was so much surprised, and I may add amused, at

12

SECTION 12

---

this discovery, that I procured a set of specimens for the herbarium, and also dug up a living plant, which I took northward to Chekiang. On comparing it with those which grow on the green tea hills, no difference whatever was observed.

It appears, therefore, that the black and green teas of the northern districts of China (those districts in which the greater part of the teas for the foreign markets are made) are both produced from the same variety, and that that variety is the *TJiea viridis,* or, what is commonly called the green tea plant. On the other hand, those black and green teas which are manufactured in considerable quantities in the vicinity of Canton are obtained from the *Thea Bohea,* or black tea. And, really, when we give the subject our unprejudiced consideration, there seems nothing surprising in this state of things. Moreover, we must bear in mind that our former opinions were formed upon statements made to us by the Chinese at Canton, who will say any thing which suits their purpose, and rarely give themselves any trouble to ascertain whether the information they communicate be true or false.

The soil of the tea districts is, of course, much richer in the northern provinces than it is in Quan- tung. In Fokien and Chekiang it is a rich sandy loam, very different from the sample which will be found noticed in the chapter on climate and soil. Tea shrubs will not succeed well unless they have a rich soil to grow in. The continual gathering of their leaves is very detrimental to theirhealth, and, in fact, ultimately kills them. Hence a principal object with the grower is to keep his bushes in as robust health as possible; and this cannot be done if the soil be poor.

The tea plantations in the north of China are always situated on the lower and most fertile sides of the hills, and never on the low lands. The shrubs are planted in rows about four feet apart and about the same distance between each row, and look, at a distance, like little shrubberies of evergreens.

The farms are small, each consisting of from one to four or five acres; indeed, every cottager has his own little tea garden, the produce of which supplies the wants of his family, and the surplus brings him in a few dollars, which are spent on the other necessaries of life. The same system is practised in every thing relating to Chinese agriculture. The cotton, silk, and rice farms are generally all small and managed upon the same plan. There are few sights more pleasing than a Chinese family in the interior engaged in gathering the tea leaves, or, indeed, in any of their other agricultural pursuits. There is the old man, it may be the grandfather, or even the great-grandfather, patriarch like, directing his descendants in the labours of the field. Many of them are in their youth and prime, while others are in their childhood. He stands in the midst of them, bowed down with age. But, to the honour of the Chinese as a nation, he is always looked up to by all with pride and affection, and his old age

Chap. X.] REMARKS ON THEIR MANAGEMENT. 191

and grey hairs are honoured, revered, and loved. When, after the labours of the day are over, they return to their humble and happy homes, their fare consists chiefly of rice, fish, and vegetables, which they enjoy with great zest, and are happy and contented. I really believe that there is no country in the world where the agricultural population are better *off* than they are in the north of China. Labour with them is pleasure, for its fruits are eaten by themselves, and the rod of the oppressor is unfelt and unknown.

In the green tea districts of Chekiang near Ning-po, the first crop of leaves is generally gathered about the middle of April. This consists of the young leaf-buds just as they begin to unfold, and forms a fine and delicate kind of young hyson , which is held in high estimation by the natives, and is generally sent about in small quantities as presents to their friends. It is a scarce and expensive article, and the picking of the leaves in such a young state does considerable injury to the tea plantations. The summer rains, however, which fall copiously about this season, moisten the earth and air, and if the plants are young and vigorous they soon push out fresh leaves.

In a fortnight or three weeks from the time of the first picking, or about the beginning of May, the shrubs are again covered with fresh leaves,and are ready for the second gathering, which is, in fact, the most important of the season. The third and last gathering, which takes place as soon as new leaves are formed, produces a very inferior kind of tea, which, I believe, is rarely sent out of the district.

This is what is called Russian tea in England.

The mode of gathering and preparing the leaves of the tea-plants is extremely simple. We have been so long accustomed to magnify and mystify every thing relating to the Chinese, that, in all their arts and manufactures, we expect to find some peculiar and out of the way practice, when the fact is, that many operations in China are more simple in their character than in most other parts of the world. To rightly understand the process of rolling and drying the leaves, which I am about to describe, it must be borne in mind that the grand object is to expel the moisture, and at the same time to retain as much as possible of the aromatic and other desirable secretions of the species. The system adopted to attain this end is as simple as it is efficacious

In the harvest seasons the natives are seen in little family groups on the side of every hill, when the weather is dry, engaged in gathering the tea leaves. They do not seem so particular, as I imagined they would have been, in this operation, but strip the leaves off rapidly and promiscuously, and throw them all into round baskets made for the purpose out of split bamboo or rattan. In the beginning of May, when the principal gathering takes place,

Chap. X.] MANUFACTURE OF TEA. 193

the young seed-vessels are about as large as peas. These are also stripped off and dried with the leaves; it is these seed-vessels which we often see in our tea, and which have some slight resemblance to young capers. When a sufficient quantity of leaves are gathered, they are carried home to the cottage or barn, where the operation of drying is performed.

The Chinese cottages, amongst the tea hills, are simple and rude in their construction, and remind one of what we used to see in Scotland in former years, when the cow and pig lived and fed in the same house with the peasant. Scottish cottages, however, even in these days, were always better furnished and more comfortable than those of the Chinese are at the present time. Nevertheless, it is in these poor cottages that a large proportion of the teas, with their high-sounding names, are first prepared. Barns, sheds, and other outhouses, are also frequently used for the same purpose, particularly about the temples and monasteries.

The drying pans and furnaces in these places are very simply constructed. The pans, which are of iron, and are made as thin as possible, are round and shallow, and, in fact, are the same, or nearly the same, which the natives have in general use for cooking their rice. A row of these are built into brick-work and chunam, having a flue constructed below them, with the grating, or rather fire-place, at one end, and the chimney, or, at least, some hole to allow the smoke to escape, at

the other. A chimney is a secondary consideration with the Chinese, and in many instances which came under my observation, the smoke, after passing below the drying pans, was allowed to escape, as it best could, through the doors and roofs of the houses, which, indeed, in China, is no difficult matter.

When the pans are first fixed, the brick-work and chunam are smoothed off very neatly round their edges and carried up a little higher, particularly at the back of the pans, at the same time widening gradually. When complete, the whole has the appearance of a row of large high-backed basins, each being three or four times larger than the shallow iron pan which is placed at its bottom, immediately over the flue. When the fire is applied, the upper part of these basins, which is formed of chunam, gets heated as well as the iron pan, though in a less degree. The drying pans, thus formed, being low in front, and rising very gradually at the sides and back, the person, whose duty it is to attend to the drying of the leaves, can readily manage them, and scatter them about over the back of the basin. The accompanying sketch, which was made on the spot, will render this description more clear.

The leaves having been brought in from the hills are placed in the cottage or drying-house. It is now the duty of one individual to light the little fire at the mouth of the flue, and to regulate it as nicely as possible. The pans become hot very

Chap. X.] FURNACES AND DRYING PANS.

soon after the warm air has begun to circulate in the flue beneath them. A quantity of leaves, from a

Furnaces and Drying Puns.

sieve or basket, are now thrown into the pans, and turned over, shaken up, and kept in motion by men and women stationed there for this purpose. The leaves are immediately affected by the heat. They begin to crack, and become quite moist with the vapour or sap which they give out on the application of the heat. This part of the process lasts about five minutes, in which time the leaves lose their crispness, and become soft and pliable. They are then taken out of the pans, and thrownupon a table, the upper part of which is made of split pieces of bamboo as represented in the annexed sketch. Three or four persons now surround the table, and the heap of tea leaves is divided into as many parcels, each individual taking as many as he can hold in his hands, and

The Rolling Process.

the rolling process commences. I cannot give a better idea of this operation than by comparing it to a baker working and rolling his dough. Both hands are used in the very same way; the object being to express the sap and moisture, and at the same time to twist the leaves. Two or three times during the operation the little bundles of rolled leaves are held up and shaken out upon the table,

Chap. X.] EXPOSURE TO THE AIR. 197

and are then again taken up and pressed and rolled as before. This part of the process also lasts about five minutes, during which time a large portion of green juice has been expressed, and may be seen finding its way down between the interstices of the bamboos. The leaves being now pressed, twisted, and curled, do not occupy a quarter of the space which they did before the operation.

When the rolling process is completed the leaves are removed from the table and shaken out for the last time, thinly, upon a large sort of screen, also made out of split pieces of bamboo, and are exposed to the action of the air. The best days for this purpose are those which are dry and cloudy, with very little sun. The object being to expel the moisture in the most gentle manner, and, at the same time, to allow the leaves to remain as soft and pliable as possible. When the sun is clear and powerful the moisture evaporates too rapidly, and the leaves are left crisp, coarse, and not in a proper state to undergo the remaining part of the process. There is no stated time for this exposure, as much depends upon the nature of the weather and the convenience of the work-people ; sometimes I have seen them go on with the remaining part of the operation without at all exposing the leaves to the air.

Having in this manner got rid of a certain part of the superfluous moisture, the leaves, which are now soft and pliant, are again thrown into thedrying pans, and the second heating commences. Again one individual takes his post at the furnace, and keeps up a slow and steady fire. Others resume their places at the different drying pansl one at each l and commence stirring and throwing up the leaves, so that they may all have an equal share of the fire, and none get scorched or burned. The process of drying thus goes on slowly and regularly. This part of the operation soon becomes more easy, for the leaves, as they part with their moisture, twist and curl, and consequently take up much less room than they do at first, and mix together more readily. The tea leaves being now rather too hot for the hand, a small and neat brush, made of bamboo, is used instead of the fingers for stirring them up from the bottom of the pan. By this means the leaves are scattered about on the smooth chunam-work, which forms the back of the drying pan, and, as they roll down on this heated inclined plane they dry slowly, and twist at the same time. During this operation the men and women who are employed never leave their respective stations, one keeps slowly feeding the fire, and the others continually stir the leaves. No very exact degree of temperature is attempted to be kept up, for they do not use the thermometer, but a slow and steady fire is quite sufficient; that is, the pan is made and kept so hot, that I could not place my hand upon it for a second of time. In order to get a correct idea of the time required to complete this second part of the process, I referred to my

Chap. X.] LENGTH OF TIME REQUIRED. 199

watch on different occasions, and at different tea farms, and always found that it occupied about an hour; that is, from the time the leaves were put into the pan after exposure to the air, until they were perfectly dry.

When the operation of drying is going on largely, some of the pans in the range are used for finishing the process, while others, and the hottest ones, are heating and moistening the leaves before they are squeezed and rolled. Thus a considerable number of hands can be employed at once, and the work goes on rapidly without loss of time or heat, the latter of which is of some importance in a country so ill provided with fuel.

The tea prepared in the manner which I have just described is greenish in colour, and of a most excellent quality. It is called by the Chinese in the province of Chekiang, *Tsaou-tsing,* or the tea which is *dried in the pan,* to distinguish it from the *Hong-tsing,* or that kind which is dried in flat bamboo baskets over a slow fire of charcoal.

This latter kindlthe *Hong-tsing* l is prepared in the following manner:lThe first process, up to the period of rolling and exposure to the air, is exactly the same as that which I have just described, but instead of being put into the drying pan for the second heating like the *Tsaou-tsing,* the *Hong-tsing* is shaken out into flat baskets, which are placed over tubs containing charcoal and ashes. The charcoal, when ignited, burns slowly and sends out a mild and gentle heat. Indeed, the onlydifference between the two teas consists in the mode of firing, the latter being dried less and more slowly than the former. The *Hong-tsing* is not so green in colour as the *Tsaou-tsing,* and I believe has rarely been sent to England. The Russian tea is dried in this manner.

After the drying is completed the tea is picked, sifted, divided into different kinds and qualities, and prepared for packing. This is a part of the operation which requires great care, more especially when the tea is intended for the foreign market, as the value of the sample depends much upon the " smallness and evenness" of the leaf, as well as upon its other good qualities. In those districts where the teas are manufactured solely for exportation, the natives are very particular in the rolling process, and hence the teas from these districts are better divided and more *even*lalthough I should doubt their being really better in quality I than they are in the eastern parts of the province of Chekiang. When they have been duly assorted, a man puts on a pair of clean cloth or straw shoes, and treads the tea firmly into baskets or boxes, and the operation is considered complete, in so far as the grower is concerned.

I have stated that the plants grown in the district of Chekiang produce green teas, but it must not be supposed that they are the *green* teas which are exported to England The leaf has a much more natural colour, and has little or none of what we call the " beautiful bloom" upon it, which is

Chap. X.] DYED TEAS FOR THE FOREIGN MARKET. 201

so much admired in Europe and America. There is now no doubt that all these " blooming" green teas, which are manufactured at Canton, are dyed with Prussian blue and gypsum, to suit the taste of the foreign "barbarians:" indeed, the process may be seen any day, during the season, by those who will give themselves the trouble to seek after it. It is very likely that the same ingredients are also used in dying the northern green teas for the foreign market; of this, however, I am not quite certain. There is a vegetable dye obtained from *Isatis indigotica* much used in the northern districts, and called *Tein-ching,* and it is not unlikely that it may be the substance which is employed.

The Chinese never use these dyed teas themselves, and I certainly think their taste in this respect is more correct than ours. It is not to be supposed that the dye used can produce any very bad effects upon the consumer, for, had this been the case, it would have been discovered before now; but if entirely harmless or inert, its being so must be ascribed to the very small quantity which is employed in the manufacture.

The following very curious and interesting experiments are extracted from a paper by Mr. Warington, of Apothecaries' Hall, published in the " Memoirs of the Chemical Society : "I

" In examining lately some samples of tea which had been seized, from their being supposed to be spurious, my attention was arrested by the varied tints which the sample of green tea exhibited, extending from a dull olive to a bright greenish blue colour. On submitting this to the scrutinising test of examination by the microscope, with a magnifying power of one

hundred times linear, the object being illuminated by reflected light, the cause of this variation of colour was immediately rendered apparent, for it was found that the curled leaves were entirely covered with a white powder, having in some cases a slightly glistening aspect, and these were interspersed with small granules of a bright blue colour, and others of an orange tint: in the folded and consequently more protected parts of the curled leaves these were more distinctly visible. By shaking the whole of the sample mechanically for a short time a quantity of powder was detached, and from this a number of the blue particles were picked out under a magnifying glass, by means of the moistened point of a fine camel's hair pencil. On being crushed in water between two plates of glass they presented, when viewed by transmitted light, a bright blue streak. This change in the method of illuminating the object was necessary for the purpose of seeing the action of the following tests : I A minute drop of a solution of caustic potash was introduced by capillary attraction between the glass plates, and the blue tint was immediately converted to a dark brown, and the original blue colour again restored by the introduction of a little dilute sulphuric acid. It was therefore evident that these particles consisted of the ferrocyanide of iron or Prussian blue. The orange granules on examination proved to be some vegetable colouring substance.

" To ascertain if possible the nature of the white powder observed on this sample, I separated some of the dust, and heated it to redness with free exposure to the air; the whole of the vegetable matter and Prussian blue was thus destroyed, and a white powder, with a slight shade of brown, was obtained. This dissolved by boiling in dilute hydrochloric acid, and when tested with solution of chloride of barium gave indications of sulphuric acid; it was then evaporated to dryness, and again acted upon by very dilute hydrochloric acid ; a trace of silica remained undissolved. Solution of ammonia being added threw down a little alumina and oxide of iron, and the ammoniacal solution, treated with oxalic acid, gave a precipitate of oxalate of lime. A second portion of the powder, after calcination, was boiled for some time in distilled water, and yielded a solution containing sulphate of lime; this latter substance, therefore, and some other body containing silica, alumina, andChap. X.] THE GREEN TEAS OF COMMERCE. 203

perhaps lime, formed the white powder observed. This substance I believe to be kaolin, or powdered agalmatolite, the figure stone of the Chinese. I venture this conjecture, not only from the ingredients found, but also from the gloss which the rubbed parts of the curled leaves always assume, and which these materials would be well fitted to produce.

" Four or five other samples of green teas were then submitted to the same method of examination, and only one of them proved to be free from these blue granules; this sample was a high-priced tea, and had been purchased about two years; it appeared covered with a very pale blue powder, instead of the white, with the blue particles interspersed, as exhibited by the others.

" Being still in doubt as to whether this powder and colouring was an adulteration practised in this country or not, I applied to a most extensive wholesale dealer of the highest respectability, and from him obtained a series of samples, each being an average from a number of original chests, and from these I gathered the following results by examination, as before, with the microscope. No. 1. Imperial. The leaf, where seen beneath the superficial coating was of a bright olive brown colour, with small filaments on its surface; it was covered with a fine white powder, and with here and there a minute bright blue particle, at times having the appearance of a stain. No. 2. Gunpowder. Similar to No. 1., but the filaments not visible: this may have arisen from the tight and close manner in which the leaf was curled. No. 3. Hyson. The same as No. 1., the blue particles being, perhaps, more frequent. No. 4. Young Hyson. The same. No. 5. Twankey. The leaf of this had more of a yellow hue, and was profusely covered with white powder, having the blue particles also more thickly strewn over the surface. It was evident, from the examination of these teas, that they arrive in this country in an adulterated or factitious state.

" On detailing what I had thus found to the friend who had favoured me with the preceding samples, he inquired if I had examined any *unglazed teas.* This appellation immediately arrested my attention, and I requested to inspect some of them, and found that they possessed externally a totally different aspect, indeed, as far as their colour was concerned, not to belike green teas. They were of a yellow-brown tint, without a shade of green or blue, but rather tending on the rubbed parts to a blackish hue. I afterwards received two samples of unglazed teas, specified as of very fine quality, accompanied by two others of the ordinary, or, as they are called, in contradistinction, *glazed* varieties, also of a very superior quality. These were, therefore, immediately submitted to examination. No. 6. Unglazed Gunpowder. It presented the same colour under the microscope as when viewed by the unassisted eye, was filamentous, and covered with a white powder, inclining to a brown tint, but no shade of blue was visible. No. 7. Unglazed Hyson. The same as No. 6. No. 8. Gunpowder glazed. Filamentous, covered with a powder of a very pale blue, and the blue granules being but rarely seen. No. 9. Hyson. The same as No. 8. No. 10. Pidding's Howqua, purchased at Lit- tlejohn's, at 8. *6d.* per catty package. This was evidently of the glazed variety; it was filamentous, and covered with a pale blue powder, interspersed with bright blue granules. No 11., entitled Canton Gunpowder. This was a splendid sample of the *glazed* variety, as far as colour was concerned; it was more thickly powdered and blued than any that I have examined, and the dust rose from it in quantity when poured from one paper to another. A great many other samples of ordinary green teas were examined, with much the same results; the cheaper teas, or those in general use, and which form the bulk of the imports, being similar to Nos. 5. and 11., and being represented by Twankeys and lower priced Hysons or Gunpowders.

" After several unsuccessful experiments, I found that with a little care the whole of this powder or facing, if I may be allowed the term, it being entirely superficial, could be easily removed from the tea, by simply agitating the sample briskly for a few seconds in a phial with distilled water, and then throwing the whole on a lawn or muslin filter, in order to strain the liquid, with the suspended matter, from the leaves as rapidly as possible. After this operation, the tea presented a totally altered aspect, as may be supposed; in fact, changing its colour from a bluish green to a bright and lively yellow or brownish yellow tint, and I found that with care it could be redried at a temperature below 212 without even uncurling theChap. X.] THE GREEN TEAS OF COMMERCE. 205

leaf, and without apparent loss of any of its characteristic qualities. When the drying was complete, the example appeared nearly as dark as the ordinary black teas, and when examined by the microscope presented a smooth surface, perfectly free from the previously observed facing, and having all the characters of black tea, with the exception of the corrugated aspect, which is common to the greater part of the teas of the latter variety, and which evidently arises from their having been exposed in the operation of drying to a much higher temperature. The greenish-coloured turbid liquid which passes through the meshes of the muslin filter was allowed to deposit the matter suspended in it, which was then washed and collected. These sediments, obtained from various samples, were submitted to the following course of chemical examination. They were, in the first instance, tested with a solution of chlorine gas in water, to ascertain if the colouring material was indigo or other vegetable colour; this substance, as we shall presently see, having been supposed by some persons to be the one employed by the Chinese for the purpose of imparting the blue tint to some of their green teas. In no case, however, that I have yet examined, have I found this to be the case; but the colouring agent has invariably proved to be the ferro- cyanide of iron or Prussian blue. The presence of this compound was next evidenced by adding a small drop of caustic potash to a little of the sediment under examination, when the green hue was instantly converted to a bright reddish brown, the original blue appearance being again restored by the subsequent addition of a little diluted sulphuric acid. The other ingredients of the facing were sought for in the manner stated in the previous part of this paper, and also by heating a part of the sediment, after calcination and free exposure to the air, with carbonate of soda, to fusion, which, in the case of sulphate of lime being present, formed sulphate of soda and carbonate of lime, and these were each subsequently tested for.

" By these means Nos. 5. 8.10. and 11. were found to be faced with Prussian blue and sulphate of lime. Nos. 6. and 7. gave no indication of Prussian blue, but of sulphate of lime only. The sulphate of lime from some samples appeared to be crystallised gypsum reduced to a fine powder, the coarser.particles still exhibiting a crystalline structure.

" Through the kindness of Mr. Greene, of the East India House, I was enabled to obtain samples of the Assam teas in a genuine condition ; No. 12. Imperial, No. 13. Gunpowder, and No. 14. Hyson. They had none of the blue granules, were very filamentous, and presented the same appearance as the unglazed varieties, but brighter in colour; the facing was apparently sulphate of lime. No. 15. Assam Hyson, of the last importation; it was of the unglazed variety, with the superficial white powder having a slight brown tint, and consisting of a minute quantity of sulphate of lime with a little alumina.

" It appears, therefore, from these examinations, that all the green teas that are imported into this country are faced or covered superficially with a powder consisting of either Prussian blue and sulphate of lime or gypsum, as in the majority of samples examined, with occasionally a yellow or orange-coloured vegetable substance ; or of sulphate of lime previously stained with Prussian blue, as in Nos. 8. and 9., and one of those first investigated ; or of Prussian blue, the orange-coloured substance with sulphate of lime and a material supposed to be kaolin, as in the original sample; or of sulphate of lime alone, as in the unglazed varieties. It is a curious question what the object for the employment of this facing can be ; whether, as when sulphate of lime alone is used, it is simply added as an absorbent of the last portions of moisture which cannot be entirely dissipated in the process of drying, or whether it is only, as I believe, to give that peculiar bloom and colour so characteristic of the varieties of green tea, and which is so generally looked for by the consumer, that the want of the green colour, as in the unglazed variety, I am informed, affects the selling price most materially. This surely can only arise from the want of the above facts being generally known, as it would be ridiculous to imagine that a painted and adulterated article, for such it must really be considered, should maintain a preference over a more genuine one."

13

SECTION 13

CHAP. XI.

TEA MERCHANTS. I THEIR VISITS TO THE TEA HILLS. I MODE OF BUY-ING FROM THE SMALL GROWERS. BLACK TEA DISTRICT IN FOKIEN. TEAS DIVIDED INTO TWO KINDS. I

PECULIAR METHOD OF PREPARING EACH. I CAUSE OF THEIR DIFFER-ENCE IN COLOUR. I FLOWERS USED IN SCENTING THE

FINER TEAS. EXPORT OF TEAS. QUANTITIES CONSUMED
BY THE CHINESE. I PRICE OF A CUP OF TEA. I MEANS OF
SUPPLYING AN INCREASED DEMAND. REMARKS ON THE TEA
COUNTRIES OF INDIA. I HISTORY OF EXPERIMENTS IN TEA CULTI-VATION. I OBSERVATIONS ON INDIAN TEA LANDS. I RESULTS. SIR JOHN FRANCIS DAVIS'S REMARKS ON DIFFERENT KINDS OF TEAS SOLD AT CANTON.

When the teas are ready for sale, the large tea merchants or their servants come out from the principal towns of the district, and take up their quarters in all the little inns or eating houses, which are very numerous in every part of the country. They also bring coolies loaded with the copper coin of the country, with which they pay for their purchases. As soon as the merchants are known to have arrived in the district, the tea growers bring their produce for inspection and sale. These little farmers or their labourers may now be seen hastening along the different roads, each with two baskets or chests slung across his shoulder on his bamboo pole. When they arrive at the merchant's abiding place the baskets are opened before him, and the quality of the tea inspected. If he is pleased with its appearance and smell, and the parties agree as to the price, the tea is weighed, the money paid down, and the grower gets his strings of copper money slung over his shoulder, and returns to his farm. But should the price offered appear too low, the baskets are immediately shouldered with the greatest apparent independence, and carried away to some opposition merchant. It, however, sometimes happens that a merchant makes a contract with some of the tea growers before the season commences, in which case the price is arranged in the usual way, and generally a part paid in advance. This, I understand, is frequently the case at Canton when a foreign resident wishes to secure any particular kind of tea.

After the teas are bought up in the district where they are grown, they are conveyed to the most convenient town, where they are assorted and properly packed for the European and American markets. Such is the system of green tea culture and manufacture which came under my own observation in the province of Chekiang.

The *black tea districts* of Fokien, which I visited, are managed in the same way as those of Chekiang.

I have already said that the species of plant which produces the black teas near Foo-chow is the very same as that found in the green tea districts of the north. Being further south, and of course in a hotter climate, the tea plant of Fokien is generally grown at a high elevation amongst the hills. At

Chap. XL] PROCESS OF DRYING BLACK TEA. 209

the risk of some little repetition I will insert an account of my visit to the tea hills of Fokien.

Every cottager, or small farmer, has two or three patches of tea shrubs growing on the hill sides, which are generally planted and kept in order by the members of his own family. When the gathering season arrives, the cottage-doors are locked, and all proceed to the hills with their baskets and commence plucking the leaves. This business, of course, only goes on during fine days when the leaves are dry.

The first gathering takes place just when the leaf-buds begin to unfold themselves in early spring. This tea is scarce and of a very superior quality, being, in fact, the same, or nearly the same, as that which is made from the young leaves in the green-tea district. The second gathering produces the principal crop of the season; the third crop is coarse and inferior.

When the leaves are brought home from the hills, they are first of all emptied out into large flat bamboo sieves, and, providing the day is not too bright, are exposed in the open air to dry *off* any superfluous moisture. When this moisture has evaporated, convenient portions of the leaves are brought in and thrown into a round flat iron pan, such as the Chinese use for boiling their rice, and are exposed to the heat of a gentle fire which is lighted below them. As soon as this heat reaches them, they give out a large quantity of moisture with a crackling noise, and they soon become soft and pliant. The person who attends to them stirs them about with his hands, and in about five minutes takes them out and puts in a fresh supply. The heated leaves are emptied out on a large round and flat bamboo sieve, which is placed upon a table at a convenient height from the ground, and the process of rolling commences. Three or four persons take a portion of the heated leaves and begin to squeeze and roll them in the manner which I have already described. This goes on for a minute or two, when each person takes his portion and examines the effects which have already been produced; it is then shaken well out upon the table, after which it is gathered up and the operation of rolling and squeezing goes on as before. This is repeated three or four times, and then the whole is shaken well out, on another large flat bamboo sieve, in such a manner as to spread it thinly upon it.

Up to this stage of the process all the leaves have been subjected to the same treatment. But the tea in this district is now divided into two classes, each of which is treated in a peculiar manner. They are called in the language of the district, *Luk-cha* and *Hong-cha*. The former seems to be a kind of mixture of black and green, and I should imagine it is only made for the use of the natives themselves; the latter is our common black tea.

The Luk-cha is prepared in the following manner:l The leaves, after being rolled and squeezed, are shaken out thinly and exposed to the air to

Chap. XI.] THE HONG-CHA, OR BLACK TEA. 211

dry. Great care is taken not to expose them in this state to much bright sunshine, and hence a tine dry day when the sun is partially obscured by thin clouds is always preferred for this part of the operation. After being exposed for an hour or two, or even longer, as the case may be, for this depends upon a variety of circumstances, such as the dryness of the air, or the convenience of the workpeople, they are brought within doors, and the drying process commences. The flat rice-pan, in which they were first heated, is so constructed that it can be taken out at the pleasure of the cottager. It is now removed, and a bamboo sieve, exactly the same size, is put into its place, and filled with the leaves. A very slow and steady fire of wood or charcoal is now kept up, and the remains of the moisture in the leaves is thus gradually and slowly evaporated. After a few minutes the sieve is lifted out and placed in one of a larger size with a closer bottom. The leaves are then well shaken up and turned over, and any of the smaller tea which falls through the open sieve, during the operation, is thus collected in the under one and carefully saved. Both sieves are now placed over the flue, and the leaves carefully watched and turned frequently, for about an hour, when the tea is considered properly fired. Sometimes, if the day is fine, it is exposed a little while to the sun before it is packed away.

The Hong-cha, or our common black tea, is prepared rather differently. In the first place thenatives seem more particular in the rolling process, especially when it is for the foreign market, although the operation is performed much in the same way. After heating and rolling, the leaves are shaken out on large screens, and subjected to the action of the open air; the natives in this, as in all other cases, taking care not to expose them to a bright and burning sun. This is a most important part of the manufacture. The black tea is left in this state sometimes for two or three days before it is fired, which, doubtless, is one cause why the colour of this tea is so much darker than those kinds which are prepared from the same plants and quickly dried.

After being exposed for a sufficient length of time to the action of the air, the leaves are taken in for the purpose of firing. Instead, however, of being heated in baskets, like the other kind, this is thrown at once into the pan. An old and experienced person takes his place at the furnace, and keeps up a slow and steady fire, while it is the duty of the younger branches of the family to keep the leaves in the pan in continual motion and prevent them from being burned. This is done by means of little hand-brushes made from the prolific bamboo, the outer flinty part being split for this purpose. The tea prepared in this manner soon becomes of a dark colour, and is quite different in appearance from the *Luk-cha*. After it has been sufficiently dried, it has, of course, to undergo the other operations of sifting, picking,

Chap. XI.] FLOWERS USED FOR SCENTING TEAS. 213

and dividing, before it is fit to be packed up for the foreign market.

From this it appears, that the black tea is rendered darker in colour, first by being longer exposed to the air in a soft and moist state ; and secondly, by being subjected to a greater degree of fire-heat. With regard to the green teas, there can be no doubt that those used by the Chinese themselves are of the genuine colour which they acquire in the drying; and that those " blooming " kinds, prepared to suit our depraved tastes, are, one and all, dyed. Morever, in conclusion, I may repeat, what I have already proved, that the black and green teas of the north are produced from the same species, the *Thea viridis,* and that the true Canton teas are manufactured from the leaves of the *Thea bohea.* It therefore follows that the black teas can be, and, in fact, are made from both species; and with regard to the green, as it is the result of a dye, the Chinese, I doubt not, could substitute for that colour either red or yellow, should our tastes change and lead us to prefer more glaring tints!

There are several different kinds of scented flowers, which are grown in particular districts, for the purpose of mixing with and perfuming the tea. Amongst these I may mention the following: | *Olea fragrans, Chloranthus inconspicuus, Aglaia odorata,* &c. I believe these flowers are dried by themselves, and afterwards mixed with the teas.

The principal tea districts of China lie between the 25th and 31st degrees of north latitude. Leaving out Quantung, which produces teas of a very inferior quality, the provinces in which tea is known to be extensively cultivated are Fokien, Chekiang, and Kiangnan. It is difficult to say what the actual quantity is which is yearly exported from these districts, owing to the large exportation in Chinese vessels to Cochin China, Siam, Borneo, and other parts of the Straits; but the following returns, for which I am indebted to Mr. Winch, of Liverpool, show very nearly the exports to other parts of the world: |

Exports to Great Britain for the year
ending 30th June, 1846 - - - 57,584,561 Ibs. United States of America for same period - 18,502,142 To the Continent of Europe for the year
ending 31st December, 1845 - - 4,051,529
Total —- 80,138,232 Ibs.

Besides these, the exports to Sydney, and other parts of Australia, amount to about 4,000,000 lbs.; and the quantity annually sent by inland transit to Russia amounts to more than 5,000,000 lbs. If we suppose the total export to be at least 90,000,000lbs., or I taking what is sent to the Straits in native vessels into account I 95,000,000 lbs., we must be very near the truth.

Although this seems a very large quantity, it must be trifling when compared with that which is consumed by the Chinese themselves. It has been

Chap. XI.] REMARKS OF SIR G. STAUNTON ON TEA. 215

justly remarked by Sir George Staunton, that " such immense quantities of tea are yearly raised in China, that a sudden failure of demand from Europe would not be likely to occasion any material diminution of price in the Chinese markets."

The consumption in the country must be very great. A Chinaman rarely drinks cold water: tea is his favourite beverage when thirsty, and it is drunk at all meals. Houses for its sale are as plentiful as our inns and beer-shops are in England. Tea-gardens (properly so called) are numerous in all the cities; every street and lane has its teahouses, which at stated periods of the day are crowded by the Chinese. Nor is it in cities only that this great consumption goes on. On the sides of country roads, on the passes over the mountains, at the Budhists' temples, and even in the most retired parts of the country, numerous public teahouses are met with for the sale of the beverage in a prepared state. A cup of tea in these places is sold for the small sum of one, or at most two " cash;" and when we remember that one hundred cash amount only to four-pence halfpenny, we then learn that the Chinese peasant can have three or four cups of his favourite tea for a sum not greater than one farthing of our money. I have no hesitation in saying that each individual in China consumes three or four times the quantity an Englishman does.

Estimating the tea-drinking population of China

Chap. XI.] QUANTITY OF TEA USED IN CHINA. 217

at 300,000,000, and supposing that each individual f consumes 6 lbs. of tea per annum, we get the large quantity of 1,800,000,000 lbs. This quantity, large as it appears to be, is very likely under the actual amount, no other unintoxicating beverage being in general use, and an ardent spirit (Samchoo) being the only other fluid refreshment that appears at their tables. According to a late calculation, the quantity consumed by each person in the island of Jersey amounts annually to between four and five pounds.

Assuming the above to be the annual consumption of the Chinese, and adding 95,000,000 lbs. as exports, we arrive at the quantity yearly manufactured in the country, which amounts to 1,895,000,000 lbs.

Since the government of this country was first pressed to reduce the import duties upon tea, the question has arisen, whether, in the event of a larger demand, the Chinese would be able to supply it without materially advancing the price of the article ? For my own part I agree with Sir George Staunton, that a sudden failure of demand from Europe would scarcely affect the native market, and consequently, as has been justly remarked by Mr. Winch I, " an increased demandfrom the same quarter would be inadequate to advance the cost of the article." I believe no one who has travelled much in China, or who has watched the market in this country, has any doubt upon the subject. And drawing our conclusions from past experience, we find, that although our demands have been yearly increasing, not only have teas not advanced in value, but we are supplied at constantly diminishing prices. " In 1846 we imported 24,000,000 Ibs. more than in 1833, while the average prices in 1846 are about one shilling per pound lower."

I make this low estimate of population purposely, as I have been informed that in some parts of the south-western provinces tea is little used.

j" Children drink nearly as much as their parents.

t The Tea Duties considered.

Were there a greater demand for teas from China, a very large quantity could easily be spared from what is actually grown for consumption in the country. As soon as the demand increased to such an extent as to be felt in the tea districts, more attention would be paid to the cultivation of the plants. Thousands of small farmers who now grow only a little more than is sufficient for the supply of their own wants, and to enable them to procure the other necessaries of life, would increase their stock, and soon contribute their share in supplying the extra demand. And with a little more capital many parts of the hill-sides could be brought under cultivation which now produce crops only of bamboos and brushwood. From these, and perhaps other sources, we may safely conclude that the Chinese could easily supply any increased demand which we are likely to make upon them from this

Chap. XI.] CULTIVATION OF TEA IN INDIA. 219

country, and supply it without ultimately advancing the prices of tea.

Our knowledge of the provinces which lie to the westward of Chekiang and Kiang-nan is defective, but if the land is hilly there is no reason why there may not be extensive tea districts there with which Europeans are unacquainted. That vast country between the parallels of latitude just mentioned, reaching from the Chusan Archipelago on the east to the Himalayan mountains on the west, possesses a climate suitable for the culture of the tea plant.

But were there any doubts of our being able to procure an almost unlimited supply of teas from China, let us turn to our own dominions in India. It may be very true that the results of tea cultivation in Assam do not seem to have been very satisfactory. All my experience of the tea districts in China goes, however, to show that the northwestern districts of the mountains of India l any of the Himalayan mountains l are much better suited for this purpose than the more southern country of Assam. The genuine and best tea plant *(Thea viridis)* is not met with in the south of China at all, and when brought down there does not succeed. Even in Fokien, where it furnishes black teas, it is necessary to plant it high up on the mountains from two to three thousand feet above the level of the sea. But even in these circumstances, what are called Ankoy teas are considered greatly inferior to those kinds which are produced much farther to the northward. Thesame results, it will therefore be observed, have taken place in China and in India.

In the Himalayas, however, we have every variety of elevation and soil, and the same climate as the most favoured tea districts of China. Dr. Royle, when superintendent of the East India Company's Botanic Garden in Saharunpore, in the year 1827 and again in 1831, recommended the districts of Kemaon, Gurhwal, and Sirmore to the Indian government as most eligible for the cultivation of tea, and in his " Essay on the productive Resources of India" stated that he " confidently looked forward not only to having tea cultivated all along these mountains, but also to its being finer flavoured than the Assam." His recommendation was put in practice in 1836, under the superintendence of Dr. Falconer, in the neighbourhood of Almorah, and also in the Deyra Doon. Tea- seeds were obtained from the Ankoy districts of China, and Chinese manufacturers were sent from the government nurseries in Assam to those of Kemaon and Gurhwal. The last report from Dr. Jamieson, who succeeded Dr. Falconer, is most satisfactory, and the samples sent home have been pronounced by the most experienced tea-brokers and others, as Mr. Ball and Mr. Hunt, to be " excellent in quality, to belong to the Oolong class of teas, and to be equal in value to Chinese teas of two shillings and three-pence and three shillings a-pound."

The plants which have produced this tea were

Chap. XL] CHEAP TEAS IN INDIA. 221

brought from the Ankoy districts, and are, therefore, what botanists call *Thea viridis*. But this species in Fokien is evidently to a certain extent deteriorated by climate; and I therefore suggest the importance of procuring a large supply of young plants from the province of Chekiang, where it evidently grows most luxuriantly. I have already said the soil in which the plant succeeds best is a well-drained, rich gravelly loam. The plantations are always made on the lower sides of the hills in the province of Chekiang, and never on the low lands. After these statements, the following questions naturally suggest themselves: | Have we the same variety of the tea plant in India which produces the best teas of China ? | Has India the advantage of cheap labour, as we are informed it has ? | Is the soil and modes of management and manufacture the same in both countries ? If these questions can be answered in the affirmative, we may confidently look forward to the same results in the end. Dr. Jamieson is of opinion, " that if cultivated on a large scale, tea could be delivered at Calcutta for *Qd.* a-pound. Some which had been produced, sold at Almorah, in the immediate vicinity of the nurseries, from 4s. to *5s.* a-pound, which is equal to the price of good China tea in Calcutta."

The advantages which would result from thesuccessful cultivation of the tea plant in India are immense. The vast population of our empire in the East would have a cheap and harmless beverage produced amongst themselves, and thousands of families would find a healthy and profitable employment in the cultivation and manufacture of tea. These results are altogether independent of the benefit which would be conferred upon our population at home.

Amongst the Chinese excellent teas are sold for about *5d.* per Ib.: inferior kinds may be had for *2d.* or *3d.* The scarce and finest teas are sold for about Is. a-pound.

In order to give the reader some idea of the different sorts of teas manufactured for the European and American markets, I cannot do better than quote some excellent remarks on this subject by Sir John Francis Davis, in his work, *"* The Chinese ' :" |

" As tea has always held so principal a place in our intercourse with China, it requires some particular consideration as an article of commerce. We have seen before, that the fineness and dearness of tea are determined by the tenderness and smallness of the leaf when picked. The various descriptions of the Black diminish in quality and value as they are gathered later in the season, until they reach the lowest kind, called by us Bohea, and by the Chinese (*Ta-cha*), ' large tea,' on account of the maturity and size of the leaves. The early leaf- buds in spring, being covered with a white silky down, are gathered to make Pekoe, which is a corruption of the Canton name *Pak-ho*, ' white down.' A few days' longer growth produce what is here styled ' black-leaved pekoe.' The more fleshy and matured leaves constitute Souchong; as they grow larger and coarser they form Congou ; and the last and latest picking is Bohea. The tea-farmers, who are small proprietors or cultivators, give the tea a rough preparation, and then take it to the contractors, whose business it is to adapt its farther

1 Charles Knight and Co., Ludgate Street, 1840.

Chap. XI.] ON TEAS SOLD AT CANTON. 223

preparation to the existing nature of the demand. The different kinds of tea may be considered in the ascending scale of their value.

" 1. Bohea, which in England is the name of a *quality,* has been already stated to be, in China, the name of a *district* where various kinds of black tea are produced. The coarse leaf brought under that name to this country is distinguished by containing a larger proportion of the woody fibre than other teas ; its infusion is of a darker colour, and as it has been more subjected to the action of fire, it keeps a longer time without becoming musty than the finer sorts. Two kinds of Bohea are brought from China: the lowest of these is manufactured on the spot, and therefore called ' Canton Bohea,' being a mixture of refuse Congou with a coarse tea called Woping, the growth of the province. The better kind of Bohea comes from the district of that name in Fokien, and, having been of late esteemed equally with the lower Congou teas, has been packed in the same square chests, while the whole Bohea package is of an oblong shape.

" 2. Congou, the next higher kind, is named from a corruption of the Chinese *Koong foo,* 'labour or assiduity.' It formed for many years the bulk of the East India Company's cargoes ; but the quality gradually fell off, in consequence of the partial abandonment of the old system of annual contracts, by which the Chinese merchants were assured of a remunerating price for the better sorts. The consumption of Bohea in this country has of late years increased, to the diminution of Congou, and the standard of the latter has been considerably lowered. A particular variety, called *Campoi,* is so called from a corruption of the original name *Kien-peoy,* ' selection I choice ;' but it has ceased to be prized in this country, from the absence of strength, I a characteristic which is stated to be generally esteemed beyond delicacy of flavour.

"3. Souchong (*Seaou-choong,* 'small, or scarce sort') is the finest of the stronger black teas, with a leaf that is generally entire and curly, but more young than in the coarser kinds. What is called ' Padre Souchong' is packed in separate paper bundles, of about half a pound each, and is so fine as to be used almost exclusively for presents. The probability is that its use in that way by the Catholic missionaries first gave rise to thename. The finest kinds of Souchong are sometimes scented with the flowers of the *Chloranthus inconspicuus,* and *Gardenia florida ;* and they cannot be obtained, even among the Chinese, except at dear prices. A highly-crisped and curled leaf called *Sonchi* has lately grown into disrepute and been much disused, in consequence of being often found to contain a ferruginous dust, which was probably not intended as a fraud, but arose from the nature of the ground, where the tea had been carelessly and dirtily packed.

" 4. Pekoe being composed mainly of the young spring-buds, the gathering of these must, of course, be injurious in some degree to the future produce of the shrub, and this description of tea is accordingly both dear and small in quantity. With a view to preserving the fineness of flavour, the application of heat is very limited in drying the leaves, and hence it is that Pekoe is more liable to injury from keeping than any other sort of tea. There is a species of Pekoe made in the Green-tea country from the young buds, in like manner with the black kind ; but it is so little fired that the least damp spoils it; and for this reason, as well as on account of its scarcity and high price, the Hyson-pekoe, as some call it, has never been brought to England. The mandarins send it in very small canisters to each other, or to their friends, as presents, under the name of *Loong-tsing,* which is probably the name of the district where the tea is made.

" Green teas may generally be divided into five denominations, which are11. Twankey; 2. Hyson-skin; 3. Hyson; 4. Gunpowder; 5. Young Hyson. Twankey tea has always formed the bulk of the green teas imported into this country, being used by the retailers to mix with the finer kinds. The leaf is older, and not so much twisted and rolled as in the dearer descriptions : there is altogether less care and trouble bestowed on its preparation. It is, in fact, the *Bohea* of green teas ; and the quantity of it brought to England has fully equalled three- fourths of the whole importation of green. ' Hyson-skin' is so named from the original Chinese term, in which connection the *skin* means the *refuse,* or inferior portion of anything; in allusion, perhaps, to the hide of an animal, or the rind of fruit. In preparing the fine tea called Hyson, all those leaves that are of a coarser, yellower, and less twisted or rolled appearance,Chap. XI.] ON TEAS SOLD AT CAXTON. 225

are set apart and sold as the refuse or ' skin-tea,' at a much inferior price. The whole quantity, therefore, depends on, and bears a proportion to, the whole quantity of Hyson manufactured, but seldom exceeds two or three thousand chests in all.

" The word Hyson is corrupted from the Chinese name, which signifies ' flourishing spring,' this fine sort of tea being of course gathered in the early part of the season. Every separate leaf is twisted and rolled by hand, and it is on account of the extreme care and labour required in its preparation that the best Hyson tea is so difficult to procure, and so expensive. By way of keeping up its quality, the East India Company used to give a premium for the two best lots annually presented to them for selection; and the tea-merchants were stimulated to exertion, as much by the credit of the thing, as by the actual gain in price. Gunpowder, as it is called, is nothing but a more carefully picked Hyson, consisting of the best rolled and roundest leaves, which give it that *granular* appearance whence it derives its name. For a similar reason the Chinese call it *Choocha,* ' pearl-tea.' Young Hyson, until it was spoiled by the large demand of the Americans, was a genuine, delicate young leaf, called in the original language *l*ru-tsein, 'before the rains,' because gathered in the early spring. As it could not be fairly produced in any large quantities, the call for it on the part of the Americans was answered by cutting up and sifting *other* green tea through sieves of a certain size ; and, as the Company's inspectors detected the imposture, it formed no portion of their London importations. But the abuse became still worse of late (as we shall presently see), for the coarsest *black* tea-leaves have been cut up, and then *coloured* with a preparation resembling the hue of green teas.

" The remission of the tea duties in the United States occasioned, in the years 1832 and 1833, a demand for green teas at Canton, which could not be supplied by the arrivals from the provinces. The Americans, however, were obliged to sail with cargoes of green teas within the favourable season ; they were determined to have these teas; and the Chinese were determined they should be supplied. Certain rumours being afloat concerning the manufacture of green tea from old black leaves, the writer of this became curious to ascertain the truth, and with some difficulty persuaded a Hong merchant to conduct

him, accompanied by one of the inspectors, to the place where the operation was carried on. Upon reaching the opposite side of the river, and entering one of these laboratories of factitious Hyson, the parties were witnesses to a strange scene.

" In the first place, large quantities of black tea, which had been damaged in consequence of the floods of the previous autumn, were drying in baskets with sieve bottoms, placed over pans of charcoal. The dried leaves were then transferred in portions of a few pounds each to a great number of cast-iron pans, imbedded in chunam or mortar, over furnaces. At each pan stood a workman, stirring the tea rapidly round with his hand, having previously added a small quantity of *turmeric* in powder, which of course gave the leaves a yellowish or orange tinge ; but they were still to be made green. For this purpose some lumps of a fine blue were produced, together with a white substance in powder, which from the names given to them by the workmen, as well as their appearance, were known at once to be *prussian blue* and *gypsum.*1 These were triturated finely together with a small pestle, in such proportion as reduced the dark colour of the blue to a light shade; and a quantity equal to a small tea-spoonful of the powder being added to the yellowish leaves, these were stirred as before over the fire, until the tea had taken the fine bloom colour of Hyson, with very much the *same scent.* To prevent all possibility of error regarding the substances employed, samples of them, together with specimens of the leaves in each stage of the process, were carried away from the place.

" The tea was then handed in small quantities, on broad shallow baskets, to a number of women and children, who carefully picked out the stalks, and coarse or uncurled leaves ; and, when this had been done, it was passed in succession through sieves of different degrees of fineness. The first sifting produced what was sold as Hyson-skin, and the last bore the name of Young Hyson. As the party did not see the intermediate step between the picking and sifting, there is reason to believe that the size of the leaves was first reduced by chopping or cutting with shears. If the tea has not highly deleterious qualities, it can only be in consequence of the colouring matter

1 Prussiate of iron, and sulphate of lime.

Chap. XI.] ON TEAS SOLD AT CANTON. 227

existing in a small proportion to the leaf1 ; and the Chinese seemed quite conscious of the real character of the occupation in which they were engaged ; for, on attempting to enter several other places where the same process was going on, the doors were speedily closed upon the party. Indeed, had it not been for the influence of the Hongist who conducted them, there would have been little chance of their seeing as much as they did."

1 The turmeric and gypsum are perfectly innocuous; but the prussian blue, being a combination of prussic acid with iron, is a poison.

14

SECTION 14

CHAP. XII.

CHUSAN ARCHIPELAGO STORM IN A SMALL BOAT. | NEARLY UPSET KIN-TANG, OR SILVER ISLAND ITS INHABITANTS.
THEIR SURPRISE ON SEEING A FOREIGNER YANG-TSE-KI AM; RIVER. | ITS NUMEROUS SAND BANKS. | OUR SCHOONER AGROUND. | NOVEL METHOD OF GETTING ASSISTANCE FROM THE CHINESE. VILLAGE OF WOO-SUNG.

OPIUM STATION. REMARKS ON THE OPIUM TRADE ITS EFFECTS UPON THE CHINESE.

In the summer of 1844 I was frequently engaged in exploring the islands of the Chusan Archipelago, more particularly that portion which lies between Chusan and the opposite shores of the main-land. It was of course necessary for this purpose to employ Chinese boats, which are not very trustworthy. The distance from Chusan to the town of Chinhae, at the mouth of the Ning-po river, is about thirty miles. A sail across a sea such as this is generally pleasant enough, because the water, which is hemmed in on all sides, is frequently as smooth as a mill-pond. Sometimes, however, the wind comes down in gusts from the openings amongst the hills, and then the little China boats are all laid nearly upon their beam-ends before the sail can be taken in.

Once, in particular, I had a narrow escape from a watery grave amongst these islands. I had engaged a boat to take me across from the city of Ning-po

Chap. XII] STORM IN A SMALL BOAT. 229

to Chusan; and, as I was in a hurry at the time, I was anxious to reach my destination as soon as possible. The wind blew rather fresh as we were going down the Ning-po river, and when we reached the town of Chinhae, at its mouth, evening had set in, and the sky had a threatening and stormy appearance. The boatmen pointed this out to me, and were anxious to remain where we were until daylight. As I was afraid of being too late for a passage in an English vessel which was then at anchor in the bay of Chusan, I would not consent to this prudent proposal, but insisted that they should proceed across without further delay. After exhausting all their arguments, they at length unwillingly got up the anchor, and we proceeded on our voyage. The land and hills on our way from Ning-po to the mouth of the river had sheltered us, and prevented me from feeling the full force of the wind; but no sooner had we passed the forts, and reached the open sea, than I found I had done a very foolish thing in urging the boatmen to take me across in such a night, and I would gladly have gone back had it been prudent or indeed possible to have done so. It was now, however, too late, for with a strong spring tide and a heavy head sea, it was impossible to get back again to Chinhae, and we therefore kept on in the direction of Chusan. " Are you not carrying too much sail in such a wind as this, and with such a heavy rolling sea?" said I to the captain of the boat, an old weather- beaten man from the province of Fokien. " Nofear, no fear," he replied in his broken Chusan English, " my can manage he." " But I think there is fear, Fokei," I replied; and the words were scarcely said, when a tremendous gust came down upon us, and at the same moment a heavy sea struck the side of our boat, and laid her fairly on her beam- ends. In an instant the boat filled in all her divisions from bow to stern. " Lower the sail, lower the sail, quick, quick," cried the helmsman, " or we shall all go to the bottom." Several of the crew flew to the sail, which fortunately came down readily, and our little craft righted once more, but rolled and plunged very heavily in consequence of the great quantity of water in her hold, and seemed as if she would go down at every plunge, and leave us exposed to the fury of the waves. We again got a few feet of sail hoisted, and kept her away before the wind. It was now dark, not a star was to be seen in the heavens, the mountains, although not distinctly visible, yet loomed through the gloom, and the only objects clearly distinguished were some lights flickering on the distant shore. The crew' now surrounded the helmsman, and besought him to try and get back to Chinhae, but I was sailor enough to know that if we attempted to put the helm down and bring the boat round, in all probability we should ship another sea, and had we done so we must have gone down. I immediately went and stood by the helmsman, and kept the crew from interfering, telling him to keep on our course and try to get under the lee of some island as soon as

Chap. XII.] KIUTANG, OH SILVER ISLAND. 231

possible. The men now began to throw off their clothes as a last resource, and so completely lost all their self-possession that no remonstrances could induce them to attend to the boat and get some of the water out of her. The captain or helmsman, however, did his duty well, and to his firmness and knowledge we, doubtless, owed our lives. Providentially the wind lulled for a short time, which enabled us to hoist more sail; and soon afterwards we got to leeward of one of the numerous small islands which are scattered over this part of the coast. As soon as we had anchored all hands began baling the water out of the boat. We were in a most pitiful condition, all our clothes and beds being completely soaked with sea water; some plants, but luckily only duplicates, which I had with me, were, of course, totally destroyed; but our hearts were light, and we were thankful that our lives had been saved. Before daylight the boat was all right again, and as the weather had moderated, we were able to proceed on our course to Chusan.

Kin-tang, or Silver Island, as it is called by the English, is a large island in this archipelago. Although near Chusan, it was seldom visited by any of the English there; but its hills and valleys were very interesting in a botanical point of view, and on that account I was in the habit of anchoring my little boat in some of its numerous bays, and exploring its botanical productions. The surprise of the simple inhabitants, many of whom had never left the island in their lives, was often verygreat when I came down unexpectedly upon their little villages. The reader will easily credit this if he will only picture to himself the surprise and astonishment with which a Chinese would be regarded were he to appear suddenly in some secluded village in the highlands of Scotland or Wales, where no such phenomenon had ever been seen before. I remember, on one occasion, that having toiled up to the top of one of the beautiful hills on the island of Kin-tang, I observed on the other side of the hill, a few yards below me, a Chinese youth engaged in cutting the long grass and bushes for fire-wood. As he was employed he did not observe me, and I approached the place where he was at work, and standing upon a rock a few feet above him, made some noise to attract his attention. He looked up. and never shall I forget the look he gave me. Had I been a being from another world he could not have been more astonished; indeed, I suppose he thought that I had fallen from the clouds, or come out from the bowels of the hills. For a second or two he stood in silent amazement, seemingly completely paralysed, and then throwing his grass-knife away, fled down the hill over rocks and stones with a rapidity hardly credible; nor did he ever look behind, until he had crossed the narrow valley, and reached the village on the opposite side. The news was soon communicated to the villagers, who rushed out of their houses and assembled in great numbers in front of their buildings. I walked slowly and quietly down towards them, and soon removed all

Chap. XII.] YAXG-TSE-KIANG KIVER. 233

their fears. My young friend the grass cutter was very shy at first, but we parted excellent friends.

The port of Shanghae is situated about 80 or 100 miles to the north-west of Chusan, the latter being in lat. 30 north, and the former in 31 20'. On leaving the Chusan group of islands, and sailing to the northward in the direction of Shanghae, we pass the Bay of Hangchow on the left, and enter the mouth of the noble Yang-tse-kiang, the " child of the Ocean," as its name implies. The country, which, up to this degree of latitude from the south, is very mountainous, now changes, and becomes perfectly level. The shores of the river are, in many places, lower than the river itself, which is kept within its bounds by large and strong embankments. The mountainous scenery disappears entirely, and even from the top of the highest mast of a ship, no hill is seen to bound the distant horizon|all the view is a vast level plain. This is what is called the valley of the Yang-tse-kiang, and is the great northern Nanking cotton district. The land is a deep rich loam, and is without doubt the finest in China, if not in the world.

At the entrance of the river, the navigation is rather difficult, particularly in thick weather, owing partly to the numerous sand-banks, which are all covered at high water, and partly to the difficulty of getting prominent land-marks. Since the opening of the trade in 1843 several ships have got entangled amongst these banks, and have been totally wrecked. When I first visited the Yangtse-kiang, it was quite a common occurrence for vessels to get aground at low water, but as the greater part of them were small opium clippers, commanded by men who knew the region well, they generally got easily off again when the tide flowed. One evening in April, we were sailing up this river with a fair light breeze, which was sending us on at the rate of six or seven miles an hour. The man at the lead was singing out his soundings; and as it was " and a half three," and "by the mark three," the captain concluded that we were in the right channel, and went below for a minute or two. The leadsman was still singing out three fathoms, when, all at once, we felt the bottom of the vessel touch the ground, and in two seconds she was hard and fast in the mud. The tide was ebbing rapidly at the time, and as one side of the schooner was, in deeper water, we were obliged to get out all the spare planking we had to prop the vessel and prevent her from falling over. The next question was, how we were to get off when the tide rose. In the course of the afternoon, we had observed a number of junks astern of us, coming up the river and bound for Shanghae. Some of these were now within a quarter of a mile, and had dropt their anchors until the commencement of the flood tide. After some consultation, the captain came to the determination of boarding one of them, and getting the people to shift their anchoring ground and come a little nearer the schooner, so that a rope might be passed from the

Chap. XU.] COMPULSORY ASSISTANCE. 235

one to the other, and our vessel hauled off when the tide was sufficiently high to float her. As I was able to speak a little Chinese, I was asked to go in the boat and explain what our object was, and likewise to tell them that they should be well paid for their trouble. The boat's crew armed themselves with cutlasses, and, in order to render the business more imposing, the captain put on an old uniform which had formerly belonged to a naval officer, and with a cocked hat on his head and a sword dangling at his side took his seat in the boat. The night was dark but fine, and we could just discern the masts of the nearest junk. In a few minutes we were alongside, and were challenged by the man who had the watch upon deck, and who at the same moment, seeing we were foreigners, ran to give the alarm, exclaiming that the *Ilong-mou- jins,* or " red-haired men," were upon them. Without further parley we sprang into the junk, and when we looked round we found her decks deserted|the watch and every body else having hid themselves below. The captain directed our men to go down the hatchways and try to get the Chinese upon deck, but he gave them strict orders to use them kindly. It was not a little amusing to see our tars going about this part of the business, which they did with right good will and glee. They soon dragged the Chinamen out of their hiding-places, and, much against their inclination, mustered them on deck. I now explained to their captain that our intentions were peaceful, but that our vessel was in very greatdanger, and that it was absolutely necessary they should get up their anchor immediately, and come to our assistance. At the same time, I told them that they should receive twenty dollars for their trouble. They now held a consultation amongst themselves, and at last came and informed us that they would render the required assistance on the following morning. This, however, would not answer our purpose, and besides we knew enough of the Chinese to be perfectly aware that this " to-morrow " would never come, and was only said to get rid of us altogether, and leave us to our fate. We therefore told them that this arrangement would not suit us, and again requested them to get up their anchor. Another consultation was held, and as it was quite evident to me that they were procrastinating, and that we might go on in this manner all night, I advised the master of our schooner to set his own men to work to heave up the Chinaman's anchor, and hoist her sail. The sailors, who were getting rather impatient, gladly obeyed these orders, and when the junk's crew saw what was going on, they also gave their assistance, so that in a few minutes we were under weigh. Having gone as near the schooner as we considered prudent, the anchor was dropped, and a strong rope made fast to the two vessels in order to draw ours off the mud when the tide rose high enough to float her. This was accomplished during the night, and we were safely anchored in three fathoms of water. At daylight, however, we found

Chap. XII.] VILLAGE OF WOOSUNG. 237

that our Chinese friends had made sail, and gone away without waiting to claim the promised reward.

The small village of AVoosung, where one of the battles was fought during the last war, stands on the banks of another river, commonly known as the " Shanghae river " by Europeans, and at the point where it falls into the Yang-tse-Kiang. This is one of the principal stations in China for the opium merchant vessels, and I believe latterly more of the drug has been sold here than at all the other stations put together.

So much has been said about this trade and opium smoking, that a few remarks upon the subject will not be out of place here. It is well known that the greater part of the opium which is brought to the Chinese coast is grown and manufactured in our East Indian possessions. Those English or American merchants who deal largely in this production employ very fast sailing vessels for bringing it from India to China, and also keep up what are called receiving ships in many of the bays or harbours along the coast of China. These receiving ships are regularly supplied by the fast- sailing vessels which bring their cargoes from India or Hongkong. The Chinese smugglers come out from the adjoining bays and towns, in small boats, well manned and armed, in order to protect their property, which is generally of great value. Silver, in the form of South American dollars or Sycee, is bartered for the opium at all those stationson the coast, where no other trade is carried on ; at other places the foreign merchants often find it advantageous to barter the opium in exchange for raw silks and teas, which are the two chief exports of the country.

The statements which have been frequently made in England, both as regards the snmggling and the smoking of Opium, are very much exaggerated. When I first went to China, I expected to find those merchants who were engaged in this trade little else than armed buccaneers, indeed, if I do not mistake, they have been represented as characters of this kind on the English stage. Instead of this, the trade is conducted by men of the highest respectability, possessed of immense capital, and who are known and esteemed as merchants of the first class in every part of the civilised world. The trade in opium, although contraband, is so unlike what is generally called smuggling, that people at a distance are deceived by the term. It may be quite true that its introduction and use are prohibited by the Chinese government, but that prohibition is merely an empty sound, which, in fact, means nothing. The whole, or at least the greater part, of the mandarins use it, and it is not at all unlikely that his Celestial Majesty himself makes one of the number of its devotees. The truth is, the Chinese government, whatever it may say, has no wish to put a stop to its introduction. It is necessary, however, to publish every now and then strong threatening edicts against it, which are only consigned to

Chap. XH.] THE OPIUM TRADE. 239

oblivion in the pages of the Peking Gazette, and have no effect whatever in restraining the Emperor's loyal subjects. It is now the opinion of all intelligent foreigners, and also many of the more enlightened amongst the Chinese themselves, that the importation of opium ought to be legalised, and that it should be admitted at a small duty, as, by this means, much of the demoralising effects of smuggling would be got rid of, and a considerable revenue would flow into the coffers of the Chinese treasury.

Many instances of the feeble kind of opposition which the Chinese government employ to stop the opium trade, occurred during my residence in the country. Sometimes an admiral, renowned for his valour, was sent with a number of war-junks to a particular station, where the opium ships were anchored, for the purpose of compelling them to leave the Chinese shores. Gongs were beat, guns were fired, at a respectful distance, however, and the junks came down with all that pomp and parade which the Chinese know so well how to assume, and which seem to form a principal part of their warlike operations. In the mean time the little opium vessels were seen quietly at anchor, apparently paying but slight attention to all these threatening demonstrations. Presently a message was sent from the admiral, ordering them to get up their anchors and stand out to sea, and never more to dare to enter the waters of his Celestial Majesty under the penalty of being completely annihilated.

A summons like this in former days might havehad some weight, but now it had none; and the only answer the messengers carried back was, " that the foreign vessels were well armed, and that they would not leave their anchorage." This was quite sufficient to cool the courage of the admiral, who was now in a dilemma; he durst not fight the " barbarians," and if he did not manage to get them out of the way, his character for courage would suffer when the affair was represented at head quarters. He therefore altered his tone, and *requested* the captains, as a great favour, to leave the anchorage and move outside for a day or two only, after which time they might return to their old quarters. This was agreed to on the part of the captains of the opium vessels, and on the following morning they got under weigh and went out to sea. The Chinese, who were on the look-out at the time, made a great noise by beating gongs and firing guns, and followed the opium ships until they were fairly outside. The admiral now sent up a report to his government to the effect that he had fought a great battle with the " barbarians," and had driven them away from the shores; or very probably he said that he had blown some of their vessels to pieces, and sunk the rest in the depths of the sea. In the mean time, even before the report was half-way to Peking, the opium vessels had quietly taken up their old anchorage, and things were going on in the usual way! Such is a specimen of the way in which affairs are managed in China.

The opium from Bengal, which consists of two

Chap. XII.] THE OPIUM TRADE. 241

kindsǀnamely, *Patna* and *Benares*ǀis always of a good quality and pure, but the Bombay *Malwa* is now so much mixed up with other ingredients, that the Chinese smuggler will not buy it until he has had an opportunity of testing its quality. This is done in the following manner: ǀ having selected the chest or number of chests which he wishes to purchase, they are opened, and he takes out three or four of the worst-looking cakes, cuts a small piece from each, and dissolves them in a copper ladle over a charcoal fire. When the opium is melted, it is poured out into a coarse paper filter. If it is not of the worst description, it readily passes through the paper into a small basin, which is placed under it. When it will not pass through the filter, the Chinese call it *Man-ling,* by which name they designate opium which is so bad, or so mixed with extraneous ingredients, that it will not dissolve in water or pass through the paper filter. This description of the drug is, of course, only bought at a very reduced price.

When the mixture passes through the filter, the paper is carefully examined, and if any sediment remains, such as sand or rubbish, with which the opium is frequently adulterated, it detracts considerably from its value. This filtered mixture is now put again into a clear copper pan, and boiled slowly over the charcoal fire, until the whole of the water is evaporated, and nothing remains but pure opium. The drug is then poured out into a small porcelain cup, and stirred round and ex-

amined with great care. At this stage of the process, colour forms the principal test of its quality, and as the smuggler stirs it round, and holds it up to the light, he pronounces it to be " *tung-kow"* if it is thick like jelly ; " *pak-chat"* if it has a whitish colour; " *hong-chat"* if it is red; and " *kong-see- pak,"* if it is opium of the first quality, or like that sent round by the East India Company.

Opium is prepared for smoking much in the same manner as I have just described, and is kept in small cups, which are made for the purpose. The smoker lays his head upon a pillow, has a lamp by his side, and with a kind of needle he lifts a small portion of the opium to the candle; and having ignited it, he puts it into the small aperture of the bowl of the pipe. The candle is applied to the bowl during the process of inhaling, and the smoke is drawn into the lungs in the same manner as an Indian or Chinese swallows tobacco. A whiff or two is all that can be drawn from a single pipe, and, therefore, those who are accustomed to the use of the drug have frequently to renew the dose.

No one who has seen any thing of the habits of the Chinese will deny that the use of opium, particularly when taken to excess, has a most pernicious effect both upon the constitution and morals of its victims. From my own experience, however, I have no hesitation in saying that the number of persons who use it to excess has been very much exaggerated; it is quite true that a very large quantity of the drug is yearly imported from India, but then we must take into consideration

Chap. XH.] UPON THE CHINESE. 243

the vast extent of the Chinese empire, and its population of 300,000,000 of people. I have often been in company with opium-smokers when travelling in different parts of the country, and am consequently able to speak with some confidence with regard to their habits. I well remember the impressions I had on this subject before I left England, and my surprise when I was first in the company of an opium-smoker who was enjoying his favourite stimulant. When the man lay down upon the couch, and began to inhale the fumes of the opium, I observed him attentively, expecting in a minute or two to see him in his " third heaven of bliss;" but no: after he had taken a few whiffs he quietly resigned the pipe to one of his friends, and walked away to his business. Several others of the party did exactly the same. Since then I have often seen the drug used, and I can assert that in the great majority of cases it was not immoderately indulged in. At the same time I am well aware that, like the use of ardent spirits in our own country, it is frequently carried to a most lamentable excess. Lord Jocelyn, in his " Campaign in China," gives the following account of its effects, which he witnessed upon the Chinese at Singapore. " A few days of this fearful luxury, when taken to excess, will give a pallid and haggard look to the face, and a few months, or even weeks, will change the strong and healthy man into little better than anidiot skeleton. The pain they suffer when deprived of the drug after long habit, no language can explain ; and it is only when to a certain degree under its influence that their faculties are alive. In the houses devoted to their ruin, these infatuated people may be seen at nine o'clock in the evening in all the different stages; some entering half distracted to feed the craving appetite they had been obliged to subdue during the day: others laughing and talking wildly under the effects of a first pipe ; whilst the couches around are filled with their different occupants, who lie languid with an idiot smile upon their countenance, too much under the influence of the drug to care for passing events, and fast merging to the wished-for consummation. The last scene in this tragic play is generally a room in the rear of the building, a species of dead-house, where lie stretched those who have passed into the state of bliss the opium smoker madly seekslan emblem of the long sleep to which he is blindly hurrying."

The population of China has been estimated lately at 367,000,000.

Opium Pipe.

15

SECTION 15

Chap. XIII.] SHANGHAE. 245

CHAP. XIII.

SHANGHAE IN 1844. | ITS GARDENS AND PLANTS. | START FOR THE HILLS IN THE INTERIOR. | CANALS AND BRIDGES. ADVENTURE WITH MY PONY. THE " TEIN-CHING," OR BLUE DYE,

FOUND. | HILLS AND THEIR VEGETATION DESCRIBED. | THE SURPRISE OF THE NATIVES ON SEEING A FOREIGNER. THEIR CURIOSITY AND HONESTY! PLANTS SENT TO ENGLAND

ANOTHER JOURNEY INTO THE INTERIOR. SOME LARGE NORTHERN CITIES NOTICED A MIDNIGHT VISIT FROM THIEVES.

THE FAR-FAMED CITY OF SOO-CHOW-FOO VISITED. | A DESCRIPTION OF IT NEW PLANTS FOUND CENTRAL POSITION

OF SOO-CHOW AS A PLACE OF TRADE. BATHS FOB THE MILLION. RETURN TO SHANGHAE.

I Again visited Shanghae on the 18th of April, 1844, and spent two or three weeks there at different times. My principal object was to see all the plants in the different northern districts as they came into flower, and it was therefore necessary that I should stay as short a time as possible in each place. I have mentioned that I purchased a collection of *Tree Poeonies* during my first visit to Shanghae in the winter of 1843, which were said to be very splendid things, and entirely different in colour from any plants of the kind which were known in England. I had of course, at that time, no opportunity of seeing their flowers, and was now, therefore, particularly anxious to get some which were in bloom, and had intended to send my old friend back again to Soo-chow for another collection, stipulating, however, that the plants should this time have blooms upon them. One morning, however, as I was going out into the country, a short distance from Shanghae, I was surprised at meeting a garden labourer with a load of Moutans all in full flower, which he was taking towards the city for sale. The flowers were very large and fine, and the colours were *dark purples, lilacs,* and *deep reds,* kinds of which the very existence had been always doubted in England, and which are never seen even at Canton. Two English gentlemen, who were excellent Chinese scholars, being with me at the time, we soon found out the name of the Moutan district; and from the state of the roots in the man's basket I was quite certain that the plants had not been more than an hour or two out of the ground, and that consequently the place where they were grown could not be more than six or eight miles from Shanghae; a surmise which I afterwards found to be perfectly correct. This was doubtless the place where my nursery friend had procured his plants in the previous autumn, and where he would have gone again had I not been lucky enough to find that I could easily go there myself. Indeed, I afterwards discovered that there was no Moutan country in the vicinity of Soo-chow, having met a man from that place in the Shanghae district, where he had come for the express purpose of buying Tree Pajonies. I now went into the Moutan district daily during the time the different plants were coming into bloom, and secured some most

Chap. XIII.] GARDENS AND PLANTS. 247

striking and beautiful kinds for the Horticultural Society.

Several very distinct and beautiful Azaleas were added to my collections at Shanghae, as -well as many other plants of an ornamental character which have not yet been described. I fully expect that many of these will prove hardy enough to thrive in the open air in England, and that others will make excellent plants for the greenhouse.

Being now well acquainted with the country in the immediate vicinity of Shanghae, I was anxious to extend my researches into the interior, particularly as far as some hills which were said to be about thirty miles distant in a westerly direction. It was extremely difficult to gain any information on this subject from the Chinese, who were particularly jealous of foreigners going any distance inland. Their suspicious feelings had also been much increased at this time by the indiscretion of some of our own countrymen, who had hired a boat and gone a considerable distance up one of the rivers, taking soundings with bamboo poles, in the manner of the Chinese. The authorities suspected that they had some particular object in view in ascertaining the depth of the river, and immediately complained to Captain Balfour, the English consul, who was consequently obliged to notice the circumstance.

Being determined, however, to make an effort to accomplish the object I had in view, I procured a pony and a pocket compass, and started off one morning early on a voyage of discovery. The hills were said to lie westerly, and in that direction I rode for eight or ten miles without seeing any thing higher than a mound of earth. The compass was my only guide both in going and also in finding my way back again; the roads were generally not more than four or six feet wide; but still the country had its highways and byways, and for a length of time I was fortunate enough to keep on the former; as long as I did so, I got easily over the numerous canals which intersect the country in all directions, because wherever these are crossed by the main road, good substantial stone bridges are erected. At last I got a glimpse of the hills in the distance, and in my anxiety to take the shortest road, I lost sight of the highway, and got entangled amongst byways and canals. I was soon in a somewhat critical position, the bridges which I was constantly crossing were old, narrow, and rotten, and the feet of my pony were every now and then getting entangled between the planks. At length we came to one much worse than the others, and although I got off and did every thing to persuade the pony to follow me over it, with great reluctance he attempted to do so, but when about the centre of the bridge, his feet got fast in the rotten planking, and in the struggle to free himself, the centre gave way; I had just time to spring to the bank, when the bridge and pony both fell into the canal. Luckily for me the poor animal swam to the side I was on, and allowed me to catch him when he got

Chap. XIH.] CURIOSITY AT SEEING A FOREIGNER. 249

out of the water: he was completely covered with mud, and my saddle and bridle were of course in a sad condition. By the assistance of some labourers who were at work within a short distance, I was soon enabled to get out of this network of canals, and regain the main road; but this was a lesson to me, and as long as I was in China, I never afterwards went off the main road when I was on horseback.

I reached a small town in the vicinity of the hills about two o'clock in the afternoon ; the pony having had nothing to eat since we left Shanghae, was much exhausted, and I was therefore anxious to procure a feed of corn for him at some of the shops. The news of the presence of a foreigner in the town spread like lightning, and I was soon surrounded and followed by some thousands of people of both sexes, young and old, who were all anxious to get a glimpse of my features and dress. Their behaviour on the whole, however, was civil and respectful, and the only inconvenience I had to complain of was the pressure of the crowd. For a few of the copper coin of the country, a boy had promised to take me to a shop where I could purchase something for the pony, and we wended our way through the crowd, which was every moment becoming more dense, towards, as I supposed, a corn or hay shop. At last, to my surprise, he came to a halt in front of an eating-house, and my guide came and asked me for money to go in and buy some boiled rice. " But I want a feed for the pony," said I. " Very well, give me the money, and I will fetch you a basin of boiled rice for him." " You had better bring him a pair of chopsticks also," said I, as I put the money into his hand. The idea of a pony eating with chopsticks delighted the crowd, and put them into high good humour: during my travels in the interior, I often found the benefit of having a joke with the natives.

My pony seemed to enjoy the meal which was set before him, and I too had some rice from the same pot. I then proceeded on foot to examine the nearest hill, and soon came to the conclusion that it would be advantageous for me to be some days in the vicinity of this place. As I could not trust the natives with the pony, which belonged to the head mandarin in Shanghae, I determined to take him home again myself, and hire a boat with which I could return by any of the numerous canals which branch all over the country, and stay as long as I pleased. I reached Shanghae late on the same evening, weary enough, having ridden at least sixty miles during the day.

A few days after this, having engaged a boat, I started early one morning, and taking advantage of the tide, which ebbs and flows over all this part of the country, I reached the hills on the same evening. The country through which I passed was rich and fertile, cotton forming the staple production of the fields in the neighbourhood of Shanghae. After passing the cotton district, I came into a tract of country in which a cruciferous

Chap. Xni.] TEIN-CHING, OR BLUE DYE. 251

plant seemed to be principally cultivated. From this plant a kind of indigo or blue dye is prepared; it is called *Tein-ching* by the Chinese. Very large quantities of this substance are brought to Shanghae, and all the other towns in the north of China, where it is used in dyeing the blue cotton cloth, which forms the principal article of dress of the poorer classes. I brought home living specimens of the plant which produces this dye, and as these are now in flower in the gardens of the Horticultural Society, the proper scientific name of the plant will soon be ascertained.

As I approached the hills the level of the country became lower, and at that time of the year (June) it was completely flooded, and rice was extensively cultivated. In general, the higher land of this vast plain is used in the cultivation of cotton and the cruciferous plant mentioned above ; while the lower lands, those which are easily flooded, are converted into rice fields. Here and there on my way I met with large trees of the *Salisburia adi- antifolia,* which are the largest and most striking trees in this part of the country. Small patches of bamboo were seen around all the villages, and groups of cypress and pine generally marked the last resting-places of the Chinese, which are scattered over all the country.

The hills were very different from any which I had seen in the more southern parts of China:they are not more than 400 feet in height, and have none of that bold and rugged character which I have formerly noticed. Here and there crumbling rocks show themselves above the sui-face, but these are not so numerous as to affect the general pastoral- looking appearance of these hills. The country is also more richly wooded than any other part near Shanghae, and, of course, contains a greater number of species of plants. One curious fact, however, came under my notice: no Azaleas were met with in this part of the country, although the hills about sixty or eighty miles to the south abound in such plants ; and, although the other plants, which accompany Azaleas on the Chusan and Ning- po hills, were here growing in all their native luxuriance, these, their more lovely companions, were not to be found. I can scarcely believe that the hills between Ning-po and Shanghae are the most northern limit for this class of plants; yet such from my own observations would appear to be the case.

It has proved to bo a new species, and has been named Isatis indigotica.

The natives in this part of the country were vastly surprised when they saw me for the first time; at the different villages and towns, men, women, and children of all ranks lined the banks of the canals as my boat passed along, and often requested me to come out in order that they might have a better opportunity of seeing me. When I left my boat for the purpose of ascending the hills, my boatmen used to make a good deal of money by allowing the people to go in and inspect my

Chap. XIII.] PLANTS SENT TO ENGLAND. 253

little cabin. A copy of the " Pictorial Times," which I happened to have with me, was greatly admired, and I was obliged to leave it amongst them. It is a remarkable fact, however, that nothing, as far as I know, was ever stolen from me at this time, although several hundred persons visited my boat in my absence. The boatmen must either have been very sharp, or the people must have had a superstitious dread of the property of a foreigner: to put it down to their honour is, I am afraid, out of the question!

Having finished my researches amongst the hills, I left this part of the country and returned to Shanghae. The " Helen Stuart," one of the first vessels which left Shanghae for England direct, was at this time ready for sea, and I availed myself of this opportunity to send some cases of plants to the Horticultural Society, which, I regret to say, arrived in very bad condition. When I had despatched these cases, I determined on another journey into the interior.

Every one who has been in China, or who is at all acquainted with Chinese history, has heard of the city of *Soo-chow-foo*. If a stranger enters a shop in Hong-Kong, in Canton, or in any of the other towns in the south, he is sure to be told, when he inquires the price of any curiosity out of the common way, that it has been brought from this celebrated place; let him order any thing superb, and it must be sent for from Soo-chow I fine pictures, fine carved work, finesilks, and fine ladies, all come from Soo-chow. I It is the Chinaman's earthly paradise, and it would be hard indeed to convince him that it had its equal in any town on earth. In addition to its other attractions, I was informed by the Chinese nursery gardeners at Shanghae that it contained a great number of excellent flower gardens and nurseries, from which they obtained all or nearly all the plants which they had for sale, and I was, therefore, strongly tempted to infringe the absurd laws of the Celestial Empire, and try to reach this far-famed place. My greatest difficulty was to meet with boatmen who would travel with me, as they were all frightened for the mandarins, who had issued very stringent orders to them after the circumstance happened which I have already noticed. They were told, that they might take foreigners down the river towards the sea, and up as far as a pagoda a mile or two above Shanghae, but on no account were they to go up the western branch of the river. This was a direct infringement on the right which had been secured to us by the treaty of Nanking, and her Majesty's consul at this port soon found it necessary and prudent to interfere in the matter. Some time after this period, when what are called the boundaries were fixed, the foreign residents were allowed to go a day's journey into the interior, that is, as far as they could go and come back again in twenty-four hours.

Having at length procured a boat, we set off on

Chap. XIII.] VISIT TO SOO-CHOW. 255

our journey, the boatmen neither knowing where I intended to go to, or how long I was to be absent from Shanghae. I simply told them we were going into the country in search of plants, and that they must take a supply of rice for several days. My Chinese servant, who always accompanied me, also informed them, that it was a common thing for me to wander about the country in search of plants, but that I was *perfectly harmless,* and would take care that they should not get into any trouble on my account. This gave them some confidence, and as the wind and tide were both in our favour we were soon a considerable distance away from Shanghae. As I knew pretty well in what direction Soo-chow lay, I took my course by a pocket compass which I always carried with me. After getting twenty or thirty miles from Shanghae, I judged it prudent to break the subject of my wishes to my companions. First of all, I took my servant aside; he was a most active fellow, and capable of persuading the others to do any thing he liked. " Now," said I to him, " I want to visit Soo-chow, and if you will persuade the boatmen to go on there, I will make you a present of five dollars when we return: besides, you may tell the men that I shall double the amount of the hire which I have already promised them." Upon this a long conference ensued, the result of which was that they determined to accept my offer.

I was, of course, travelling in the Chinese costume; my head was shaved, I had a splendid wig and tail, of which some Chinaman in former days had doubtless been extremely vain ; and upon the whole I believe I made a pretty fair Chinaman. Although the Chinese countenance and eye differ considerably from those of a native of Europe, yet a traveller in the north has far greater chance of escaping detection than in the south of China, the features of the northern natives approaching more nearly to those of Europeans than they do in the south, and the difference amongst themselves also being greater.

In China, the canal is the traveller's highway, and the boat is his carriage, and hence the absence of good roads and carriages in this country. Such a mode of conveyance is not without its advantages, however little we may think of it in England; for as the tide ebbs and flows through the interior for many miles, the boats proceed with considerable rapidity; the traveller, too, can sleep comfortably in his little cabin, which is, in fact, his house for the time being.

The canal, after leaving Shanghae, leads in a northerly direction, inclining sometimes a little to the west; branches leading off in all directions over the country. Some very large towns and walled cities were passed on our route, at one of which, named *Cading,* we halted for the night just under the ramparts. I spread out my bed in my little cabin, and went to sleep rather early, intending to start by times with the tide next morning,

Chap. XIII.] MIDNIGHT THIEVES. 257

and get as far as possible during the ensuing day. But, as my countryman says,|

" The best laid schemes of mice and men gang aft agee ;"

and I awoke during the night by the cool air blowing in upon my head through one of the windows of the boat, which I had shut before I went to rest. I jumped up immediately and looked out, and through the darkness I could discern that we were drifting down the canal with the tide, now coming in contact with some other boat, which had been fastened up like ourselves for the night, and now rubbing against the branches of trees which hung over the sides of the canal. I lost no time in awaking my servant and the boatmen, who rubbed their eyes with astonishment, and exclaimed that some robber must have boarded us. This had never struck me before, but when I called for a light, I found that all my clothes, English and Chinese, were gone. Our visitor, whoever he had been, after taking possession of all the cabin contained, cut the rope by which we were fastened, and shoved us off into the centre of the canal, along which we had drifted a considerable way before I awoke. Fortunately for me, the few dollars I had with me were in my Chinese purse beneath my pillow.

" What shall we do," said my servant when we had made the boat fast again to some others on the side of the canal, " your clothes are all gone ?"

" Do," said I, laughing; " I think the best

thing we can do is to go to bed again until daylight." This being agreed to, we were soon all once more sound asleep. When morning dawned, I sent my servant into the town of Cading with a few dollars, which procured me another dress, and we proceeded on our journey.

The city of Cading *is* large and fortified, although the walls and ramparts are in a state of decay. It is evidently a very ancient place. Here a large quantity of the celebrated carving is done, for which the Chinese in the north are so well known. After leaving this town, the canal, which was narrow, continued in a northerly direction for a few miles, and then, all at once, our little boat shot out of it into a broad and beautiful canal, resembling a lake or broad river, running nearly east and west, and probably connecting itself with the Yang-tse-kiang river, somewhere between Woosung and Nanking. The scenery here is extremely striking; the broad and smooth canal bears on its waters hundreds of Chinese boats of all sizes, under sail, and each hurrying to its place of destination; pagodas here and there are seen rearing their heads above the woods and Buddhist temples, which are scattered over this wide and extensive plain. One of these temples crowns a solitary little hill, named *Quin-san,* which at certain seasons of the year is visited by crowds of people from Soo-chow and the neighbouring towns: the whole country, as far as the eye can reach, is one vast rice-field; and every where the

Chap. XHi.] SOO-CHOW VISITED. 259

pleasing clatter of the water-wheels falls upon the ear, and hundreds of happy and contented Chinese peasants are seen engaged in the cultivation of the soil. After continuing its westerly course for some distance, the canal divided, and the branch we took soon led us to another town named *Ta- tsong-tseu.* It is a place of great size, walled and fortified like Cading and Shanghae, and is probably larger than the latter, although perhaps not so populous. A great number of large old junks are moored on the canal round the walls, apparently used as dwelling-houses, being now unfit for any other service. This town, too, like Cading, is evidently in a decaying state, judging from the dilapidated condition of the houses and fortifications, but teems with an immense population of men, women, and particularly children.

On approaching Soo-chow some hills were seen, bounding the level plain, which I afterwards found were some few miles west from the town itself. The whole country here, as well as near Cading, is one vast rice-field. Many females are employed in driving the water-wheels, generally three or four to each wheel: these ladies have large feet, or rather their feet are of the natural size; indeed, if they were cramped in the usual way it would be impossible for them to work on the water-wheel- Small feet, however, are general amongst the lower classes who work in the fields, for of the hundreds whom I observed hoeing the cotton, orengaged in other agricultural operations, but a small proportion had feet of the natural size.

A few miles on the east of Soo-chow there is a large and beautiful lake, twelve or fifteen miles across, through which the boats from Sung-Kiang- foo and other places in that direction approach the city. After passing this lake the canal, which had widened considerably, now began to contract; bridges here and there were passed, villages and small towns lined the banks, and every thing denoted the approach to a city of some size and importance. It was a delightful summer's evening on the 23d of June, when I approached this far- famed town. The moon was up, and with a fair light breeze my little boat scudded swiftly, its masts and sails reflected in the clear water of the canal; the boats thickened as we went along, the houses became more crowded and larger, lanterns were moving in great numbers on the bridges and sides of the canal, and in a few minutes more we were safely moored, among some hundreds of other boats, under the walls of this celebrated city. Having taken all the precautions in our power against another nightly visitor, my servant, the boatmen, and myself, were soon fast asleep.

With the first dawn of morning I was up, and dressed with very great care by my Chinese servant, whom I then despatched to find out the nursery gardens in the city, in order to procure the plants which I wanted. When he had obtained this information he returned, and we proceeded

Chap. XiH.] SOO-CHOW VISITED. 261

together into the city, in order to make my selections.

When I left the boat, I confess I felt rather nervous as to the trial I was about to make. Although I had passed very well as a Chinaman in the country districts, I knew that the inhabitants of large towns, and particularly those in a town like this, were more difficult to deceive. My old friends, or I should rather say my enemies, the dogs, who are as acute as any Chinaman, evidently did not disown me as a countryman, and this at once gave me confidence. These animals manifest very great hatred to foreigners, barking at them wherever they see them, and hanging on their skirts until they are fairly out of sight of the house or village where their masters reside.

As I was crossing the bridge, which is built over the moat or canal on the outside of the city walls, numbers of the Chinese were loitering on it, leaning over its sides, and looking down upon the boats which were plying to and fro. I stopped too, and looked down upon the gay and happy throng, with a feeling of secret triumph when I remembered that I was now in the most fashionable city of the Celestial Empire, where no Englishman, as far as I knew, had ever been before. None of the loiterers on the bridge appeared to pay the slightest attention to me, by which I concluded that I must be very much like one of themselves. How surprised they wouldhave been had it been whispered to them that an Englishman was standing amongst them.

The city of Soo-chow-foo, in its general features, is much the same as the other cities in the north, but is evidently the seat of luxury and wealth, and has none of those signs of dilapidation and decay which one sees in such towns as Ning-po. A noble canal, as wide as the river Thames at Richmond, runs parallel with the city walls, and acts as a moat as well as for commercial purposes. Here, as at Cading and Ta-tsong-tseu, a large number of invalided junks are moored, and doubtless make excellent Chinese dwelling-houses, particularly to a people so fond of living on the water. This same canal is carried through arches into the city, where it ramifies in all directions, sometimes narrow and dirty, and at other places expanding into lakes of considerable beauty; thus enabling the inhabitants to convey their merchandise to their houses from the most distant parts of the country. Junks and boats of all sizes are plying on this wide and beautiful canal, and the whole place has a cheerful and flourishing aspect, which one does not often see in the other towns in China, if we except Canton and Shanghae. The walls and ramparts are high, and in excellent repair, having considerable resemblance to those of Ning-po, but in much better order. The east wall, along the side of which I went all the way, is not more than a mile in length, but the north and south are much longer, thus making the city a parallelogram. That part of the city

Chap. XIII.] NEW PLANTS FOUND. 263

near the east gate, by which I entered, is any thing but splendid ; the streets are narrow and dirty, and the population seems of the lowest order, but towards the west the buildings and streets are much finer, the shops are large, and every thing denotes this to be the rich and aristocratic part of the town. The city gates seem to be well guarded with Chinese soldiers, and all the streets and lanes inside are intersected at intervals with gates, which are closed at nine or ten o'clock at night. The Governor General of the province resides here, and keeps those under his control in excellent order.

The number of nursery gardens in this city had been exaggerated by my Chinese friends at Shanghae, but nevertheless there were several of considerable extent, out of which I was able to procure some new and valuable plants. Among these I may notice in passing a white *Glycine,* a fine new double yellow rose, and a *Gardenia* with large white blossoms, like a Camellia. These plants are now in England, and will soon be met with in every garden in the country. The Soo-chow nurseries abounded in dwarf trees, many of which were very curious and old, two properties to which the Chinese attach far greater importance than we do in England.

The ladies here are considered by the Chinese to be the most beautiful in the country, and, judging from the specimens which I had an opportunity of seeing, they certainly deserve their high character.Their dresses are of the richest material, made in a style at once graceful and elegant; and the only faults I could find with them were their small deformed feet, and the mode they have of painting or whitening their faces with a kind of powder made for this purpose. But what seemed faults in my eyes are beauties in those of a Chinaman, and hence the prevalence of these customs.

Soo-chow-foo seems to be the great emporium of the central provinces of China, for which it is peculiarly well fitted by its situation. The trade of Ning-po, Hang-chow, Shanghae, and many other towns on the south, Ching-kiang-foo, Nanking, and even Peking itself on the north, all centres here, and all vthese places are connected either by the Grand Canal, or by the hundreds of canals of lesser note, which ramify over all this part of the empire. Shanghae, from its favourable position as regards Soo-chow, will doubtless become one day a place of vast importance, in a commercial point of view, both as regards Europe and America.

I remained for several days in this city, and its neighbourhood, when, having done all that was possible under the circumstances, I set out on my way back to Shanghae. When I arrived, I was obliged to go on shore in my Chinese dress, as the English one had been stolen by my midnight visitor. The disguise, however, was so complete, that I was not recognised by a single individual, although I walked up the street where I was well known, and even my friend Mr. Mackenzie, with

Chap. XIII.] BATHS FOR THE MILLION. 26

whom I was staying, did not know me for the first few minutes after I sat down in his room.

In the town of Shanghae, as well as in many other large Chinese towns, there are a number of public hot water bathing establishments, which must be of great importance as regards the health and comfort of the natives. I will describe one which I passed daily during my residence in Shanghae. There are two outer rooms used for undressing and dressing; the first, and largest, is for the poorer classes; the second, for those who consider themselves more respectable, and who wish to be more private. As you enter the largest of these rooms, a placard which is hung near the door informs you what the charges are, and a man stands there to receive the money on entrance. Arranged in rows down the middle and round the sides of both rooms are a number of small boxes or lockers, furnished with lock and key, into which the visitors put their clothes, and where they can make sure of finding them when they return from the bathing room, which is entered by a small door at the farther end of the building, and is about 30 feet long and 20 feet wide; the water occupying the whole space, except a narrow path round the sides. The water is from 1 foot to 18 inches deep, and the sides of the bath are lined with marble slabs, from which the bathers step into the water, and on which they sit and wash themselves: the furnace is placed on the outside, and the flues are carried below the centre of the bath.

In the afternoon and evening this establishment is crowded with visitors, and on entering the bath room, the first impression is almost insupportable ; the hot steam or vapour meets you at the door, filling the eyes and ears, and causing perspiration to run from every pore of the body ; it almost darkens the place, and the Chinamen seen in this imperfect light, with their brown skins and long tails, sporting amongst the water, render the scene a most ludicrous one to an Englishman.

Those visitors who use the common room pay only six copper cash; the others pay eighteen, but they have in addition a cup of tea and a pipe of tobacco from the proprietors. I may mention that one hundred copper cash amount to about 4rf. of our money ; so that the first class enjoy a hot water bath for about one farthing! and the other a bath, a private room, a cup of tea, and a pipe of tobacco for something less than one penny!

16

SECTION 16

CHAP. XIV.

CHINESE COTTON CULTIVATION. | YELLOW COTTON. | DISTRICT WHERE IT GROWS. | COTTON COUNTRY DESCRIBED. | SOIL.

| MANURE, AND MODE OF APPLICATION. | PRECEDING CROPS.

| TIME OF SOWING. METHOD. | RAINS SUMMER CULTIVATION. EARLY RAIN ADVANTAGEOUS. TIME OF REAPING

AND GATHERING. COTTON FARMERS AND THEIR FAMILIES. DRYING AND CLEANING PROCESS DESCRIBED. MARKETING. INDEPENDENCE OF THE SELLER. CROWDED STREETS IN 8HANGHAE DURING THE COTTON SEASON. WAREHOUSES AND PACKING. | HOME CONSUMPTION. | STALKS USED FOR FUEL.

The Chinese or Nanking cotton plant is the *Gossy- pium herbaceum* of botanists, and the " *Mie who,* " of the northern Chinese. It is a branching annual, growing from one to three or four feet in height, according to the richness of the soil, and flowering from August to October. The flowers are of a dingy yellow colour, and, like the Hibiscus or Malva, which belong to the same tribe, remain expanded only for a few hours, in which time they perform the part allotted to them by nature, and then shrivel up and soon decay. At this stage the seed pod begins to swell rapidly, and when ripe, the outer coating bursts and exposes the pure white cotton in which the seeds lie imbedded.

The yellow cotton, from which the beautiful Nanking cloth is manufactured, is called " *Tze miewho,*" by the Chinese, and differs but slightly in its structure and general appearance from the kind just noticed. I have often compared them in the cotton fields where they were growing, and although the yellow variety has a more stunted habit than the other, it has no characters which constitute a distinct species It is merely an accidental variety, and although its seeds may generally produce the same kind, they doubtless frequently yield the white variety, and *vice versa.* Hence, specimens of the yellow cotton are frequently found growing amongst the white in the immediate vicinity of Shanghae; and again a few miles northward, in fields near the city of *Poushan* on the banks of the Yang-tse-kiang, where the yellow cotton abounds, I have often gathered specimens of the white variety.

The Nanking cotton is chiefly cultivated in the level ground around Shanghae, where it forms the staple summer production of the country. This district, which is part of the great plain of the Yang-tse-kiang, although flat, is yet several feet above the level of the water in the rivers and canals, and is consequently much better fitted for cotton cultivation than those flat rice districts in various parts of the country, I such, for example, as the plain of Ning-po, I where the ground is either wet and marshy, or liable at times to be completely overflowed. Some fields in this district are, of course, low and marshy, and these are cultivated with rice instead of cotton, and regularly flooded

Chap. XIV.] SOIL, MANURE, AND CULTURE. 269

by the water-wheel during the period of growth. Although the cotton land is generally flat, so much so, indeed, that no hills can be seen from the tops of the houses in the city of Shanghae, it has nevertheless a pleasing and undulating appearance, and, taken as a whole, it is perhaps the most fertile agricultural district in the world. The soil is a strong rich loam, capable of yielding immense crops year after year, although it receives but a small portion of manure.

The manure applied to the cotton lands of the Chinese is doubtless peculiarly well fitted for this kind of crop. It is obtained from the canals, ponds, and ditches which intersect the country in every direction, and consists of mud which has been formed partly by the decay of long grass, reeds, and succulent water plants, and partly by the surface soil which has been washed down from the higher ground by the heavy rains. Every agricultural operation in China seems to be done with the greatest regularity, at certain stated times, which experience has proved the best, and in nothing is this more apparent than in the manuring of the cotton lands. Early in April the agricultural labourers, all over the country, are seen busily employed in cleaning these ponds and ditches. The water is first of all partly drawn *off,* and then the mud is thrown up on the adjoining land to dry, where it remains for a few days until all the superfluous water is drained out of it, and is then conveyed away and spread over the cotton fields.Previous to this, the land has been prepared for its reception, having been either ploughed up with the small buffalo plough in common use in the country, and then broken and pulverised by the three-pronged hoe, or, in those instances where the farms are small and cannot boast of a buffalo and plough, it is loosened and broken up entirely by manual labour. When the mud is first spread over the land, it is, of course, hard or cloggy, but the first showers soon mix it with the surface soil, and the whole becomes pulverised, and it is then ready for the reception of the cotton seed. Road- scrapings and burnt rubbish are saved up with care, and used for the same purpose and in the same manner.

A considerable portion of the cotton lands either lie fallow during the winter months, or are planted with those crops which are ready for gathering prior to the sowing of the cotton seed. Frequently, however, two crops are found growing in the field at the same time. Wheat, for example, which is a winter crop, is reaped in the Shanghae district generally about the end of May, while the proper time for putting in the cotton seed is the beginning of that month or the end of April. In order, therefore, to have cotton on the wheat lands, the Chinese sow its seeds at the usual time amongst the wheat, and when the latter is reaped, the former is several inches above ground, and ready to grow with vigour when it is more fully exposed to the influence of sun and air. The Shanghae season |

Chap. XIV.] TIME AND METHOD OF SOWING. 271

that is, from the late spring frosts to those in autumn | is barely long enough for the production and ripening of the cotton, as it is easily injured by frost, and the Chinese farmer is thus obliged, in order to gain time and obtain two crops from his ground in one year, to sow its seeds before the winter crop is ready to be removed from the ground. When it is possible to have the first crop entirely removed before the cotton is sown it is much preferred, as the land can then be well worked and properly manured, neither of which can otherwise be done. The method of sowing one crop before the preceding one is ripe and removed from the land is very common in this part of the country; and even in autumn, before the cotton stalks are taken out of the ground, other seeds are frequently seen germinating and ready to take the place of the more tender crop.

In the end of April and beginning of May | the land having been prepared in the manner just described | the cotton seeds are carried in baskets to the fields, and the sowing commences. They are generally sown broad-cast, that is, scattered regularly over the surface of the ground, and then the labourers go over the whole surface with their feet and tread them carefully in. This not only embeds the seeds, but also acts like a roller to break and pulverise the soil. Germination soon commences, the seeds rooting first in the manure which had been scattered over the surface of the land. In some cases the seed, instead of being sown broadcast, is sown in drills or patches, but this mode is less common than the other. These patches are often manured with bruised oil-cake, which is the remains of the cotton seed, after its oil has been extracted. The rains, which always fall copiously at the change of the monsoon which takes place at this season of the year, warm and moisten the earth, and the seeds swell, and vegetation progresses with wonderful rapidity. Many of the operations in Chinese agriculture are regulated by the change of the monsoon. The farmer knows from experience, that when the winds, which have been blowing from the north and east for the last seven months, change to the south and west, the atmosphere will be highly charged with electric fluid, and the clouds will daily rain and refresh his crops.

The cotton fields are carefully tended during the summer months. The plants are thinned where they have been sown too thickly, the earth is loosened amongst the roots, and the ground hoed and kept free from weeds. If the season is favourable, immense crops are obtained owing to the fertility of the soil, but if the weather happens to be unusually dry from June to August, the crop receives a check which it never entirely recovers, even although the ground, after that period, should be moistened by frequent showers. 1845 was a season of this kind, and the crop was a very deficient one compared with that of the previous year. The spring was highly favourable, and the plants looked well up to the month of June, when the dry

Chap. XIV.] RAINS I SUMMER CULTIVATION. 273

weather set in, and gave them a check which they never recovered. Abundance of rain fell later in the season, but it was then too late, and only caused the plants to grow tall and run to leaf, without producing those secretions which ultimately go to the formation of flowers and seed.

The cotton plant produces its flowers in succession from August to the end of October, but sometimes, when the autumn is mild, blooms are produced even up to November, when the cold nights generally nip the buds, and prevent them from forming seed. In the autumn of 1844 this happened on the night of the 28th of October, when the thermometer sunk to the freezing point, and then ice was found on the sides of the canals and ponds.

As the pods are bursting every day, it is necessary to have them gathered with great regularity, otherwise they fall upon the ground and the cotton gets dirty, which of course reduces its value in the market. Little bands of the Chinese are now seen in the afternoon in every field, gathering the ripe cotton, and carrying it home to the houses of the farmers. As the farms are generally small, they are worked almost entirely by the farmer and his family, consisting sometimes of three or even four generations, including the old grey-haired grandfather or great-grandfather, who has seen the crops of fourscore years gathered into his barns. Every member of these family groups has a certain degree of interest in his employment; the harvest is

their own, and the more productive it is, the greater number of comforts they will be able to afford. Of course there are many cotton farms of larger size, where labourers are employed in addition to the farmer's family, but by far the greater number are small and worked in the way I have just described. It is no unusual sight to see the family goats, too, doing their share of the work. Several of these animals are kept on almost every farm, where they are, of course, great favourites with the children, and often follow them to the cotton fields. Although the children with their little hands can gather the cotton as well as their elders, they are not strong enough to carry it about with them, and it is amusing to see their favourites the goats, with bags slung across their backs, receiving the deposits of cotton, and bearing it home to the houses, evidently aware that they too are working for the general good.

However fine the crop may be, the Chinese are never sure of it until it is actually gathered in. Much depends upon a dry autumn, for, if the weather is wet after the pods begin to burst, they drop amongst the muddy soil, and are consequently much injured, if not completely destroyed. When the cotton reaches the farmyard, it is daily spread out on hurdles raised about four feet from the ground, and fully exposed to the sun. As the object is to get rid of all the moisture, it is of course only put out in fine weather, and is always taken into the house or barn in the evening.

Chap. XIV.] COTTON|CLEANING AND MARKETING. 275

When perfectly dry, the process of separating it from the seeds commences. This is done by the well-known wheel with two rollers, which, when turned round, draws or sucks in the cotton, and rejects the seeds. It is a simple and beautiful contrivance, and answers well the end for which it is designed. The cotton is now sent to market, and a portion of the seeds are reserved for the next year's crop.

Early in the fine autumnal mornings, the roads leading into Shanghae are crowded with bands of coolies from the cotton farms, each with his bamboo across his shoulders and a large sack of cotton swung from each end. With these they hurry into the town, for the purpose of disposing of them to the merchants, who have numerous warehouses from which they send the cotton to the other provinces of the empire. These coolies or small farmers | for many of them bring their own produce to market themselves|are very independent in their dealings. Having reached the first warehouse, the cotton is exposed to the view of the merchant, who is asked what price he intends to give for that particular quality; and should the sum offered be below the owner's expectations, he immediately shoulders his load and walks away to another merchant. At thi season it is almost impossible to get along th streets near the sides of the river where the cotton warehouses are, owing to the large quantities of this commodity which arc daily brought in from the country. It is bought up by the large cottonmerchants, who empty it out in their warehouses, and then repack it in a neat and compact manner before it is conveyed on board the junks.

Before the cotton is converted into thread for the purpose of weaving, it is cleaned and freed from knots by the well-known process common in our possessions in India. This is done by an elastic bow, the string of which being passed under a portion of the cotton placed on a table, throws it in the air by the vibration which is kept up by the workman, and separates the fibre without at all breaking or injuring it. At the same time the wind caused by the sudden vibrations carries off the dust and other impurities. After this process the Chinese cotton is particularly pure and soft, and is considered by good judges not to be surpassed by any in the world. It is much superior to that imported to China from Hindostan, and always commands a higher price in the Chinese market.

Every small farmer or cottager reserves a portion of the produce of his fields for the wants of his own family. This the female members clean, spin, and weave at home. In every cottage throughout this district the traveller meets with the spinning-wheel and the small hand-loom, which used to be common in our own country in days of yore, but which have now given way to machinery. These looms are plied by the wives and daughters, who are sometimes assisted by the old men or young boys who are unfit for the labours of the field. Where the families are numerous and industrious, a much

Chap. XIV.] COTTON|STALKS USED FOR FUEL. 277

greater quantity of cloth is woven than is required for their own wants, and in this case the surplus is taken to Shanghae and the adjacent towns for sale. A sort of market is held every morning at one of the gates of the city, where these people assemble and dispose of their little bundles of cotton cloth. Money is in this manner realised for the purchase of tea and other necessaries which are not produced by the farms in this particular district.

When the last crops are gathered from the cotton fields, the stalks are carried home for fuel. Thus every part of the crop is turned to account: the cotton itself clothes them, and affords them the means of supplying themselves with all the necessaries of life ; the surplus seeds are converted into oil; the stalks boil their frugal meals: and the ashes even|the remains of all|are strewed over their fields for the purposes of manure. But even before this takes place, the system I have already noticed I of sowing and planting fresh crops before the removal of those which occupy the land I is already in progress. Clover, beans, and other vegetables are frequently above ground in the cotton fields before the stalks of the latter are removed. Thus, the Chinese in the northern provinces lengthen by every means in their power the period of growth; and gain as much as they possibly can from the fertility of their land. The reader must bear in mind, however, that the soil of this district is a rich deep loam, which is capable of yielding many crops in succession without the aid of a particle of manure. Nature has showered her bounties on the inhabitants of this part of the Chinese empire with no sparing hand; the soil is not only the most fertile in China, but the climate is capable of rearing and bringing to perfection many of the productions of the tropics, as well as the whole of those found in all the temperate regions of the globe.

17

SECTION 17

Chap. XV.] CLIMATE OF CHINA. 279

CHAP. XV.

CLIMATE OF CHINA SUMMER AND WINTER. I TEMPERATURE
OF HONG-KONG|OF SHANGHAE MONSOONS. TYPHOONS.
SIGNS OF THEIR APPROACH. I DESCRIPTION OF A TYPHOON
WITNESSED BY THE AUTHOR. EFFECT PRODUCED UPON
VEGETATION. RAINS. WET AND DRY SEASONS. METEOROLOGICAL TA-
BLE.

In order to understand Chinese agriculture, a knowledge of the climate of the
country is of course necessary. The dominions of the Emperor of China stretch over
twenty-three degrees of latitude I from 18 to 41 north, and from the 98 to the 123 of
east longitude ; thus including both tropical and temperate regions in its vast extent.
Being placed on the east side and forming part of the large continent of Asia, it is
liable to extremes of temperature I to excessive heat in summer, and extreme cold in
winter I which are unknown in many other parts of the world within the same parallels
of latitude. One of our best writers upon China makes the following very sensible
remarks on this subject:I"Although Peking is nearly a degree to the south of Naples|the
latitude of the former place being 39 54', of the latter 40 50' I

Davis's " Chinese."

the mean temperature of Peking is only 54 of Fahrenheit, while that of Naples is 63. But the thermometer at the Chinese capital sinks much lower during the winter than at Naples, so in summer does it rise somewhat higher; the rivers are said to be frozen for three or four months together, from December to March; while during the last embassy in September, 1816, we experienced a heat of between 90 and 100 in the shade. Now it is well known that Naples, and other countries in the extreme south of Europe, are strangers to such a degree of long continued cold, and not often visited by such heats. 'Europe,' observes Humboldt, ' may be considered altogether as the western part of a great continent, and therefore subject to all the influence which causes the western sides of continents to be warmer than the eastern; and at the same time more temperate, or less subject to *excesses* of both heat and cold, but principally the latter.' "

From my own tables, kept by Newman's best registering thermometers, I find that at Hong-kong, in the months of July and August | the two hottest months in the year|the mercury frequently stood as high as 90, and one day at 94 Fahr. in the shade. The minimum was generally about ten degrees lower than the maximum. In the winter, from December to March, the thermometer frequently sinks nearly down to the freezing point, and sometimes, although rarely, snow has fallen at Canton and on the adjacent hills. The influence of

Chap. XV.] SUMMER AND WINTER. 281

the sea, however, in this part of the empire, has a tendency to check the extremes of both heat and cold; but these are much greater in the northern interior. The northerly winds in the winter and spring months are severely cold in the south of China; indeed, I have suffered more from cold at Hong-kong and Macao in the month of February, than I have ever done in England.

At Shanghae, in the province of Kcangsoo, in latitude 31 20' north, the extremes of heat and cold arc much greater than what we experienced in the southern provinces. Through the kindness of Dr. Lockhart, who kept up my meteorological tables during my absence in different parts of the country, I have obtained a very complete set of observations for nearly two years. From these it appears that in July and August the heat is the greatest; the thermometer in the shade sometimes standing for several days at 100 of Fahrenheit. The heat during these days was almost insupportable to Europeans, who, when I was in Shanghae, were obliged to live in Chinese houses, which, from their construction, were ill calculated to exclude the heat. In the end of October the thermometer sometimes sinks as low as the freezing point. In the evening of the 28th of that month, in 1844, the remains of the cotton and other tropical plants which are cultivated in the fields during the summer, were destroyed by frost. December, January, and February are the coldest months inthe year, the cold then being quite as severe as it is with us in the south of England. In the winter of 1844-45 the thermometer sunk as low as 26 Fahrenheit. On the night of the 18th of December, and again on January the 4th, the index was left at 24. But that winter, according to Chinese accounts, was peculiarly mild, so much so, that the usual supply of ice could not be procured. In ordinary years the ponds and canals are frequently frozen several inches in thickness, and afford a plentiful supply of ice. I have, therefore, little doubt that in most years the thermometer may be found at least twenty degrees below the freezing point, or at 12 of Fahrenheit, and perhaps even lower. Snow frequently falls, but the sun is too powerful to allow it to lie long on the ground.

If we except the extremes of heat and cold just noticed, the climate of Shanghae may be pronounced as fine as any in the world. Even the cold in winter is highly advantageous to the natives, and still more so to Europeans and Americans, as it strengthens their constitutions, and enables them to withstand the effects of the excessive heat. The months of April, May, and June are delightful; and although the sun is hot in the middle of the day, in the afternoon the air is soft and agreeable, and the evenings cool and pleasant. The autumnal months are generally of the same description ; the wind then is cool and bracing, and the sky is much clearer than in England. The sun, for days, and some-

Chap. XV.] MONSOONS AND TYPHOONS. 283

times for weeks together, rises in the morning, runs his course, and sets again in a clear and cloudless sky.

The prevailing winds blow from the south-west from the end of April to the middle of September ; during the remaining portion of the year they are northerly and easterly: thus forming what are called the south-west and north-east monsoons. These monsoons blow with great regularity in the south of China, but are more variable towards the north. In the latitude of Chusan or Shanghae, although the monsoons prevail, the wind, not unfrequently, blows from other quarters. In the end of the summer season, that is, from July to October, the country is frequently visited by those dreadful gales called by foreigners typhoons. The name is a corruption of the Chinese word *Ta-fung* or " great wind." These storms commit the most fearful ravages both by land and sea. The barometer gives warning some hours before the gale commences, and, therefore, foreign ships can always send down their masts and yards, and, if possible, remove to a safe anchorage. Where that is not to be had, they have the dreadful alternative of standing out to sea. The Chinese, without the aid of the barometer, can always tell when the *Ta-fung* is coming on by the following signs. The wind, which blows from the south-west in the typhoon season, changes and blows from the north or north-east, becoming gusty and gradually increasing in strength, the sky lowers and looks wild, the sea rolls in upon the beachwith a dead heavy swell, and every thing portends a coming storm. When these signs appear, the fleets of fishing-boats on the coast take their nets in, crowd all sail, and make for the shore as fast as they can, where the boats are hauled up on dry land, or into some creek which is sheltered from the force of the winds and waves. The coasting junks, which are ill fitted for bad weather, lose no time in getting into some sheltered port where they can ride out the storm in safety. And, luckily, as a safeguard from the fury of these winds, nature has provided a great number of excellent well-sheltered harbours on the coast of China, all of which are well known to the pilots who are employed on board the junks.

During my residence in China, I witnessed two of these terrific gales I once at sea, and once on shore. Luckily, in the first instance, we were able to run into a deep bay, and with three anchors down rode out the gale in perfect safety. The other occurred on the 21st and 22d of August, 1844, when I was at Ningpo. I observed the Chinese running about in great consternation, and calling to each other that the " great wind " was coming, and to make preparations for it. Mats and rattan work, which had been placed over the doors and windows to afford shade from the sun, were hastily removed, and many of the houses, which were known to be in a weak state, were, in a rapid way, propped up and strengthened. Nor were the husbandmen less busy in the fields. The heads of the tall millet,

Chap. XV.] WITNESSED BY THE AUTHOR. 285

being nearly ripe, were quickly cut, and the long stalks left to be reaped at another time. Millet is so heavy when nearly ripe, that had it been left exposed to the wind it must have been dashed to pieces, and the crop entirely lost. Crops on the sides of the rivers and canals were removed where it was possible to do so; otherwise, they would have been blown into the water, and carried away far beyond the reach of their owners. All the fruit which was nearly ripe was hastily gathered from the trees, unnecessary branches were cut away, and others tied up and supported.

The gale gradually increased in force until daylight on the morning of the 22d, when it seemed to be at its height. In Mr. Mackenzie's house, where I was staying at the time, we passed a fearful night. The wind howled and whistled round the roof, every blast seemingly more fierce than that which preceded it, until I really thought we should have the building down upon us and be buried in the ruins. At daylight the rooms presented a dismal appearance; all the floors, chairs, and tables were covered with dust and pieces of broken tiles and mortar which had been shaken out of the roof. As the storm still raged with unabated fury, Mr. Mackenzie and myself, glad to escape from the wreck by which we were surrounded, went out to see what effect the gale was producing on the other places in the vicinity. The wind was so powerful, that it was next to impossible to keep our feet; in fact, we were frequently blown off the path, and were obligedto scramble back to it again on our hands and knees. The river, which is generally beautiful and smooth, had now risen and completely overflowed its banks, having been forced back by the strength of the wind, and was as rough as the sea itself. The whole country was one vast sheet of troubled water, for the branches of the river, and the numerous canals by which it is intersected, had all overflowed their banks, and had spread in the low paddy fields. Most of the small boats were safe, as they were either in sheltered creeks, or drawn up beyond the reach of the water, but many of the large wood-junks which frequent this port were not so fortunate. These had been moored off the city, having, as usual, a large portion of their cargo lashed to their sides. In many instances, the combined force of the winds and waves snapped the lashings, strong as they were, and the spars of wood floated from their sides, and were either carried away by the force of the stream, or thrown on shore. Hundreds of the Chinese were now ready to seize the wood as it floated to land, and with a total disregard to the " rights of property " conveyed it at once to their own houses. No mandarin or other government officer interfered to prevent this, and the Chinese servants of the English Consul and other foreign residents actually brought a considerable quantity to the houses of their masters, and seemed surprised when reproved for their dishonesty. The English of course honourably returned the spoil to its owners, much to the surprise

Chap. XV.] WITNESSED BY THE AUTHOR. 287

of the Chinese. On the opposite side of the river, we observed great numbers engaged in the same lawless occupation. The city walls, here, run parallel with the river, and these rascals were coolly hoisting the wood over the walls and ramparts, assisted by their friends inside the city: nor was this attempted to be checked.

At about nine o'clock in the morning, the wind, which commenced from the north, had veered round to the east and south, but still raged with fearful power. On retracing our steps, which we had some difficulty in doing, owing to the flooded state of the country, and the force of the wind, we encountered a family group in the fields surrounding a coffin, which the wind seemed inclined to carry off in spite of all their efforts to fasten it to the ground. It is customary in this part of the country to place the remains of the dead upon the surface of the ground, sometimes supporting the coffins on short stakes, to raise them a few feet from the earth. In this instance the poor people were actually fighting with the winds, but were at last able to secure the remains of their relative, and allow him to sleep the long sleep of death in peace. At this time the barometer stood at 28 30', but the wind was still blowing a perfect gale until about mid-day, when it gradually became less violent. In the evening, although the sky still looked wild, it was evident the gale had passed away, and the wind was then blowing from the south-west. The river soon returned to its former limits, boats began to sail upand down, and business, which had been entirely suspended, went on again as usual. Altogether, the typhoon lasted nearly twenty-four hours.

The following morning was calm and beautiful, but the scene was one of ruin and devastation. The streets were strewed with broken tiles and mortar; many of the houses were completely unroofed, walls were blown down, and every thing evinced the violence of the storm. In the fields the change was still more striking; but two days before the trees and hedges were green, the gardens were gay with flowers, and every thing bore the happy smiling aspect of summer; now vegetation had changed from green to withered sickly brown, flowers had faded, trees were torn up by the roots and broken and shattered, and many of the crops were completely ruined.

The accounts which reached us from sea after this typhoon proved that the loss of life had been very great. For many days after the gale had ceased, our vessels on the coast frequently met with large portions of wreck floating about, the remains of Chinese junks, which told a fearful tale. An English vessel on her way to Chusan was obliged to cut away her masts, and was towed into the harbour a day or two afterwards by one of the government steamers. Mr. Shaw, one of her passengers, informed me that during the typhoon they had a perfect calm for some time, and that then the wind veered round to a different quarter, and blew with increased violence. This is not unfrequently

Chap. XV.] EFFECTS OF THE TYPHOON. 289

the case, and during these short lulls the vessels roll and labour in a dreadful manner, owing to the heavy swell of the sea, as they are then entirely at its mercy, and have nothing to steady them.

In the preceding year, this part of the country was twice visited by typhoons, viz. on the 1st of September and 1st of October. In the island of Chusan, where they were particularly violent, the most disastrous effects were produced upon the crops. The little streams in the island were swollen into large rivers, and carried away every thing before them. The crops of entire fields, chiefly paddy, were in some instances swept away, and in others sanded completely up, and rendered useless. The patched-up houses of our officers, who held the island at the time, suffered severely. During the typhoon of 1844, a house built on the beach by one of the officers was actually lifting up, and would doubtless have been carried away by the force of the wind, but fortunately Brigadier Campbell, who was passing at the time, gave the alarm, and ordered out a number of men from the barracks, who held it down until it was rendered more secure.

The wet and dry seasons in the southern and tropical parts of China are more decided in their character than they are in the northern portions of the Empire. At Hong-kong and in the provinces of the south, the winter season, that is, from October to March, is generally dry, more particularly in November, December, and January. The most wet

months in the year are those near the change of the monsoons, in May and June, and again in September, when the rains fall in torrents, probably owing to the stagnation produced in the atmosphere by the change in the direction of the winds.

The author before quoted explains this on the following principles. He says: I " The north-east monsoon, which commences about September, blows strongest during the above period, and begins to yield to the opposite monsoon in March. About that time the southerly winds come charged with the moisture which they have acquired in their passage over the sea through warm latitudes ; and this moisture is suddenly condensed into thick fogs as it comes in contact with the land of China, which has been cooled down to a low temperature by the long-continued northerly winds. The latent heat given out, by the rapid distillation of this steam into fluid, produces the sudden advance of temperature which takes place about March; and its effect is immediately perceptible in the stimulus given to vegetation of all kinds, by this union of warmth with moisture. With the progressive increase of heat and evaporation those rains commence, which tend so greatly to mitigate the effects of the sun's rays in tropical climates. In the month of May the fall of rain has been known to exceed twenty inches, being more than a fourth of all the year, and this keeps down the temperature to the moderate average marked for that month."

Chap. XV.] METEOROLOGICAL TABLE.

The following table, made from observations kept by the late Mr. Beale at Macao for a number of years, shows the amount of the average monthly fall of rain in inches:
I

Thermometer. , .s C 3 S3S B §tt & Range.||Osj S.II'!C O 3 H !" 4) jinl'e 1iFromToSg5 PSJanuary574551H652930-230-675February -584551-5683330-121-700March716065-5794530-172-150April766972-5845930-045-675May787375-5 866929-8911-850June847981-5,897429-8711-100July888486948129-847-750August868384-59079I29-869-900September-847981-58875 I 29-9010-925October767073856030-045-500November-686164-5794830-142-425December-635257-5694030-250-975Annual Means74-166-7 70-481-3 57-6, 30-03 Total rain, 70-625.

In the north the rains also fall copiously at the change of the monsoons, more particularly in spring, at which time they are of the greatest utility to the crops, which are sown or planted about that time. Those parts of China, however, which are included in the temperate zone, cannot properly be said to have a wet and dry season in the same sense as these terms are generally understood in the tropics. The winter months, which are dry at Hong-kong, are far from having the same character at Shanghae, for example, where heavy and continued falls of rain

18

SECTION 18

and snow are of frequent occurrence. In fact, the climate of Northern China has a greater resemblance to that of the south of England or France, than it has to that of the southern parts of the Chinese Empire ; and, although hotter, used always to remind me of the beautiful summers we have in England once in every ten and twelve years. The sky is for days and weeks together without a cloud, and in the evening a heavy dew falls and refreshes vegetation.

These remarks will assist the reader to understand more fully the theory and practice of Chinese agriculture, which form the subject of the following chapter.

Chap. XVI.] CHINESE AGRICULTURE. 293

CHAP. XVI.

CHINESE AGRICULTURE. I EXAGGERATED STATEMENTS REGARDING ITS ADVANCEMENT. SOIL OF THE HILLS. TEA LAND.

SOIL OF THE PLAINS. I SUMMER CROPS RICE AND ITS CULTIVATION. I CHINESE PLOUGH AND HARROW. I NUMBER OF CROPS PRODUCED. I METHOD OF OBTAINING TWO CROPS OF

RICE IN SUMMER IN THE PROVINCE OF CHEKIANG RICE

HARVEST. I TERRACE CULTIVATION DESCRIBED. I THE TEIN- CHING PLANT, FROM WHICH THE NORTHERN INDIGO IS OBTAINED.I SUMMER HILL CROPS. I CULTIVATION OF SWEET
POTATOES. I EARTH-NUTS WINTER CROPS. I CELEBRATED
SHAN-TUNG CABBAGE. I OIL PLANT.IWHEAT, BARLEY, ETC.
IRIPENING OF WINTER CROPS. I MANURES TWO PLANTS
CULTIVATED FOR THIS PURPOSE I THEIR CULTIVATION AND
MODE OF APPLICATION, A MANURE FOR MIXING WITH SEEDS
IITS UTILITY.IOTHER MANURES IN COMMON USE. I MANURE
TANKS. NIGHT SOU, AND URINE MODE OF APPLICATION.
SUCCESSION AND ROTATION OF CROPS.

The profession of agriculture in China has been highly honoured and encouraged by the government of the country, from the earliest times down to the present day. The husbandman ranks higher here than he does in any other country in the world, and the Emperor himself marks his sense of the importance of agriculture, by engaging in its operations at the commencement of every season. In his character of " Son of Heaven," or mediator between the gods and his subjects, he devotes three days to solemn fasting and prayer, after which heproceeds to a field, and with his own hands holds the plough, and throws a portion of the rice seed into the ground, thus showing the importance which government attaches to industry in the cultivation of the earth, that there may be plenty on the land to supply the wants of the teeming population.

The progress and advancement of the Chinese in agriculture as an art has been, however, greatly exaggerated by many who have adverted to this subject in their writings. The Chinese government has been always so jealous of foreigners entering the country, that those who were probably able to form a correct opinion on the subject were prevented from doing so, and were led away by the fertility of their imaginations; while, on the other hand, the Roman Catholic missionaries who travelled and resided in the interior were evidently ignorant of the art itself, as well as of the progress it had made in other countries. But it must also be borne in mind that whilst agriculture has been advancing rapidly towards perfection amongst the nations of the western world, the Chinese in this, as with most other things, have remained stationary, and hence there must be a much greater disparity between us and them now than there was when the early writers upon China published their works. To these writers, and more particularly to those who kept on faithfully copying their works, we must attribute the erroneous opinions which have been generally held by us in every thing relat-

Chap. XVI.] SOIL OF THE HILLS. 295

ing to the agriculture of the Chinese. I have no doubt that, as a nation, they surpass the natives of India and other half-civilised states in this art, as they do in most other peaceful accomplishments; but it is ridiculous, now, at least, to compare them for a moment with our intelligent farmers in England or Scotland. As well might we compare their coasting junks with the navy of England, or their merchants with ours, whose ships are met with on every sea, and whose commercial operations extend to every quarter of the world. In order, however, that the reader may form an opinion for himself, I will describe in detail what passed under my own eye connected with this subject, during my travels of nearly three years in the country. In that space of time I had an opportunity of seeing repeatedly the various methods of cultivation and their results, both in the north and in the south; all of which were carefully noted in my journal at the time.

I will begin with the southern provinces. These are, of course, tropical, and differ from those in the north in many respects, both with regard to soil and the nature of the plants cultivated.

The soil of the mountains in the south of China is of the poorest description. Rocks of granite are seen every where protruding themselves above the scanty vegetation, whilst the soil itself is composed of dry burnt clay mixed with particles of granite in a decaying or disintegrated state. This soil, naturally so poor, is kept so by the practice of periodically cutting and carrying off the long grass and stunted bushes for firewood. Sometimes the natives set fire to this upon the mountains, for the purpose of affording a scanty manure, but nevertheless the soil is miserably sterile. Almost all the hilly portions of the south of China are in a state of nature, " *stern and wild,"* where the hand of man never attempts agricultural operations, and where it is almost impossible he ever can. Here and there, near the base of the hills, the far-famed terrace cultivation may be seen, where the natives grow small patches of rice and other vegetables, such as sweet potatoes and earth-nuts, but the portion of land in this part of the country used for such purposes bears but an extremely small proportion to the vast tracts in a wild state.

At Amoy and over all that part of the province of Fokien the mountains are even more barren than those of Quantung. On some of the hills on the island of Amoy, the traveller may wander for miles and scarcely see even a weed. On every side there is nothing but masses of dark crumbling granite, and red burnt-looking clay. This, however, seems the northern boundary of the most barren part of China. When we reach the river Min, near Foo-chow-foo, there is a great change visible in the vegetation of the hills, caused, of course, by the richer nature of the soil. This remark applies to the northern portion of Fokien and to the whole of the province of Chekiang. I have ascended hills near the mouth of the Min at least 3000 feet above

Chap. XVI.] TEA LAND. 297

the level of the sea, which were under cultivation to the summit. The soil here was composed of a gravelly loam; and though far from rich, it contained more vegetable matter or humus, and was also much deeper. The addition of vegetable matter rendered the soil sufficiently fertile to repay the Chinese farmer for the labour expended in bringing the crops to maturity. Some of the hills are of course much more productive than others. The tea districts, for example, both in the province of Fokien and Chekiang, are not only more fertile, but are very different from what they are generally supposed to be. One of the most accredited accounts of China gives the following analysis of the soil of these districts:l" The tea soil of China consists almost entirely of siliceous sand in a minute state of divisionl84 per cent, of sand, a quantity of carbonate of iron and alumina, *and only* 1 *per cent, of vegetable matter."* Where or how this analysis could be obtained, I have no means of knowingl most probably from the black tea districts near Canton; but it is certainly very far from being a correct one if meant to apply to the rich soil of the great tea districts.

But even here, and over all the most fertile mountain districts of Central China, it would be ridiculous to assert, as some have done, that the whole or even the greater part is under cultivation. On the contrary, by far the greater part lies in a state of nature, and has never been disturbed by the hand of man. I am anxious to state this fact in express terms, in order to set those right who havebeen led to believe that every inch of land in the empire, however bleak and barren, is under cultivation, having given way to Chinese industry and skill! I myself, before I visited China, was under the same impression; but the first glance at the rugged mountainous shores soon convinced me of my error. Unfortunately, our opinions of a distant unknown country are apt to go to extremes, either fancying it entirely barren, or else a paradise of fertility.

The *soil of the valleys* or plains varies quite as much in different provinces as it does in the hills. The level of these valleys or plains is generally very low; in many instances below that of the rivers and canals. In the south the soil consists of a strong stiff clay mixed with a small portion of sand, but containing scarcely any vegetable matter or humus. This is its composition about Canton and Macao, and in fact over all the provinces of the south, unless perhaps in the vicinity of large towns, where its natural character has been altered to a certain extent by the influence of manure. Where the hills lose their barren character, four or five hundred miles to the northward from Hongkong, a visible change takes place also in the soil of the valleys and plains. In the district of the Min, for example, instead of being almost entirely composed of strong stiff clay, it is mixed with a considerable portion of vegetable matter, and is an excellent strong loam, not unlike that which we find in some of our best wheat lands in England and

Chap. XVI.] CHINESE PLOUGH. 299

Scotland, and capable of producing excellent crops. As a general rule it may be observed, that the lower the valleys are, the more the soil approaches in its nature to the stiff clay of the south, and *vice versd*. For instance, the Shanghae district is several feet higher above the level of the rivers and canals than that of Ning-po, and the soil of the latter consists more of a stiff clay and has less vegetable matter in its composition, and is far from being so fertile as the cotton district of Shanghae.

Rice being the chief article of food is, of course, the staple production of the country, more particularly in the south, where two crops of it can easily be raised in the hot months, besides another crop of some more hardy vegetables in winter.

The ground is prepared in spring for the first crop of rice, as soon as the winter green crops are removed from the fields. The plough, which is commonly drawn by a buffalo or bullock, is a rude implement; but probably answers the purpose much better than ours would, which has been found to be too heavy and unmanageable for the Chinese. As the land is always flooded with water before it is ploughed, this operation may be described as the turning up a layer of mud and water, six or eight inches deep, which lies on a solid floor of hard stiff clay. The plough never goes deeper than this mud and water, and consequently the ploughman and his bullock in wading through the field find a solid footing at this depth below the surface. The waterbuffalo generally employed in the south is well adapted for this work, as he delights to wallow amongst the mud, and is often found swimming and amusing himself in the canals on the sides of the rice fields. But it seems a most disagreeable and unhealthy operation for the poor labourer, who nevertheless goes along cheerful and happy. After the plough comes the harrow; this is chiefly used to break and pulverise the surface of the soil or to bury the manure. Hence it has not long perpendicular teeth like ours; but the labourer stands upon the top of it, and presses it down upon the muddy soil while it is drawn along. The object of both plough and harrow is not only to loosen the earth, but to mix up the whole until it forms a puddle and its surface becomes smooth and soft. In this condition it is ready to receive the young rice plants.

Several of our ploughs have been sent out to China, and offered to the native farmers *gratis,* but they will not use the

Previously to the preparation of the fields the rice seed is sown thickly in small patches of highly manured ground, and the young plants in these seed-beds are ready for transplanting when the fields are in a fit state to receive them. Sometimes the Chinese steep the seeds in liquid manure before they sow them ; but although this practice is common in the south, it is not general throughout the empire.

The seedling plants are carefully dug up from the bed and removed to the fields. These fields are now smooth, and overflowed with water to the depth of three inches. The plants are put in, in patches, each containing about a dozen plants, and

Chap. XVI.] NUMBER OF CROPS. 301

in rows from ten to twelve inches apart each way. The operation of planting is performed with astonishing rapidity. A labourer takes a quantity of plants under his left arm, and drops them in bundles over the land about to be planted, as he knows, almost to a plant, what number will be required. These little bundles are then taken up, and the proper number of plants selected and plunged by the hand into the muddy soil. The water, when the hand is drawn up, immediately rushes into the hole, and carries with it a portion of soil to cover the roots, and the seedlings are thus planted and covered in without further trouble.

In the south the first crop is fit to cut by the end of June or the beginning of July. Before it is quite ripe, another crop of seedlings is raised on the beds or corners of the fields, and is ready for transplanting as soon as the ground has been ploughed up and prepared for their reception. This second crop is ready for cutting in November.

In the latitude of Ning-po, 30 north, the summers are too short to have the land cropped in the same way in which it is done in the south. The farmers here manage to have two crops of paddy in the summer by planting the second crop two or three weeks after the first, in alternate rows. The first planting takes place about the middle of May, and the crop is reaped in the beginning of August, at which time the alternate rows are only about a foot in height, and are still quite green. After the early crop is removed, the ground is stirred up and manured, and the second crop having now plenty of light and air, advances rapidly to maturity, and is ready for the reaping-hook about the middle of November.

About one hundred miles further north, in the Shanghae district, the summers are too short to enable the husbandman to obtain a second crop of rice, even upon the Ning-po plan, and he is therefore obliged to content himself with one. This is sown at the end of May, and reaped at the beginning of October.

A large quantity of rain always falls at the change of the north-east monsoon in May. This is of the utmost importance to the farmer, not only as regards his rice crops, but also as to many other operations at this season of the year. We are accustomed to hear a great deal of the machine-like regularity which pervades all the operations of the Chinese; but a little investigation of the circumstances in which they are placed|at least in so far as agriculture is concerned|will convince us that their practice is regulated, not so much by caprice and those " Mede and Persian " laws, as by the laws of nature herself, upon which the success of the varied operations of agriculture mainly depend. Thus the crops of rice and cotton are sown on the low lands, and the sweet potatoes are planted on the hills, year after year, exactly at the same time. But this regularity is not the effect of prejudice, nor in obedience to the imperial orders; it is simply the result of experience, which has taught the farmer that this is the proper time for these

Chap. XVI.]

IRRIGATION.

operations, because there will then be a continuance of frequent and copious showers, which will moisten the earth and the air until such time as the young rootlets have laid hold of the soil and are capable of sending up sufficient nourishment to the stems.

During the growth of the rice, the fields are always kept flooded when water can be obtained. The terraces near the base of the hills are supplied by the mountain streams, and the fields which are above the level of any adjoining river or canal are

Water-wheel Tor Irrigation.

flooded by the celebrated water-wheel, which is in use all over the country. These machines are of three kinds. The principle in all of them is the same, the only difference being in the mode of applying the moving power; one is worked by the hand, another by the feet, and the third by an animal of some kind, generally a buffalo or bullock. The rice lands are kept flooded in this way until the crops are nearly ripe, when the water is no longer necessary. It is also necessary, or at least advantageous, to go over the ground once or twice during the summer, and stir the soil up well amongst the roots, at the same time removing any weeds which may have sprung up. If the weather is wet, the fields retain the water for a considerable time, and then it is not an uncommon sight to see the natives wading nearly up to the knees in mud and water, when they are gathering in the harvest.

When ripe, the crops are cut with a small instrument, not very unlike our own reaping-hook, and are generally thrashed out at once in the fields where they have grown. Sometimes, however, and more particularly in the north, the paddy is tied up in sheaves, and carried home before it is thrashed; indeed every thing in the northern agriculture of the Chinese has a great resemblance to what is practised in Europe.

The *terrace cultivation* of China has been noticed by nearly all writers upon this country, and, like most other subjects, it has been either much exaggerated or undervalued. It appeared to me to be carried to the greatest perfection on the hill sides adjacent to the river Min near Foo-chow-foo; at least I was more struck with it there than any where else. On sailing up that beautiful river, these terraces look like steps on the sides of the mountains, one rising above another, until they sometimes reach six or eight hundred feet above

Chap. XVI.] TERRACE CULTIVATION. 305

the level of the sea. When the rice and other crops are young, these terraces are clothed in luxuriant green, and look like a collection of gardens among the rugged and barren mountains. The terrace system is adopted by the Chinese, either for the purpose of supplying the hill-sides with water where paddy is to be grown, or to prevent the heavy rains from washing down the loose soil from the roots of other vegetables. Hence these cuttings are seen all over the sides of the hills, not exactly level like the rice terraces, but level enough to answer the purpose of checking the rains in their descent down the mountain. For the same reason, the sweet potato and some other crops which are grown on the hills are always planted in ridges which run cross-ways, or horizontally; indeed, were the ridges made in a different direction, the heavy rains which fall in the early summer months would carry both the loose soil and crops down into the plains.

Rice is grown on the lower terrace ground, and a stream of water is always led from some ravine and made to flow across the sides of the hills, until it reaches the highest terrace, into which it flows and floods the whole of the level space. When the water rises three or four inches in height, which is sufficiently high for the rice, it finds vent at an opening made for the purpose in the bank, through which it flows into the terrace below, which it floods in the same manner, and so on to the lowest. In this way the whole of the rice terraces are kept

continually flooded, until the stalks of the crops assume a yellow ripening hue, when the water being no longer required, it is turned back into its natural channel, or led to a different part of the lull, for the nourishment of other crops. These mountain streams, which abound in all parts of the hilly districts, are of the greatest importance to the farmer; and as they generally spring from a high elevation in the ravines, they can be conducted at pleasure over all the lower parts of the hills. No operation in agriculture gives him and his labourers more pleasure, than leading these streams of water from one place to another and making them subservient to their purposes. In my travels in the country the inhabitants often called my attention to this branch of their operations, and I pleased them much when I expressed my admiration at the skill with which they executed it. The practice is not confined to the paddy fields: for I remember once, when superintending the planting of some large trees and shrubs in the garden of Messrs. Dent and Co. in Hong-kong, after I had given them a large supply of water at the time they were put into the ground, I desired the gardener to repeat the dose next morning. But, on the following day, when I returned to the spot, I was surprised to find a little stream divided into many branches, and meandering amongst the roots of the newly planted trees. As there was no stream there before, I went up to examine its source, and found that it had been led from a neighbouring ravine; a work more easy than car-

Chap. XVI.] SUMMER CKOPS. 307

rying a large supply of water in buckets, and at the same time more effectual.

Several other summer crops are cultivated in the low lands. In the southern provinces, for instance, we find large quantities of the *Nelumbium specioswn* grown for its roots, which are much esteemed; the *Trapa bicornis,* the castor oil plant, *Scirpus tuberosus, Convolvulus reptans,* and several other vegetables, for which there is a great demand in all Chinese towns. The sugar-cane, also, is extensively grown both in the provinces of Quantung and Fokien, and probably in other parts of the empire.

In the district of Kiangsoo my attention was directed to a plant called *Tein-ching*, which is largely cultivated by the inhabitants for the sake of its blue dye. In the southern provinces a great deal of indigo *(Indigofera)* is grown and manufactured, in addition to a large quantity which is annually imported from Manila and the Straits. In the north, however, the plant which we call indigo is never met with, owing, I suppose, to the coldness of the winters; but its place is supplied by the *Tein-ching (Isatis indigotica)* the leaves of which are prepared in the same manner as the common indigo. The colour of the liquid at first is a kind of greenish blue, but, after being well stirred up and exposed to the air, it becomes much darker. I suppose it is thickened afterwards by evaporation; but this part of the process did not come under my observation. I am very much inclined to believe that this is the dye used to colour the green teas which are manufactured in the north of China for the English and American markets: this, however, is only conjecture.

The summer productions of the hilly country are, of course, different from those of the plains. From the province of Fokien northward, to the great valley of the Yang-tse-kiang, the hills are amongst the most fertile in China. They are frequently terraced in the manner I have described, and their staple productions, if we except the rice which is grown on the lower terraces, are sweet potatoes and earth-nuts *(Arachis hypogaea)*. In the southern provinces, when the winters are mild, the roots of the sweet potato frequently remain in the ground all the winter. In the north the cold is too severe, and consequently the natives are obliged to dig up and protect the roots. In April those roots whtfch have been saved for " seed " are planted thickly in beds near the houses or in the corners of the fields. They begin to push out their young shoots immediately, and these are ready to be taken off by the beginning of May. In the mean time the ground on the hill-sides has been prepared, and horizontal ridges or drills formed about two feet apart. About the 10th or 12th of May these cuttings are taken off and planted, and seem to grow as readily as couch grass. It is astonishing how well they succeed, considering the little care expended upon them; but we must keep in mind that this is the commencement of the rainy season at the change of the monsoon, that the sky is generally cloudy, that scarcely

Chap. XVI.] RIPENING OF THE WINTER CROPS. 309

a day passes without frequent showers, and that consequently the air is saturated with moisture. The earth-nuts are grown most extensively in the southern provinces, more particularly in Fokien; while the sweet potatoes are better a little farther north, where they form the chief hill crop.

The *winter crops* in the neighbourhood of Macao and Canton consist of large quantities of our European vegetables, such as potatoes, peas, onions, and cabbages, which are grown for the supply of the Europeans who reside at Hong-kong or Canton. Our potatoes are generally planted here in October, which is considered the best time to insure a good crop, but as they always sell well in the markets, the growers manage to keep up a succession during the greater part of the year. Several varieties of the cabbage tribe, which seem indigenous to China, are grown extensively in the fields at this season both in the south and north. These never produce a solid heart like our cabbages, and are of no value when imported to England; but the celebrated *"Pak-tsae,"* or white cabbage of Shantung and Peking, is a very different plant; it is never grown in the south of China, but is produced in the summer months in the north. Large quantities of this delicious vegetable are brought south every autumn, in the junks which sail at the commencement of the north-east monsoon in October.

In the northern provinces the principal winter productions are wheat, barley, peas, beans, the cabbage oil plant, and various other vegetables of lesser note. These crops are grown on the hills as well as on the low lands, and on the ground which produces sweet potatoes in summer. In the Nanking district they are generally sown or planted in October upon those lands which produce rice or cotton during the summer months. Frequently the sowing takes place before the cotton or the dry summer crops have been removed from the ground, and the young plants are seen coming up amongst these crops, and ready to take their place when they are removed. This is done in order to give a longer season for the ripening of the different crops, and is very generally practised in the northern districts. The wheat and barley ripen in Fokien in April, and in the neighbourhood of Shanghae about the middle of May. About Chinchew and Amoy the wheat crops are so poor that the labourers pull them up by the hand, in the same manner as we do in our moorlands in England and Scotland. They are of course much better in the rich district of Shanghae, but the varieties of both wheat and barley are far inferior to ours ; and as the Chinese sow them too thickly, they are generally much drawn, and the heads and corn small. The beans and peas seem to be exactly the same as our field kinds, and are certainly indigenous to the northern parts of China. Very large quantities of the cabbage tribe are cultivated for the sake of the oil which is extracted from their seeds. They are planted out in the fields in autumn, and their seeds are ripe in April and May, in time to be removed

Chap. XVI.] PLANTS CULTIVATED FOR MANURE. 311

from the land before the rice crops. It must not be supposed, however, that the whole of the land is regularly cropt in this manner, and that, as some writers inform us, it never for a moment lies idle, for such is not the case.

In the island of Chusan, and over all the rice country of Chekiang and Keangsoo, there are two plants cultivated in the winter months, almost exclusively for manure, the one is a species of *Coro- nilla;* the other is *Trefoil,* or clover. Large ridges, not unlike those on which gardeners grow celery, are thrown up on the wet rice fields in the autumn, and the seeds of the plants are dropt in, in patches at five inches apart, on the surface of the ridges. In a few days germination commences, and long before the winter is past the tops of the ridges are covered with luxuriant herbage. This goes on growing until April, when it is necessary to prepare the ground for the rice. The ridges are then levelled, and the manure plants are scattered in a fresh state over the surface of the ground. The fields are flooded, and the plough and harrow are employed to turn up and pulverise the soil. The manure, thus scattered over the ground and half-buried amongst mud and water, commences to decay immediately, and gives out a most disagreeable putrid smell. This mode of manuring is generally adopted in all the rice lands in this part of China, and the young paddy doubtless derives strong nourishment from the ammonia given out in the decomposition of this fresh manure.

Fire-wood is so scarce in the country that a great portion of the straw, cotton stalks, and grass, which would go to manure the fields, are used for firing, and, therefore, the plan of growing manure for the land is forced upon the farmers by necessity. The plan of using manure in a fresh state, instead of allowing it first to decay, has doubtless been found from long experience to be the best for the young paddy. The Chinese farmer is not a chemist; he knows little or nothing of vegetable physiology, but his forefathers have hit accidentally upon certain systems which are found in practice to succeed, and to these he himself adheres, and hands them down unchanged to his children.

When the first crop of rice is cut, the second, which has been planted in the alternate rows, is left to grow and ripen in the autumn ; the ground is stirred up, and the stubble and part of the straw of the first crop is immediately worked up with the mud and water between the rows: this decays in the same manner as the trefoil in spring, and affords manure to the second crop. Prawns and fish of various kinds are frequently used for the same purpose and in the same way.

Burnt earth mixed with decomposed vegetable matter is another highly esteemed manure, and is common in all the agricultural districts. During the summer months all sorts of vegetable rubbish are collected in heaps by the road-sides, and mixed with straw, grass, parings of turf, &c., which are set on fire and burn slowly for several days, until all the

Chap. XVI.] MANURE FOK MIXING WITH SEEDS. 313

rank vegetable matter is decomposed, and the whole reduced to a rich black earth. It is then turned over several times, when it presents the same appearance as the vegetable mould used in gardens in England. This manure is not scattered over the land, but reserved for covering the seeds, and is applied in the following manner. When the seed time arrives, one man makes the holes, another follows and drops in the seeds, and a third puts a handful of this black earth on the top of them. Being principally vegetable matter, it keeps the seeds loose and moist during the period of germination, and afterwards affords them nourishment. This manure is useful mechanically as well as chemically in a stiff soil, like that of the low lands of China, where the seeds are apt to be injured in the process of germination. The young crop thus planted acquires a vigour in its first growth, which enables it to assimilate the matter which forms the strong stiff soil, and to strike its roots firmly into it.

What is commonly known by the name of oilcake, is broken up and used in the same manner as the vegetable earth, and is also scattered broadcast over the land. The oil-cake is the remains or refuse of the seeds of several different plants, such as the tallow tree, various kinds of beans, and the cabbage formerly mentioned. There is a great demand for this manure in all parts of the country, and it forms a very considerable branch of trade both by sea and land. Bones, shells, old lime, soot,ashes, hair, and all kinds of rubbish, are also eagerly bought up by the farmer for the purpose of manure.

In the Fatee gardens near Canton the proprietors have a curious kind of rich mud, which they cut up into small square bits, and sell at a very high price for the growing of plants in pots. This is obtained chiefly from the ponds and lakes in the vicinity, where the *Nelumbium spedosum* grows. This soil is so much esteemed, that the price for the best kind is 1 dollar for 3 peculs, and for the second 1 dollar for 4 peculs. The inferior sort has been frequently sent to England in plant cases from Canton.

For crops in a vigorous growing state no kind of manure is so eagerly sought after as night soil; and every traveller in China has remarked the large cisterns or earthen tubs which are placed in the most conspicuous and convenient situation for the reception of this kind of manure. What would be considered an intolerable nuisance in every civilised town in Europe, is here looked upon by all classes, rich and poor, with the utmost complacency ; and I am convinced that nothing would astonish a Chinaman more, than hearing any one complain of the stench which is continually rising from these manure tanks. Almost every Chinese town is placed on the banks of a river or canal, and the water is generally led not only round the walls, thus forming a kind of moat, but also through many parts of the city. Long clumsy boats are placed in different departments of A Chinese pecul is equal to 133 lbs.

Chap. XVI.] MODE OF USING NIGHT SOIL. 315

the town, into which the night soil and urine are emptied and conveyed from thence into the country. The fields in the neighbourhood of cities are generally supplied with it by coolies, who go every morning to market loaded with the produce of their farms. Each brings home two buckets of this manure, slung at the ends of his bamboo pole. In England it is generally supposed that the Chinese carry the night soil and urine to these tanks, and leave it there to undergo fermentation, before they apply it to the land. This, however, is not the case; at least, not generally. In the fertile agricultural districts in the north, I have observed that the greater part of this stimulant is used in a fresh state, being of course sufficiently diluted with water before it is applied to the crops. And there can be little doubt that in this the Chinese are perfectly right, as the manure must be much more efficient in this state than when a great portion of its ammonia has passed off into the air. The Chinese, as far as I could learn, have no mode of disinfecting their manure, but they seemed to be perfectly aware, that if allowed free access to the air a great loss must result, owing to the gases which are given out and dissipated. Without waiting, then, for fermentation or putrefaction, this manure is at once applied to the growing crops. On the afternoons, or on cloudy days, the labourers are seen carrying water from the nearest pond or canal to the manure tank, for the purpose of diluting its contents. This being done, they fill their buckets, attaching one to each end of their bamboo in the usual way, and carry them *off* to their destination. When this is reached, each man takes a small wooden ladle having a long bamboo handle, and with this he scatters the liquid over the growing crop. A strong stimulant like this would probably in other circumstances have an injurious effect; but, by using it only when the crops are young and luxuriant, they assimilate its gases, and a most marked effect is produced upon their growth and productiveness. This kind of liquid manure is generally applied to wheat, barley, and all the cabbage tribe, and other garden vegetables; but not to rice, which is always flooded during its growth.

This manure is sometimes used after putrefaction and fermentation have taken place, and even in this state it is very efficient. In the gardens near Canton it is often dried and mixed with the soil taken from the bottom of the Lotus ponds, and used for growing plants in pots, or for enriching any particular tree which may be a favourite in the garden.

Although the land is sometimes allowed to lie idle for some months, yet there is no regular system of fallowing, nor is the rotation of crops much known or practised. Indeed, as regards the low lands, the soil being a kind of stiff, strong clay, capable of yielding many crops of rice in succession, without being in any way burthened or impoverished, no such mode of cultivation is necessary.

SECTION 19

My first visit to Chusan in 1843 was during the autumn and winter, but in 1844 I had an opportunity of exploring this beautiful island, at intervals, from the commencement of spring, until the close of the season. At this time the first impression regarding the unhealthiness of the climate had been entirely removed, and the island was looked upon as the most healthy in the Chinese seas.

It will be recollected that when the island was first occupied by our troops, the mortality was so great that the place was pronounced by every one to be the most unhealthy in China. Many a brave soldier fell a victim to the malignant fever whichprevailed at the time. No regiment suffered more than Her Majesty's 26th, the " Cameronians," who were encamped on a green hill which overlooked the city, and which certainly appeared to be the most healthy spot which could have been selected for the purpose. That place still bears the name of the " Cameronian Hill," and is now thickly strewed with the graves of our countrymen.

It soon became evident, that this great mortality proceeded from other causes than the paddy fields which surrounded the city of Tinghae. Invalids from Hong-kong and Amoy were sent here to recover their health; and the difference in the appearance of the troops stationed in Chusan, from those in Hong-kong, was most marked. Dr. Maxwell of the Madras army, who was a most excellent judge in such matters, has often expressed his opinion, that, with good medical skill and ordinary care, this beautiful island might have been rendered one of the most healthy stations for our troops in the East. Indeed, every one now seemed to regret that we had not secured Chusan as a part of the British dominions for the protection of our trade in China, instead of the barren and unhealthy island of Hong-kong; and some even went so far as to recommend that means should still be taken by our government to accomplish this desirable end. The time, however, for doing this had gone by, and I believe that every right-thinking person would have seen with regret any power exercised by a great and exalted nation like England to in-

Chap. XVII.] TREATY WITH CHINA. 319

fringe a solemn treaty which had been entered into with a nation so utterly powerless as the Chinese; and most assuredly nothing less than this I no negotiations or promises I would have induced the Chinese to give up an island like Chusan, which commands the central and most important parts of their empire. That we committed a blunder and made a bad bargain is quite certain, but having done so, we must abide by the consequences. Had we retained Chusan, it would not only have been a healthy place for our troops and merchants, but it would also have proved a safeguard to our trade in the north, which must ultimately become of greater importance than that at Canton. Moreover, we should have been in a central position as regards a large and important part of the world, which must sooner or later open its ports to our commerce. I allude of course to Japan and Corea, both of which are only a few days' sail from Chusan, and are still in a great measure sealed countries to Europeans. These regrets, however, are vain.

In the event of another war taking place between England and China, it might then be a question whether or not Chusan should be retained. The propriety of this would be questionable, and could only be justified on the ground of necessity. Equally important alterations in the treaty would be: first, to insist on having an ambassador at Pekin ; secondly, to allow our merchants to trade at any of the ports of the empire; and thirdly, to break down those absurd regulations regarding boundaries, which are altogether unnecessary, and which only tend to give the native population a false idea of the character of foreigners. If foreigners break the laws, let them be seized by the Chineseauthorities and punished, or delivered over to the nearest British consul. The latter proceeding would be necessary only in the southern districts, where the people are much prejudiced against us : in the north we have only to fear that the Chinese authorities would allow the criminals to escape altogether. These alterations would, I am convinced, place our relations with this vast empire upon a much more satisfactory basis.

Chusan in spring is one of the most beautiful islands in the world. It reminds the Englishman of his own native land. In the mornings the grass sparkles with dew, the air is cool and refreshing, the birds are singing in every bush, and flowers are hanging in graceful festoons from the trees and hedges.

The new plants of the island, some of which I had discovered in the preceding autumn, I now saw in flower for the first time. Early in spring the hill-sides were covered with a beautiful Daphne with lilac flowers *(Daphne Fortuni* Lindl.) ; *Azalea ovata* Lindl., certainly one of the finest and most distinct plants of this kind which I have introduced, also grows wild on the hills, and was in full bloom at this period. A fine new Buddlea *(B. Lindleyana)* had a most graceful appearance, as its long spikes of purple flowers hung in profusion from the hedges on the hill-sides, often side by side with the well-known *Glycine sinensis.* Another plant, certainly one of the most beautiful shrubs of Northern China, the *Wdgela rosea,* was first discovered in the garden of a Chinese mandarin near the city of Tinghae on this island. This spring it was loaded with its noble rose-coloured flowers, and was the admiration of all

Chap. XVH.] GARDENS OF THE MANDARINS. 321

who saw it, both English and Chinese. I have great pleasure in saying that all these plants and many others, natives of Chusan, are now growing in our gardens in England.

Ning-po is about 40 miles west from Chusan, and is situated on the mainland. My visits to it at different times during this summer were attended with much less difficulty than in the preceding autumn. I was now beginning to speak a little Chinese, and was perfectly acquainted with the town, and the whole of the places where the different mandarins' gardens and nurseries were situated. The mandarins were particularly inquisitive at this time about every thing which related to the movements of the English, or other foreigners, who were likely to establish themselves at their port; and I soon perceived that, as we were able to keep up a conversation together in Chinese, my visits were very agreeable to them. The nurserymen, too, having found out that my money was as valuable to them as that which they received from their own countrymen, threw aside their shyness, and were all anxiety to sell me any plants I wanted.

The gardens of the mandarins were extremely gay, particularly during the early months of the year: and, what was of more importance to me, contained a number of new plants of great beauty and interest. On entering one of the gardens on a fine morning in May, I was struck with a mass of yellow flowers which completely covered a distant part of the wall. The colour was not a common yellow,

but had something of buff in it, which gave the flowers a striking and uncommon appearance. I immediately ran up to the place, and, to my surprise and delight, found that it was a most beautiful *neto double yellow climbing rose*. I have no doubt, from what I afterwards learned, that this rose is from the more northern districts of the empire, and will prove perfectly hardy in Europe. Another rose, which the Chinese call the *"jive-coloured,"* was also found in one of these gardens at this time. It belongs to the section commonly called China roses in this country, but grows in a very strange and beautiful manner. Sometimes it produces self-coloured blooms|being either red or French white, and frequently having flowers of both on one plant at the same time|while at other times the flowers are striped with the two colours. This will also be as hardy as our common China rose. *Glycine sinensis* is often grown on a flat trellis in front of the summer-house, or forms a kind of portico, which affords a pleasing shade. Entwined with one of these trees, I found another variety, having very long racemes of pure white flowers, which contrasted well with the light blue of the other. I obtained permission from the old Chinese gentleman to whom it belonged (my old friend Dr. Chang) to make some layers of this fine plant, and I am happy to say that one of these is now alive in the garden at Chiswick.

The Horticultural Society having sent me out some small optical instruments to be given as

Chap. XVII.] MANNERS OF CHINESE LADIES. 323

presents, I presented some of them to the Doctor, with which he was much pleased, and offered in return to let me have whatever cuttings or plants from his garden I might wish to possess.

We are generally led to believe that ladies of rank in this country are never seen by visitors. It is quite true that Chinese custom, in this respect, differs entirely from ours; and that the females here, like those of most half-civilised or barbarous nations, are kept in the background, and are not considered as on an equality with their husbands. For example, they do not sit at the same table; when a " sing-song" or theatrical performance is got up, they are put in a place out of view, where they can see all that is going on and yet remain unseen. But for all this they are not entirely secluded from society ; at least they used frequently to honour me with their presence, and crowd round me with the greatest curiosity. At first they used to be extremely shy, and only took sly peeps at me from behind doors and through windows; by and by, however, their strong curiosity conquered their bashfulness, and then they used to stand and look on very composedly. They generally, however, kept at a little distance, and whenever a movement was made towards where they stood, they pretended to be vastly frightened, and ran away; but they soon came back again.

To Mr. Mackenzie, one of our merchants at Ning-po, and also to Mr. Thom, Her Majesty's consul, I was greatly indebted for their kindnessand hospitality. They did every thing in their power to forward my views, and to both these gentlemen I take this opportunity of rendering my best thanks.

After having spent the summer in the districts of Ning-po, Chusan, and Shanghae, I returned to the last-mentioned place, where my plants were all collected, intending immediately to sail for Hongkong, and send a portion of them home to England ' but the exposure to the sun during the summer was now beginning to affect my health, and when I landed at Shanghae I was laid up with a severe attack of fever. Providentially this happened when I was amongst my English friends ; and, as I had the means of procuring excellent medical advice, I recovered in the course of a fortnight, and was able to proceed to sea, where the change of air completed my cure. I reached Hong-kong in November, and forthwith made preparations for sending my collections home in several vessels, which were at anchor in the bay at this time.

During the summer which had now passed by, I had had frequent opportunities of inspecting the tombs of the Chinese both in the northern and southern districts. In the south, the natives form no regular cemeteries or churchyards, as we do in Europe, but the tombs of the dead are scattered all over the sides of the hills, the most pleasant situations being generally selected. The more wealthy individuals often convey their dead a considerabe distance, and employ a kind of fortune-teller, whose

Chap. XVTL] BKST SITUATIONS FOR TOMBS. 325

duty it is to find out the most appropriate resting- place. This man goes with the corpse to the place appointed, and of course pretends to be very wise in the selection of the spot, as well as in the choice of the soil with which the ashes of the dead are to mingle in after years; and upon trial, should the particular earth appear unsuitable, he immediately orders the procession off to some other place in the neighbourhood, where he expects to be more successful. I believe many of the Chinese have this important point settled before they die; for one day when one of our principal merchants went to call on old Howqua, the late Hong merchant at Canton, a tray was brought into the room with several kinds of earth upon it, which the old man examined with great care, and then fixed on the one in which he wished to be buried.

A situation on the hill-side is also considered of great importance, especially if it commands a view of a beautiful bay or lake. But I believe that of all places the one most coveted is where a winding stream, in its course, passes and then returns again to the foot of the hill where the grave is to be made. The director of the ceremonies, with a compass in his hand, settles the direction in which the body is to lie, which is another point of great importance. An intelligent Chinese, with whom I was acquainted, informed me that this fortuneteller of the dead is often very eloquent in his descriptions of the future happiness of those who obey his directions; he informs them that they ortheir children, or some one in whom they are much interested, shall enjoy riches and honours in after life, as a reward for the attention and respect they have paid to the remains of their fathers; that as the stream which they then behold when standing around their father's grave flows and returns again in its windings, so shall their path through life be smooth and pleasant until they sink into the tomb hoary with years, respected, beloved, and mourned by their children.

These men are generally great rogues, and play upon the prejudices of the people. It frequently happens, that after a corpse has been interred for some time, they call upon the relatives, and inform them, that for some cause which they affect to explain, it is absolutely necessary to remove and re- inter it. Should the relations object to this, the answer is, " Very well, I don't care; but your children and relations will also be regardless of your remains when you die, and you will be miserable in your graves."

The feelings of the poor deluded people are thus wrought upon, and a further sum of money is extracted for finding a more suitable grave.

The late Mr. Lay, during one of his rambles amongst the hills on the banks of the river Min, was present at one of these ceremonies, and the relatives of the deceased crowded round him and consulted him as to the site of the grave, under the impression that he was well versed in such matters. He remarks in his journal, that " much good or much

Chap, XVTl.] FOKMS OF TOMBS, 327

evil is thought to betide the survivors from a right or wrong position. Keangse practitioners in this ' *te le*' and lfung shwuy,' or soothsaying from the influence of the earth's local modalities, get large moneys by the trade; but as they do not agree amongst themselves, the people are fain to ask counsel of a stranger."

In my travels in the south of China I often came upon graves in the most retired places amongst the hills ; they were all more or less of the same form, namely, a half circle cut out of the hill-side, having the body interred behind it. Sometimes, indeed generally, there were several of these half-circles with a succession of terraces in front of the grave; and in the burying-places of the more wealthy, the semicircles were built of brick or stone, and on a more extensive scale. In the centre of the semicircle, and of course near the body, the grave-stone is placed with its inscription. M. Callery, an excellent Chinese scholar, informed me that these inscriptions are always of the most simple kind, merely stating the name of the deceased, that he died in such a dynasty, in such a year. This is the plain and unflattering tale which the Chinese tombstone tells. In some instances | I cannot tell if in all | after the body has decayed, the bones are dug up, and carefully put into earthenware vessels, which are then placed on the hill-side above ground. These, as well as the graves, are visited at stated times by the relatives. They go first to the grave of the patriarch, or father of the tribe, and then to thoseof the other members of the family in rotation, where they perform their devotions, and offer incense. They afterwards dine together when the ceremonies are over.

I was once or twice in the wild mountain districts in the interior, at the time when the natives visited the tombs. Even the most retired parts had their visitors, and it was both pleasing and affecting to see the little groups assembled round the graves, paying the tribute of affection to those whose memory they revered and loved. The widow was seen kneeling by the grave of her lost husband; children, often very young, shedding tears of sorrow for a father or mother; and, sometimes, an old man whose hair was white with age, was there mourning the loss of those whom he had looked to as the support of his declining years. All were cutting the long grass and weeds which were growing round the tombs, and planting their favourite flowers to bloom and to decorate them.

Near Amoy, this scattered mode of interring the dead has been departed from, and perhaps necessarily, in consequence of the large population; in the country, however, I sometimes found tombs in retired and inaccessible parts of the hills here, as well as in the more southern provinces ; but these were evidently the property of the wealthy inhabitants.

As the traveller proceeds northward, the circular form of the tombs is less common, and they become more varied in their appearance. In Chusan, Ning-po, and various other places in that district, a

Chap. XVH.]

COFFINS EXPOSED.

great number of the coffins are placed on the surface of the ground and merely thatched over with straw. I met with these coffins in all sorts of places, l on the sides of the public highway l on the banks of the rivers and canals l and in woods and other retired parts of the country. Sometimes the thatch was completely off, the wood rotten, and the remains of the Chinamen of former days exposed to view. On one hill-side on the island of Chusan, skulls and bones are lying about in all directions, and more than once, when wandering through the long brushwood in this place, I have been entangled by getting my feet through the lid of a coffin.

Tombs on the Island of Chuian.

I believe that the wealthy in these districts generally bury their dead, and some of them build very chaste and beautiful tombs. There are three orfour very fine ones in the island of Chusan, where the paving in front of the mound which contains the body is beautiful, and the carving elaborate; the whole of the stone-work is square, instead of circular as in the tombs in the south of China. Here, as at homeland I believe in every part of the worldltrees of the pine tribe are generally planted in the burying-grounds. Lord Jocelyn, in his "Campaign in China," mentions such places in the following beautiful and appropriate language : l" Here and there, as if dropped at random upon the sides of the hills, were clumps of pine trees, and peeping through their thick foliage, the roofs of houses and temples diversified the scene. Amongst many of the beautiful groves of trees which here invite the wanderer to repose, spots are selected as the resting-places of mortality; and gazing on those tranquil scenes, where the sweet clematis and fragrant flowers help to decorate the last home of man, the most careless eye cannot fail to mark the beauties of the grave."

In the Shanghae district I have frequently visited large houses which seem to have been built by the rich expressly as mausoleums. In these houses I generally found a coffin in one of the principal rooms, and an altar, with all the trappings of idolatry, where incense on high days is burned to the memory of the deceased, and various other ceremonies are gone through by the relatives. These houses or temples are generally surrounded by a pine wood, and sometimes the body is buried out of

Chap. XVH.] COFFINS KEPT IN HOUSES. 331

doorslthe altar and records only being kept in the temple, where a servant with his family is always placed to look after them.

When the English first established themselves at Shanghae, some of them had thoughts of taking houses in the country that their families might enjoy retirement and fresh air. One day towards the end of 1843, I accompanied a gentleman of my acquaintance on an errand of this kind. When we had proceeded about six or eight miles from Shanghae, we observed a good-looking house in a wood hard by, and determined to pay it a visit and see whether the occupant would be inclined to let it. As we drew near, all was still and quiet; not even our old enemies, the dogs, appeared to dispute our approach. When the Chinese l who always followed us in considerable numbers wherever we went I saw us approaching the house, they stood still at a little distance, watching our proceedings with a great degree of interest. We knocked at the door of the mansion, and then stood at one side so that the porter might not see that his visitors were the *Hong-mou-jins,* or red-haired race, as they are pleased to call the English; for we well knew that if we were seen, the door would not be opened. In a few seconds we heard the sounds of feet, and then a voice summoned us to know our business. We mumbled something in Chinese, and the poor man, quite unconscious of his danger, threw open the door. I shall never forget the look of mingled fear and astonishment which he gave us as we quietly walked into the court; at the same time the group of natives outside were indulging in hearty laughter at the way in which he had been entrapped.

The court-yard, where we now were, was neatly paved, and the whole of the house appeared to be in excellent repair. As we were led from room to room by our terrified guide, every thing appeared quite suitable for a country residence, at least as good as one could expect in such an out-of-the-way place, and my friend remarked that it was the best he had yet seen, and that he should certainly make an effort to get possession of it. At last we came to what appeared the principal room: " Ah, this shall be my drawing-room," said my companion, " but what is that?" added he in the same breath. I looked in the direction in which he pointed, and a large massive coffin met my eye. We then discovered that we were in one of those places set apart for the remains of the dead.

During one of my journeys in the interior, I met with a very curious tomb near the town of Sung- kiang-foo. It was placed on the side of a hill, in a wood, and evidently belonged to some very wealthy or important personage of that city. From the base of the hill to where the tomb stood, about halfway up, the visitor ascended by a broad flight of steps, on each side of which were placed a number of figures carved in stone. As far as I can recollect, the following was the order in which the figures were placed; first, a pair of goats or sheep,

Chap. XVH.] FLOWERS FOK THE GRAVES. 333

one on each side; second, two dogs; third, two cats ; fourth, two horses saddled and bridled; and fifth, two most gigantic priests; the effect of the whole being most strange and imposing. There is another tomb of the same description near Ning-po, but on a much smaller scale.

The flowers which the Chinese plant on or among the tombs are simple and beautiful in their kind. No expensive camellias, moutans, or other of the finer ornaments of the garden, are chosen for this purpose. Sometimes the conical mound of earthlwhen the grave is of this kindlis crowned with a large plant of fine, tall, waving grass. At Ning-po wild roses are planted, which soon spread themselves over the grave, and, when their flowers expand in spring, cover it with a sheet of pure white. At Shanghae a pretty bulbous plant, a species of *Lycoris,* covers the graves in autumn with masses of brilliant purple. When I first discovered the *Anemone Japonica,* it was in full flower amongst the graves of the natives, which are round the ramparts of Shanghae; it blooms in November, when other flowers have gone by, and is a most appropriate ornament to the last resting-places of the dead.

The poor, as well as the rich, often keep their dead in their dwelling-houses for a long time: I should imagine, from the numerous coffins which I met with in such circumstances, that many are thus kept for years. The coffins are remarkably thick and strong, and the joints so carefully cementedthat no unpleasant smell is emitted during the decay of the body.

Much of the respect which is paid by the Chinese to the memory of their deceased relatives may doubtless be a mere matter of form, sanctioned and rendered necessary by the custom of ages, but I am inclined to think that a considerable portion springs from a higher and purer source, and I have no doubt that when the Chinese periodically visit the tombs of their fathers to worship and pay respect to their memory, they indulge in the pleasing reflection, that when they themselves are no more, their graves will not be neglected or forgotten I but will also be visited by their children and grandchildren, in whose hearts and affections they will live for many, many years after their bodies have mouldered into dust.

Tomb of a Mandarin's wife.

SECTION 20

Chap. XVIII.] PLANTS SHIPPED FOU ENGLAND. 335
  CHAP. XVIII.
  Plants Shipped For England. Sail Fob Manila Natural
  Productions And Exports. Passport Annoyances The
  Interior Of Luzon|Its Lag Una. Early Morning In The
  Philippines.|Valuable Plants Procured. The "queen
  Of Orchids." Natural Habits Of Air-plants. Lawless
  Banditti Of The Interior. A False Alarm. | Monkeys
  More Harmless Than Men. A Night At Dolores With
  The Padre. | Volcanoes In The Philippines. | General Appearance Of The Country.
Leeches Not Very AgreeAble Companions. Return To Manila And Ship Plants
  For England. Sail For The North Of China. |" A Man
  Overboard"| His Recovery By A Gallant Boat's Crew.| Arrive In The North.

The collections of plants and seeds which I had made during the summer and autumn of 1844 arrived in safety at Hong-kong, and I lost no time in shipping them for England. All the living objects were planted as usual in "Ward's cases," well guarded with iron bars and placed upon the poops of the largest vessels I could find then at anchor in the bay. I always took care to divide my collections into three or four parts for the purpose of sending them by different ships, so that if any thing happened to one portion, the others had a chance of reaching England in safety. The last shipment at this time was made on the 31st of December. As it was then winter in the northern provinces, andas nothing could be done in the south, I determined to go over to the Philippine Islands for a few weeks, and accordingly sailed for Manila in the beginning of January, 1845.

See an account of these in the Appendix.

The voyage from Hong-kong to Manila at this season is generally made in six or eight days, as the monsoon is fair. I need not give any description of the town, which is well known as being the chief Spanish settlement in the Philippines. The inhabitants are principally Spaniards, Indians, Chinese, and there are a few English mercantile establishments. The chief productions and exports are sugar, coffee, rice, cheroots, and indigo. The beautiful cloth generally known by the name of *Pinia,* which is made from the fibre of the pineapple plant, is manufactured and embroidered by the natives and is sold in the shops. A kind of hemp, the produce of a species of *Musa,* is also made into ropes and cables; it is highly prized, and in much demand amongst the shipping in the East. The cigar manufactory, a government monopoly, is one of the largest establishments in the town; almost the whole of the labour in it is performed by women and girls. When I landed, it happened to be the hour when the workpeople were coming out of the factory, and the streets were crowded with females. As I was not aware of the circumstance, I began to think that the women must form the chief part of the population.

As I had no object in remaining in the town, I applied to the authorities for a passport to enable me

Chap. XVIII.] PASSPORT ANNOYANCES. 337

to proceed at once into the interior of the island. The traveller, if he is not well acquainted with the customs of the place, is exposed to much annoyance from the Spanish regulations regarding passports. Some new regulations had been established just before my arrival, and I found that I could not land without either having a passport, or getting some well-known merchant to become surety for my conduct. Having landed, a second passport was necessary to enable me to remain on the island, another before I could go into the interior, and a fourth when I wished to leave the country. These passports had to be signed by different individuals, and at different offices; and if the slightest informality occurred, the party was turned back or the vessel detained. I was much indebted to Messrs. Butler, and Messrs. Holliday, Wise, and Co., English merchants at Manila, who rendered me every assistance in their power.

Having at length got over these difficulties and engaged some guides and servants, our baggage was put into a Banca or boat, and we started for the Laguna, a large lake in the interior, and the source of the river on which the town of Manila stands. We had to cross the lake; and we were strongly advised to do so at night, as it is generally smooth at this time. We soon perceived the value of this advice. The Bancas are built long and narrow for swiftness, as they have often to make way against a rapid current, which flows down the river. Outriggers are fixed to the sides of the boats, to enable the Indians to run out and balance them when the wind comes down in strong puffs, and when without these they would be often thrown on their beam ends and capsized.

When I awoke in the morning we were half-way across the lake, and day was just dawning. Those who have never been in eastern tropical countries can form no idea of the beauty and freshness of early morning in the Philippines. The broad sheet of water through which we were swiftly passing was smooth as glass, and shone like a mirror ; there was not a breath of air to disturb it. The shores of the lake were rich in vegetation; trees and bushes dipping their luxuriant branches into the water, and crowning the summit of every hill. In this beautiful region winter is unknown, for here "the trees ever blossom, the beams ever shine."

As soon as the sun began to appear above the horizon, the whole surface of the lake was put in motion by the breeze which then began to blow, and which gradually increased until it became a pretty strong gale. Our sail was close-reefed, and all the crew except the man at the helm stood on the outriggers to balance the boat, walking out or in as the wind waa more or less powerful. In less than half an hour the lake was covered with waves rolling like those of the sea. Every now and then we took one on board, and were soon, as well as our beds and baggage, completely drenched with water. Luckily we were near our destination on the opposite shore, where we soon arrived in safety.

Chap. XVm.] PURCHASE OF ORCHIDS. 339

I counsel all travellers to beware of crossing the Laguna by day, and I took good care to avoid doing so on my return.

Having landed I made the best of my way to the farm of Don Inego Gonzales de Azaola, whom I had met in Manila, and who had kindly offered me the use of his house in the interior. My chief object in visiting this part of the country was to procure, if possible, a supply of the beautiful orchid *(Phalccnopsis amalnlis),* which Cuming had sent home a few years before, but which was still extremely rare in England. His Grace the Duke of Devonshire purchased the first plant, for which he gave the large sum of one hundred guineas.

As I had very little time to spare, I was anxious to make the most of my opportunities. I made an Indian's hut in the wood my head quarters, where I held a sort of market for the purchase of orchids. The Indians knew the hour at which I should return to the hut, and on my arrival I generally found the ground in front strewed with orchids in the state in which they had been cut from the trees, and many of them covered with flowers. The *Phalcenopsis,* in particular, was singularly beautiful. I was very anxious to get some large specimens of the plant, and offered a dollar, which was a high sum in an Indian forest, for the largest which should be brought to me. The lover of this beautiful tribe will easily imagine the delight I felt, when one day I saw two Indians approaching with a plant of extraordinary size,

having ten or twelve branching flower-stalks upon it, and upwards of a hundred flowers in full bloom. " There," said they, in triumph, " is not that worth a dollar?" I acknowledged that they were well entitled to the reward, and took immediate possession of my prize. This plant is now in the garden of the Horticultural Society of London; and although it was a little reduced, in order to get it into the plant case at

Manila, is still by far the largest specimen in Europe. This beautiful species may be well called the " Queen of Orchids."

The air-plants are not found so frequently in the dense shaded parts of the forests as in the edges of the woods, on trees by the road-sides, and in exposed situations. I found the genus *Aerides* very often in the most dense parts of the woods, but never a single plant of *Phalcenopsis.* The latter was commonly found growing on the branches of the Mango in the cleared parts of the woods, near the cottages of the Indians, and sometimes on the very tops of high trees, where it was fully exposed to the sun. I confess this fact was quite contrary to the opinion I had formed of the habits of these plants; for I expected to have found them principally in damp shaded forests, where the sun's rays could seldom penetrate; but such is not the case, at least in the Philippine Islands.

Having ransacked the country around Inego's farm, I now set off, accompanied by my servants and some other Indians, to St. Pablo and Dolores. Dolores is a small village in a wild part of

Chap. XVUI.] BANDITTI OF THE INTERIOR. 341

the country, where the natives bear a very bad character, having frequently attacked and robbed travellers. During our progress my companions related a great many stories of this kind, and were evidently not a little frightened. The roads were only narrow lanes, leading through dense thickets of brushwood, and the locality was certainly an excellent one for lawless characters of eveiy description to do exactly as they pleased in. On one occasion, when I had gone a little way ahead of the party, something alarmed them, and the whole set took to their heels and ran off in another direction. I rode back after the fugitives, and being well armed explored the ground in every direction to find out the cause of their alarm, but could discover nothing, and at length I persuaded them to return and pursue the journey. Shortly after this, however, a wild-looking Indian stepped out of the forest, and stood eyeing us narrowly as we passed him on the road. He had a short matchlock in his hand, and evidently belonged to the band of freebooters who infested this part of the country. I passed him in a very slow and deliberate manner, taking care to watch his motions, and to let him see that I and some of my party were well armed, and prepared for any attack. After looking at us in silence for a minute or two, he jumped into the jungle and disappeared.

As our path winded through the jungle, we sometimes could only see a very short distance either before or behind us. At one of these bends we heard a noise amongst the bushes, as if a number of men were advancing rapidly towards us, and naturally concluded that we were about to be attacked. A halt was instantly called, and then the question was whether we should advance or recede. As I had no time to lose I looked to my fire-arms and determined to proceed. Accordingly I rode forward a few paces to reconnoitre, and saw a numerous band, not of robbers or freebooters, but I I hope my courteous reader will not laughIof monkeys ! There must have been several hundreds of these animals on the trees, jumping about from branch to branch, and evidently enjoying themselves vastly. As we passed amongst them they commenced chattering and making all sorts of faces at us.

At length we reached the little village of Dolores, and as in duty bound, I immediately went to pay my respects to the Padre. His house was a small miserable hut, little better than those of the Indians which surrounded it, and poorly furnished.

He received us kindly, and told us that we were welcome to the shelter his house afforded, and that although he had little to offer us in the way of luxuries, he should do every thing in his power to make us comfortable. At the same time he informed us we were in a dangerous neighbourhood, and that he could not answer for the security of the ponies or baggage. The servants and Indians who accompanied me were accommodated in another house which was building for the Padre, and the ponies

Chap. XVIH.] ENTERTAINED BY THE PADRE. 343

were tied up there, and a watch set over them. The Indians mounted guard by turns; they were well armed; and as they were much frightened, there was no danger of their neglecting their duty. I was told in the morning, that they had been roused several times during the night; but I fancy imagination had something to do with it, as I found that every thing belonging to us was perfectly safe. In the evening, after dark, the worthy Padre did every thing in his power to amuse me. He had an old pianoforte which had found its way by some means into this wild mountain district, but I presume it had never been tuned since its first arrival, for it was sadly out of order. On this he played a number of Spanish and Italian airs, accompanying the instrument with his voice. After exhausting his own stock of songs he sent for his servant-boy and the head man of the village, who were musicians, and got up a sort of concert. The Padre played on the pianoforte, the boy on the fife, and the other on the clarinette. It must be confessed, however, that the music was not very harmonious.

The greater part of the following day was spent in exploring the surrounding country, and in the afternoon I bade the hospitable priest adieu, and started for St. Pablo, which was situated in a more civilised part of the country. There, also, and indeed wherever I went, the priests were most kind and hospitable.

The Philippine Islands must, at one time, have been a complete nest of volcanoes. With one exception, they are now all inactive ; but traces of them were met with at every step of our progress through the higher districts of the country, in the form of circular pools of stagnant water, and masses of lava which still emit a most disagreeable odour when they are stirred up. On the top of a high hill, near St. Pablo, I came unexpectedly on the remains of a still more recent volcano. The trees in its vicinity were in a most unhealthy state, many of their roots and branches being decayed. Sometimes I sunk nearly up to the knees amongst burnt- looking earth, which emitted a strong sulphureous smell; and, as none of the natives were with me, I was sometimes afraid of getting into the mouth of the crater, and going down altogether.

The Island of Luzon, of which Manila is the capital, is very like Java and other parts of the straits. It is very hilly, but extremely fertile, and affords a most striking contrast to the barren shores of the south of China which I had just left. Large crops of rice are produced on the low lands which are capable of being flooded. Sugar and tobacco are grown on such ground as would produce good wheat in England ; and coffee and chocolate trees are planted on the sides of the hills. The Manila mango is considered one of the finest in the world, not inferior to that which is produced near Bombay. Cocoa- nuts, plantains, bananas, and other tropical fruits abound, and are to be had in great perfection. Besides these oranges are also cultivated; but they are inferior to those of China and Europe; indeed,

Chap. XVIII.] AKNOYED BY LEECHES. 345

as might be expected, all the fruits, natives of more northern latitudes, which we find in these islands, are far surpassed by the same kinds which grow in climates more congenial to their nature. The vine is largely cultivated, but it produces grapes of a very inferior quality.

The mountainous portions of the country are for the most part in a state of nature, being covered with trees, and with brushwood ; which in some places is so thick that I had to employ the Indians to cut a way through it with small billhooks which they kept for the purpose. In other parts, the tops of the tall trees form a mass so dense, that no ray ever shines through them. The ground on the sides of these mountains is always in a moist and slimy condition; and is the habitation of millions of leeches. In my first excursion to the mountains I observed the feet and legs of the Indians, who were cutting a path for me, covered with blood, and at first I fancied that they must have wounded themselves with the thorny shrubs which they were cutting. On inquiry, however, I found that it was the leeches that were doing the mischief, and in a very little time I had a good many specimens of their powers upon my own skin. There were two species, one a small linear one, and the other nearly round. Whenever the former fixed upon the Indians, they invariably pulled it oiF, but they never interfered with the little round one. I found that the reason for this was, that the latter, if taken off by force, would leave a very painful wound; butthat, if allowed to suck until it was full, it would drop off, of its own accord, and leave scarcely a mark; the other species might be taken off with impunity. At first, when they fixed themselves upon me, which they did through my stockings, I set to work to pull them off, without regard to species, although warned by the natives of the impropriety of doing so. In a short time my legs were covered with blood, and the wounds annoyed me with a kind of itching soreness for several days afterwards.

With the exception of the Orchids, the Philippines are not very rich in plants of an ornamental kind. As far as I had an opportunity of judging, the vegetation of Luzon bears a great resemblance to the island of Java and the other parts of the Malay Archipelago. The country is, however, very rich in birds and shells, and many of the land species of the latter are extremely valuable. Mr. Cuming, who is well known in this part of the world, made very large collections of them, and has already distributed them over the greater part of Europe and America.

After spending about three weeks in the interior of Luzon, and having procured a fine supply of the beautiful *Phalcenopsis,* and several other Orchids, I returned to the town of Manila, and shipped a portion of them to England. These, I am happy to say, arrived in excellent order; and upon reference to the garden-lists on my return, I find that no fewer than forty-five specimens of this lovely plant

Chap. XVIII.] "A MAN OVERBOARD." 347

I the " Queen of Orchids " I had been distributed amongst the Fellows of the Horticultural Society of London.

The time which I had allotted for this excursion having expired, I sailed for my old station in the north of China, and arrived there on the 14th of March, 1845. On going up the coast, we had to contend with the north-east monsoon, and " beat to windward," during the whole of the passage. One afternoon when it was nearly dark, and when the sea was running very high, one of the men who was out on the bowsprit lost his hold, owing to the heaving of the vessel, and fell into the sea. The cry of " A man overboard ! " I that peculiar cry amongst sailors which, once heard, can never be forgotten, made me rush on deck. The schooner was going at the rate of at least eight knots, but her helm was instantly put down, and her way stopped. A hand was sent aloft to keep his eye upon the poor fellow, whose head was seen every now and then as he rose upon a wave, and in a few seconds the schooner was close at his side. A rope was thrown out to him, and every one thought that he would be able to lay hold, and be drawn in over the side. Probably from exhaustion he unfortunately missed it, and the schooner shooting ahead at the time, he was again left to the mercy of the waves. As a last resource the boat was lowered: and although rather a dangerous service, several gallant fellows stepped into it and pulled in the direction signalled to them from the ship. Those on board were in a state of the most painful suspense. When we caught a glimpse of the man from time to time, he was evidently sinking, and in a few more seconds all must have been over with him. The boat was nearly lost to us in the closing darkness, and the men told us that they were on the point of returning to the ship without getting a glimpse of their poor messmate, when they saw his head raised above a wave close by; and pulling towards him, they caught him by the hair, and drew him into the boat. When brought on board he was in a most exhausted state, but the usual remedies being applied he recovered in the course of the night.

SECTION 21

It was the commencement of spring when I returned to the north of China. In this season of the year no country can be more agreeable or healthy than this. The air is bracing, the sky generally clear, and the mornings are delightfully cool. Before long, vegetation progressed with wonderful rapidity, far surpassing any thing of the kind I had ever witnessed in England. By the middle of April, deciduous trees and shrubs were covered with leaves, barley was in full ear, and the oil plant *(Brassica sinensis)* was seen forming masses of golden yellow, on the hill-sides and on the plains, where the air was perfumed with the fragrance of its blossoms.

My object during this summer was to make a complete collection of all my finest plants, for the purpose of taking them home under my own care. I lost no time, therefore, in visiting all my former acquaintances, mandarins, and nurserymen I and made my selections when the plants were in bloom. *Tree-peonies, Azaleas, Viburnums, Daphnes, Roses,* and many other plants, all new to Europe, and of great beauty, were from time to time added to this collection. As many of these plants could be only verified by the colour of their flowers, it was absolutely necessary that I should visit the different districts three or four times during the spring, and consequently that I should lose as little time as possible in travelling from one place to another. Shang- hae, Chusan, Ning-po, and many other parts of the interior, all lying wide of each other, had some object of interest which demanded my presence and attention.

The distance from Ning-po to Shanghae is about a hundred miles. I had completed my researches in the Ning-po district, and was very anxious to get to Shanghae as soon as possible, in order to see some Azaleas in bloom, which I was anxious to add to my collections. In another fortnight their flowers would have been all faded, and it would then have been impossible to identify the different varieties. There were two routes from Ning-po to Shanghae, one for the foreigners and the other for the natives. The *legal* road was to go across to Chusan, then garrisoned by the English, a distance of thirty or forty miles, nearly due east, and then take the

Chap. XIX.] JOUKNEY TO SHANGHAE. 351

chance of finding some vessel about to sail for Woosung or Shanghae. I knew that if I took this line, in all probability I should have to wait for eight or ten days in Chusan before such an opportunity would occur, a delay which would have entirely defeated the object which I had in view. I determined, therefore, to go by the interdicted route, and take my chance of consequences.

The journey overland was a very interesting one. When I reached the town of Chinhae, at the mouth of the Ning-po river, I found that some small junks were to sail that evening for Chapoo, and I lost no time in securing a passage on board one of them. I was surprised at my success thus far, as I had anticipated my greatest if not my only difficulty would have been in making a start. I found afterwards that I was indebted for this to my Chinese servant, who happened to be a native of Chinhae and knew the captain of the junk. He persuaded him that there was no harm in my going by that route; and, at all events, that he could easily land me at Chapoo, and that nobody would know how I had come there.

In the evening, after many delays on account of wind and tide, and also with the view of securing more passengers and cargo, we lifted our anchor and set sail. In crossing the bay of Hangchow, the tide runs very rapidly, and the Chinese junks and boats never go across without a fair or leading wind. I shall never forget the strange and motley group of passengers who were my fellow-travellers in thislittle vessel. We were all huddled together in the centre cabin, and our beds were spread down on each side, merely leaving room for us to walk down the middle. Some of the passengers were respectable merchants, but even these had something filthy and disagreeable about them. Little insects whose names sound harsh to " ears polite," were charitably supported in great numbers amongst the warm folds of their dresses. The first thing I did when my bed was spread down was to surround it with my trunks, gun-case, and another box or two, to prevent, if possible, any visitors of this description from leaving their rightful lord and master, and taking up their quarters with me. With all my care it was next to impossible to keep myself apart from the Chinese, owing to the motion of the little vessel which sometimes sent us rolling from one side to the other. A great part of the night was spent by the Chinese in smoking opium and tobacco. When morning dawned, the scene which the cabin presented was a strange one. Nearly all the passengers were sound asleep. They were lying in heaps, here and there, as they had been tossed and wedged by the motion of the vessel during the night. Their features and appearance, as seen in the twilight of a summer morning, were striking to the eye of a foreigner. I almost fancied that I could read the characters of the different beings who lay stretched before me. There was the habitual opium-smoker |there was no mistaking him|his looks were pale and haggard, his breathing quick and disturbed,

Chap. XIX.] CHINESE TRAVELLING. 353

and so thin was he, that his cheek bones seemed piercing the skin. Some seemed care-worn with business, and others again apparently slept soundly with hearts light and joyous. All had the fore part of their heads shaved, and their tails lay about in wild confusion.

We were now far on our way across the bay, having had a fair wind and tide during the greater part of the night, and the hills near Chapoo were already visible on the horizon to the northward. All hands were soon busily engaged in getting breakfast ready. A Chinese sea breakfast consists chiefly of rice, fish, and vegetables. The proprietors of the junk provide food for the passengers, for which they charge a small sum from each, independent of the passage-money. If the passengers do not choose to have breakfast, or dinner, they are not required to pay for it. When breakfast was ended, some began to smoke opium and others tobacco, after which most of them went to bed again and were soon fast asleep. The Chinese when travelling do little else than eat, smoke, and sleep. During the whole time I was travelling in the country, I never remember seeing one Chinese engaged in reading.

About eleven in the forenoon we came to anchor in a muddy bay abreast of the city of Chapoo, where many of the junks are high and dry at low water. I had my luggage put into a small boat and rowed for the shore. " You had better take off your shoes and stockings, and draw up your trousers," said one of the Chinese boatmen as we were

getting near the landing-place. The prudence and necessity of this advice were soon apparent; for when the boat touched the beach, I found that I had to walk a quarter of a mile up to the knees in mud, before I could get on firm ground. Now came the critical part of my expedition. When I had got through the mud, I inquired for the nearest spring and commenced my ablutions; making no attempt to disguise myself, as I was dressed in the common English garb. Long before I had finished washing, I was surrounded by some hundreds of the natives, who seemed perfectly astonished at the sight of an Englishman, although this place had been attacked and taken during the late war. All sorts of inquiries were made regarding me; " where had I come from?"

"where was I bound for?" "what were my objects ?" and a hundred other questions were put to me, or to those who accompanied me. All were, however, quite civil, and did not attempt to annoy me in the slightest degree. I now walked to some hills near the city, and inspected their vegeta tion. On the way I visited some temples which had been battered down by our troops during the war, and which still remained in the same ruinous condition. Hundreds of people followed me to the hills, the view from which is one of the finest I ever saw in this country. Here it is that the hills of the south end, and the wide plain of the Yang- tse-kiang commences. On one side, looking towards the south and west, mountains are seen towering in all their grandeur; whilst on the northern side, the

Chap. XIX.] SHOPS AND TRADE. 355

eye rests on a rich and level plain, watered by its thousand canals, and dotted all over with towns and villages peopled with an immense number of industrious and happy human beings. Chapoo and the country which surrounds it may well be called the garden of China.

After inspecting the hills, I went down into the Tartar city of Chapoo. The suburbs are large and populous, but the walled city itself is not very extensive. It is a square, and the circuit of the walls is not more than three miles; they seem very old, and are surrounded by a moat, which also serves the purpose of a canal. Here the Tartar troops and their families reside, living entirely apart from the Chinese inhabitants of the town.

The streets, houses, and shops are of the same kind as those which I have already described. Indeed, so like is one town in China to another, that, if a traveller well acquainted with the northern cities, was set down blindfolded in one of them, he would have the greatest difficulty in saying whether it was Chapoo, Ning-po, or Shanghae. I observed in the shops a considerable quantity of Japanese goods, which are brought annually to this place by the junks which trade with Japan.

By the time I had examined all the chief objects of interest, it was late in the afternoon, and I began to think of leaving the city and taking the road for Shanghae. I had already taken measures by means of my servant to find the part of the canal from which the Shanghae boats started, and thither procecded with the intention of engaging a boat. A numerous crowd had surrounded and accompanied me, during the whole of the day ; but now that I was on the eve of taking my departure, it was greatly augmented. Every street, lane, window, and house-top was crowded with human beings ; all, however, perfectly harmless and civil. When I reached the canal and attempted to speak with one of the boatmen, the crowd pressed after me in such numbers, that the boat, had I got on board, would probably have been swamped. The poor boatmen were so frightened, that no reward which I could hold out would induce them to give me a passage. They begged and prayed me not to enter their boats, as some accident would happen from the number of persons whom nothing could prevent from crowding in after me.

I was now in a dilemma, and I scarcely knew how to get out of it. At last I determined, much against my inclination, to go to the mandarins. It is a bad plan to have any thing to do with Chinese officials when it can be possibly avoided, but in this case there was no help for it ; so, having inquired for the residence of the superintendent of boats, I set off to call upon him, followed, of course, by an immense mob. As we were going to his house, my servant came up to me and requested that I would not tell the mandarin that he was in my service, or that he had any thing to do in bringing me there. As I could speak the language sufficiently well to make myself understood, I did not

Chap. XIX.] VISIT TO A MANDARIN. 357

need him as an interpreter, and I was of course anxious not to bring him or his relations into any scrape on my account.

When we reached the mandarin's house, the doors were thrown open, and I walked boldly into the reception-room. It was a most difficult matter for the servants to keep out the crowd, but they accomplished the task partly by threats, and partly by whips, which they used rather more freely than we should approve of in England. This, however, is a common mode of punishing the rabble in China, and when they know they deserve it they take it very quietly.

" Tell your master I want to see him," said I in a lofty tone to one of the attendants, who immediately went into an inner apartment and returned with the mandarin himself, clothed in his most imposing robes of office, I hat, button, peacock feather, and all. I made him several very low bows, which he most politely returned. " I am in a great hurry," said I, " to go on to Shanghae, and have been trying to engage a boat for that purpose, but cannot succeed without your assistance. Will you have the goodness to aid me ? " After repeating after me what I had said, as is the invariable custom in Chinese conversation, he put the following question to me: " How old are you ? " This may seem strange, but it is considered complimentary by the Chinese, and is generally amongst the first questions they put. I thanked him for his inquiry, told him my age, and then asked his, and again proposedthe question regarding the boat. Upon this he promised to send one of his servants to get one, and in the mean time invited me to take some cake and tea, which were immediately set before me. The gun which I had with me was an object of great curiosity to the old man, more particularly the locks and percussion-caps, which he told me he had never seen before. During the time I was discussing the cake and tea, he asked me a multiplicity of questions; such as, where had I come from last ? who had told me there was a road to Shanghae this way? &c. &c., some of which I answered, and some I found it convenient not to understand. At last, through some blunder on the part of my servant, it became known that he belonged to me; a circumstance which was immediately communicated to the mandarin, who sent for him and subjected him to a close and searching examination.

While this was going on, the mandarin of the highest rank in the city arrived, having been sent for by his brother in office to hold a conference regarding me. These worthies, after a long consultation in a private room, came out and informed me, in the blandest manner, that they intended to give me a free passage across the country to Shanghae, in a boat belonging to themselves, and that, to add more to my comfort, they would send another boat to convey my servant and luggage. This seemed at first sight remarkably kind ; but I had been long enough in the celestial empire to

Chap. XIX.] OBJECT OF THIS CIVILITY. 359

be aware of the necessity of looking narrowly into their motives, in order to counteract any evil designs they might think proper to hide under their assumed kindness and civility. In this instance their motives were perfectly plain to me, and were simply these: I According to the treaty of Nanking, if any Englishman was found beyond the boundaries which were to have been fixed at each of the five ports, he was liable to be seized by the authorities and brought to the nearest British Consul, who, in these circumstances, was obliged to impose a very heavy fine upon the transgressor; and therefore, if I had accepted their *kind* offers, I should have found, on my arrival at Shanghae, that I was a prisoner instead of a guest, and should, in all probability, have been handed over as such to the British Consul. On the other hand, if I hired my own boat, and went unaccompanied by any of the mandarin's people, I was perfectly safe, according to the strict letter of the treaty, even although a complaint were lodged against me on my arrival at Shanghae. Nothing would have been done in the matter by the British Consul unless I had been *bond fide* taken up beyond the boundaries, which was not likely to happen; as the Chinese officials are extremely cautious in all matters of this kind, in order to avoid getting themselves into trouble.

I immediately determined that I would not be outdone in politeness, and therefore, with many bows and reiterated thanks, I told them that I could not think of accepting so much gratuitous kindness, as I was able to pay my own expenses; and that all I required of them was simply permission to hire a small boat, with three or four men, which would enable me to get on to Shanghae. They still kept on pressing their offer upon me, which I continued as firmly to refuse. Another long private conference between them was now held, which, I suppose, ended in a determination to try what effect could be produced on my servant, who was accordingly sent for. He was desired to tell me that the distance between Chapoo and Shanghae was very great, and that the roads were infested with bands of robbers who were sure to attack us ; and that they could not answer for the consequences unless another boat and some of their own soldiers went along with us for protection. " Tell them," said I, " that I have made up my mind to travel in my usual way, and that no arguments which can be used will induce me to change my opinion, and that the arms which I have shown them are quite sufficient to repel the attacks of any robbers whom I may meet on the road." As a last resource, they sent an officer and his servant to me, who said that they were going to Shanghae, and would be extremely obliged if I would allow them to accompany me. I was obliged to meet even this *civil request* with a refusal; and the mandarins, finding that they must either use force or allow me to have my own way, finally gave up the contest.

Chap. XIX.] PING-IIOO. 361

A boatman now made his appearance, and announced that he was ready to proceed to Shanghae. When I rose to take my leave, I found that all the servants and retainers had been ordered out for the purpose of keeping off the crowd and seeing me safely into the boat. The two mandarins accompanied me, and we marched off to the canal in grand style. The crowd which had assembled was immense, but they were all perfectly quiet and civil. When we reached the landing-place, I thanked my two friends for their kindness, and bade them adieu: then stepping into the boat she was pushed out into the stream, and we soon left the crowd and the Tartar city far behind us.

The country through which we passed was perfectly level, highly cultivated, and more richly wooded than any of the lowlands which I had visited before. It was getting dark when we reached a town of considerable size, named Ping- hoo, which is distant only a few miles from Chapoo, and I determined to remain there for the night. When the morning dawned I roused the Chinamen, and we proceeded on our journey. We now passed through an extensive silk district, where the mulberry-tree was the principal object of cultivation. The natives at this time (May 18th) were busily employed in gathering the leaves and feeding the silkworms with them.

The mulberry-trees are all grafted, and produce very fine thick leaves. I obtained a plant, which is now alive in England, in order to determine theparticular variety, and whether it is different from the kinds which are used for the purpose in Europe. It is not yet, however, in a sufficiently advanced state for this to be ascertained. One thing, however, is certain, that the silk produced in this district is considered as being amongst the finest in China; but whether this is owing to the particular variety of mulberry-tree used in feeding the worms, or to climate or soil, still remains to be ascertained. If the plant should prove a different species or variety from that which is cultivated in the south of Europe, it may be a matter of some importance to introduce it to the plantations of Italy, as Chinese silk is much heavier in the thread than the Italian, and is used in the manufacture of those fabrics requiring lustre and firmness.

The trees, or rather bushes, are planted in rows, the banks of the canals being a favourite situation; and they are not allowed to grow more than from four to six feet in height. The natives set to work with a pair of strong scissors, and cut all the young shoots off close by the stump; they are then either stript of their leaves, or taken home in bundles and stript afterwards. Before this operation takes place, the plants seem in a high state of health, producing vigorous shoots and fine large and thick shining leaves. After the leaves have been taken off, the bushes look like a collection of dead stumps, and in the middle of summer have a curious wintry appearance; but the rain, which falls copiously, and the fertility of the soil, soon

Chap. XIX.] SILK DISTRICTS. 363

revive a succulent plant like the mulberry. The Chinese seem very particular in stirring up the earth amongst the roots of the bushes immediately after the young branches and leaves have been taken off, and the plantations appear to have great attention paid to them.

The farms are small, and are generally worked by the family and relatives of the farmer; who not only plant, graft, and cultivate the mulberry, but also gather the leaves, feed the silkworms, and wind the silk off the cocoons.

During my progress through the silk district, I visited a great number of cottages, where the worms were feeding. They are commonly kept in dark rooms, fitted up with shelves, placed one above another, from the ground to the roof of the house. The worms are kept and fed in round bamboo sieves, placed upon these shelves, so that any one of the sieves may be taken out and examined at pleasure. The poor natives were greatly surprised when they saw a foreigner coming amongst them, and generally supposed that I intended to rob them of their silkworms. In all the villages where I went to, they uniformly denied that they had any feeding-roomsïalthough the leaves and stems of the mulberry about their doors told a different tale; and they never failed to direct me to go on to some other part of the country, where they assured me I should find them. Before we parted, however, they generally gained confidence, and showed me their collections of worms, as well as their mode of managing them.

After passing through the Hang-chow silk district, and keeping on in an easterly direction, we reached, late in the evening, a large town named Sung-kiang-foo, which is about 30 miles to the west of Shanghae, and stopped for the night under its ramparts. By daybreak the next morning we were again on our road, and reached Shanghae on the afternoon of the same day. Having taken up my abode in the house of my friend, Mr. Mackenzie, I was surprised in going down stairs next morning to find one of my Chapoo acquaintances|the officer already mentioned|in close conversation with the Chinese servants; but I now cared very little about the matter, knowing perfectly how the business must end. There was no doubt that the whole affair had been reported to the Taoutae, or head mandarin of Shanghae, and that he would be obliged, for his own sake, to take some little notice of it.

A day or two afterwards I had the honour to receive the following letter from H. B. M. Consul, and a translation of a note which had been sent to him by the Taoutae: |

H. B. M. Consulate,

"Shanghae, 21st May, 1845.

" Sir | The annexed translation of a note received this morning from the Taoutae is transmitted to you for an explanation, which I request may be afforded as soon as possible. I have the honour to be, Sir, yours, &c. " G. Balfouk,

" H. B. M. Consul for Shanghae."

Chap. xix.] Mandarin's Letter. 363

The enclosed ran as follows : |

"I have just heard that a merchant of your honourable nation, Fortune, and his attendant, Linguist ye Mingchoo, were coming from Tinghae to Shanghae, and met with a breeze at sea, when the vessel drifted to Chapoo; that the local officers in Chekiang then protected and sent them on along the coast, and that they are living at the Ming-le Warehouse. I would, therefore, trouble the honourable Consul to make inquiry of what ship he is the merchant, and let me know. This is written wishing you daily happiness."

" *(True Translation.)* (Signed) W. H. Medhurst,

"Interpreter."

When I perused this document I could not but admire the cunning of the old man. He knew perfectly well that it did not contain one word of truth: that I was not coming from Tinghae, but from Ning-po; that I met with no breeze at sea except that which had quietly brought us to the desired port; and, lastly, that I had not been sent along the coast, but had had a very pleasant journey through the interior of the country. I saw at once that the object of the good old Taoutae was to allow me to deny the truth of his statements; and, upon the principle that no man is bound to criminate himself, I sent the following answer to Her Majesty's Consul, which was doubtless perfectly satisfactory to the Taoutae, and just what he wanted: |

" Sir | I have the honour to acknowledge the receipt of a letter from you of yesterday's date, to which is annexed a translation of a note you had received from the Taoutae of Shanghae, concerning which you request an explanation may be afforded as soon as possible. In answer to this, I beg to inform you that the circumstances noticed in the Taoutae's letter do not apply to me, and he is, therefore, mistaken, or has been misinformed. I have the honour to be, Sir, yours," &c.

I need scarcely say that I heard no more of the matter, and from this I concluded that my answer must have been considered highly satisfactory. I arrived in Shanghae in good tune to transact the business I had in hand, and not a little pleased at having so successfully accomplished my " overland" journey.

SECTION 22

CHAP. XX.

SAIL FOB FOO'CHOW-FOO ON THE RIVER MIN. NOVEL MODE OF
ENGAGING A PILOT. ENTRANCE TO THE RIVER. SCENERY ON
ITS BANKS. I BRIDGE OF FOO-CIIOW-FOO. CHINESE CHAIRMEN.
INSULTS RECEIVED FROM THE NATIVES. I CITY AND SUBURBS.
I NATIVE TRADE. I FISHING CORMORANTS. I BANK NOTES.I
CHARACTER OF THE NATIVES. THE LADIES, AND THEIR
FONDNESS FOR FLOWERS. POPULATION REMARKS ON FOO- CHOW-
FOO AS A PLACE OF FOREIGN TRADE GOVERNMENT
SPIES. I GARDENS AND NURSERIES. I DECEIT OF THE MANDARINS. I
LEAVE FOO-CHOW-FOO FOR THE TEA HILLS. I
MOUNTAIN SCENERY DESCRIBED BLACK-TEA DISTRICTS. I
FLORA OF THE HILLS. I AGRICULTURE OF THE DISTRICT. I NATIVE
FRUIT CLIMATE AND TEMPERATURE.

When I had finished my business in Shanghae, I left that city, and sailed for *Foo-chow-foo,* on the river Min. Foo-chow-foo is the capital of the province of Fokien, situated in 25 30' N. latitude, near the celebrated Bohea hills, and about half way between Chusan and Canton. On approaching the entrance to the Min, we anchored under the lce of some islands named the White Dogs, for the purpose of procuring a fisherman who could pilot the vessel into the river, as the entrance is rather difficult for a stranger, having been until very lately but imperfectly surveyed. Going to the shore for that purpose in the ship's boat, we found a small fishing village inhabited by men and boys, most of whom had a piratical and forbidding appea ran cc. It seems that these people only come here at certain periods of the year to fish; and when the season is past, they move to more comfortable quarters on the main-land. Xo women are ever allowed to inhabit the island.

Having picked out the most weather-beaten man we could find, we asked him if he knew the passage to the Min, and if he could take a vessel in which drew three fathoms of water. He immediately answered in the affirmative; but when we wanted him to come on board, he altered his mind and hesitated, probably because he had not confidence in us; or, it might be, he was frightened at the consequences, not knowing how his conduct would be viewed by the authorities. Mr. Shaw, Captain Freeman, and myself, now held a conference as to what was to be done. A ship and a valuable cargo were at stake; the numerous and dangerous sandbanks near the mouth of the river were visible; and as the man only refused us his service through fear and ignorance, we concluded that, as " necessity has no law," there could be no great harm in taking him against his will. We accordingly pulled alongside his little junk, and took him and it off to the ship, where he very soon got over all his fears.

The Chinese are certainly a strange and unaccountable race. Never in my life did I witness greater apathy than was shown by this boat's crew when we took them off to the ship. Their companions too I for there were several boats in the little bay Iscarcely even looked at us, or manifested the

Chap. XX.] ENTER THE RIVER MIN. 369

least surprise, when they saw our men board the boat, get her anchor up, and hoist her sail.

The next morning our pilot got the ship under weigh, and took us into the river Min by a passage not marked in our charts; he evinced the most perfect acquaintance with the depth of water at every part, and at last anchored us in safety abreast of a small temple, a few miles from the mouth of the river. Before we came to the most dangerous point, where we had to pass between two sand-banks, the captain very quietly informed him, that if he made any mistake and got the ship aground, he should have his tail cut offIa punishment very nearly the greatest which can be inflicted on a Chinaman. When told, he shrugged up his shoulders, gave a sly look, and said; " Very well, we shall see by and by." The anchorage being reached in safety, the old man thought it was now his time for a joke, and, turning triumphantly round with his tail in one of his hands, exclaimed, " Now, what about the tail? is it to be cut off, or not? or are you satisfied ?"

The passage by which we entered the river is called by the natives the *Woo-hoo-mun,* or "the five tiger gate;" and here we saw a most singular rock, or island, which is cleft, as it were, into five pyramids, and is much revered by the Chinese sailor. In fact, he seems to look upon it as representing the gods of the ocean, and he fails not to offer up his thanks and his offerings every time he passes by it on returning from the sea. The

Chinese are often taunted with their indifference to the religion which they profess; and yet the earnest and devout manner in which they burn incense, and worship at their holy places, would put to the blush many of the professors of a holier and purer faith.

The scenery at the mouth of the Min and towards Foo-chow-foo is striking and beautiful. The river itself varies much in width and depth, according to the district through which it flows. Near its mouth, and at some parts where the country between it and the hills is flat, it is not less than a mile in width; but at other parts, where the mountains come almost to the water's edge, the river is narrow, deep, and rapid. There are two or three such places between the mouth of the Min and the city of Foo-chow-foo. The whole of this district is hilly, many of the mountains being at least 3000 feet high; and at this season of the year when thunder-storms were almost of daily occurrence, the effects produced by them amongst these mountains were grand and sublime.

It is evident that the Chinese greatly dreaded our visiting this place during the war. I observed that forts had been built on all the most commanding positions on the sides of the river; but most of them were now without guns, and had already become dilapidated.

The little town and fortress of *Mingan,* a few miles up the river, is beautifully situated on a hill sloping down to the water; and the position is so strong by nature, that, if manned with English

Chap. XX.] RIVER SCENERY. 371

troops, it could defend the pass against the strongest force.

A few miles below the city the river is blocked up, almost all the way across, with stones and old junks, which are covered at high water. I believe the *intended* plan of defence was to wreck all our vessels on this barrier, and destroy our men by batteries erected near it!

On the banks of the river are numerous temples, or joss houses, built in the most romantic and beautiful situations. A fig-tree *(Ficus nitida)* | a kind of Banyan|is a great favourite with the priests, and is always found growing beside the temples, where its dark green leaves and wide- spreading branches afford an agreeable shade from the fierce rays of the sun. About nine miles below Foo-chow-foo, a pretty little pagoda stands on an island on the left bank of the river; near this is the anchorage for large vessels which it would not be prudent to take up to the town. All the low hills are neatly terraced and cultivated with sweet potatoes and earth-nuts, and on the more fertile of the mountains cultivation is carried on at least 2500 feet above the level of the sea. But many of the mountains are quite barren; bare rocks of granite are showing themselves over their surface, from amongst which springs are almost always flowing, and when the water accumulates in the glens between the hills, it forms numerous beautiful cascades, as it tumbles down into the Min. Some parts of the region are well wooded, at leastfor China; and viewing the scenery as a whole | the beautiful river, winding its way between mountains, its islands, its temples, its villages and fortresses|I think, although not the richest, it is the most romantic and beautiful part of the country which has come under my observation.

The city and suburbs of Foo-chow-foo stand in an opening amongst the hills, about twenty miles from the mouth of the Mm. The river runs through the suburbs, which are connected by the celebrated bridge called the *Wan-show,* or " myriads of ages," which was always said to consist of one hundred arches. It is not an arched bridge at all; but is nevertheless a wonderful structure, being about two thousand feet in length, and having fifty strong pillars of stone, with large slabs of granite reaching from the one to the other, and forming the top of the bridge. During the rains the river rushes through these divisions with great rapidity; and as the bridge has evidently stood for many ages, it is a proof of the substantial manner in Avhich it was originally built.

Leaving the ship at the mouth of the Min, Mr. Shaw, Captain Freeman, and myself started in a native boat to go up to the city. When we were getting into the boat, our old friend the pilot, who by this time had become quite at home amongst us, came and begged us to give him a passage as far up as the first town we were to pass on our way. We inquired why he did not go back again to his fishing at the White Dog island. His reply

Chap. XX.] CHINESE CHAIRMEN. 373

was, " I should get robbed by pirates of all the money you have given me for pilotage. I must first make sure of it by depositing it in the hands of a friend of mine in the town; after that is done, I shall return to the island."

We were nearly two days in getting up to the city, owing to the rapidity of the stream, caused .by the late heavy rains. We landed near the bridge already noticed, and immediately inquired for the house of the English Consul, who, we were informed, lived in a temple situated within the city, and about three miles from the landing-place. As nearly the whole of the streets in the suburbs were under water at the time, in some parts to the depth of four feet, it was impossible to walk this distance; nor was it necessary to make the attempt, for chairmen surrounded us in great numbers, and were as determined on putting us into their chairs as a London conductor is to have passengers for his omnibus. We willingly yielded to their solicitations, and got into chairs and set *off* for the consular residence. The people here had seen but few foreigners, and were particularly impertinent and annoying. Hundreds followed us and crowded round the chairs; " Quang-yanga, quang-yanga," |their term for foreigners|was rung in our ears from all sides, and frequently other appellations of a much worse signification. Our Chinese servants, who walked by our side, were attacked and reviled for having any connection with us. In one of the streets the water was so deep that I was obliged tostand up on the seat of the chair, and even then it reached my feet. Here the crowd became very abusive, and commenced throwing water over us. At first our servants bore this treatment pretty well; but their patience was at last exhausted, and they turned upon the assailants. The scene was now both amusing and disagreeable. Luckily I happened to be a little in advance, and was therefore pretty well out of the mele'e; but Captain Freeman came in for his full share of it, and was completely soaked through. When we got within the city walls we were not molested further, owing, I suppose, to the greater strength of the police.

The city is walled and fortified upon the same plan as Ning-po and Shanghae, and is at least eight or nine miles in circumference, having as usual east, west, north, and south gates. At various points on the walls, as well as above the gates, guard-houses are erected, each containing guns; some of which, according to the writings on them, were cast about the commencement of the last war. A small area between the south and north gates is not built upon; but the greater part of the space within the walls is densely covered with houses. There are two rather handsome pagodas, and some small hills on which temples are built, and where a good view of the town and suburbs may be obtained. On one of these hills the British Consul has his residence.

The streets in all Chinese cities have much the same appearance: some are a little wider than others, and have better and more attractive shops ; but by

Chap. XX.] NATIVE TRADE OF FOO-CHOW-FOO. 375

far the greater part of them are narrow and dirty, and Foo-chow-foo certainly forms no exception to the general rule. A large trade appears to be carried on here in copper, judging from the number of shops filled with manufactured articles of that metal, particularly of gongs, of which I observed an immense number of all sizes. This copper is brought here principally in junks from Loo-choo. They also bring a considerable quantity of gold. Both metals are said to be originally the exports of Japan. I went on board two of these junks at the mouth of the Min, which were bound to Loo-choo, and were loaded with tea-oil, which they told me they had taken in exchange for their copper. A great quantity of iron is manufactured here, and wiredrawing is carried on extensively. The great export trade of the port, however, is in wood, which is floated down the Min in large quantities, and covers many acres in the suburbs near the river side. Hundreds of junks from Amoy, Ning-po, Chapoo, and some even from as far north as the province of Shan-tung and the bay of Pee-che-lee, are constantly employed in this trade. The wood is chiefly a sort of common pine, employed in the building of houses, and it is generally cut into lengths suited to that purpose before it is shipped. Good planks of fine hard wood can also be had in any quantity at this place. The wood junks are loaded with great skill, a great part of their cargo being lashed to their sides, thus making them about three times their ordinary width.

Banking is carried on to a greater extent in Foo- chow-foo than in the other towns which I have visited. Paper notes are a common medium of exchange, in which the people have the greatest confidence, preferring them to dollars or " cash." Some of the notes are as low as four hundred cash|about eighteen pence English money; others are for very large sums.

The people here are generally much cleaner in their habits, and appear to be a more active race, than those in the northern towns. In fact, they approach more nearly to the natives of Canton than to any other, in these respects. I was much surprised to find them consuming beef, and even milk, in considerable quantities ; articles which are never used by the inhabitants of the other districts where I have been : indeed, every where else the Chinese were wont to express their astonishment when they saw the English using such articles of food.

The ladies of Foo-chow-foo are particularly fond, of flowers | artificial as well as natural|for the decoration of their hair. The rustic cottage beauty employs the more large and gaudy, such as the red Hibiscus; while the refined damsels prefer the jasmine, tuberose, and others of that description: artificial flowers, however, are more in use than natural ones.

The population of Foo-chow-foo has been estimated at about half a million; and I have no doubt that if the suburbs and numerous villages in the vicinity be taken into account, the number is not over-stated. Up to the time when I left China,

Chap. XX.] FOREIGN TRADE. 377

little or nothing had been done here in the way of trade, and I cannot help thinking that its advantages in this respect have been greatly over-rated. It is never likely to be a place of as great importance to England as the more northerly port of Shanghae; and for this very simple reasonlthe physical nature of the country is against it. The whole of the surrounding region is mountainous ; the rivers are rapid and in some places shallow, and are often liable to rain-floods. There are consequently many impediments in the way of a free transmission of goods into the interior of the country. Foo-chow-foo was supposed to possess great advantages, owing to its being near the Bohea or black tea district; and it was thought at one time that it might form the great emporium for the export of this article to Europe and America. This opinion, however, has hitherto proved fallacious, and I believe it is now ascertained that the black teas can be brought more readily to Shanghae or Ning-po than to Foo-chow-foo: especially since the Bohea teas have sunk in estimation, and other districts to the northward, having taken the place of the Bohea hills, are now furnishing the black teas of commerce.

In addition to all these disadvantages the natives seem a lawless and turbulent race, having all the characteristics of those in the Canton province, and, like them, being inveterate in their hatred of foreigners, and full of conceit as to their own importance and power. Several very serious disturbances have taken place at the port since it was opened to the British.

After paying our visit to the English Consul, vre returned to the suburbs to look out for a house where we could put up during our stay. When we got back to the river, we found all our luggage and servants already safely lodged in the house of a person who had been ordered by the mandarins to lodge us and look after us. We were glad to get in-doors from the insulting crowd, and were consequently not very particular as to quarters. We soon found, however, that we were very strictly watched, and that we could not move any where without the fact being communicated to the mandarins.

My first object was to find out all the gardens and nurseries in the district. The late G. Trades- cant Lay, Esq., the first consul here, who took a great interest in botanical pursuits, had unfortunately left this place for Amoy. All was, therefore, up-hill work, as it used to be in the more northern towns when I first visited them. After a great deal of exertion and annoyance, I found out a number of gardens and nurseries, both in the town and in the surrounding country; and obtained a few new plants.

The valley of the Min was still flooded in many parts, and travelling over it was a very serious matter. One morning I started for a place at a considerable distance in the country, accompanied by a guide and a Coolie. I took the Coolie that he

Chap. XX.] DECEIT OF MANDARINS. 379

might carry me over those low flats which were known to be still flooded. We got on pretty well for some time; but the tide beginning to rise, I soon found that I must either retrace my steps or make up my mind to disregard the water, as the whole of the paths in our route were flooded. Unwilling to return, I went on, often wading up to my middle; the same thing occurred during several successive days, and this under a burning sun, with a temperature of at least 95 Fahr. in the shade. Few constitutions could stand this with impunity; and I suffered severely for it afterwards.

I was now anxious to proceed further into the country, particularly into the hilly black tea district; but the mandarins, who were informed of all my movements by their spies, did every thing in their power to dissuade me from making the attempt. They told the Consul, and induced him to believe them, that their only reason for wishing to prevent my going into the interior was, that the natives were in a state which made it unsafe for a foreigner to trust himself amongst them; that by and by they would communicate with the magistrates in the district to which I wanted to go, and that after this was done I might proceed with safety. But I had had too much to do with the Chinese authorities in various parts of the country to place any reliance in what they said, more particularly when I knew that they had some end to gain. In the present instance, their object was to procrastinate matters from day to day until I shouldbe obliged to leave the district. When the Chinese have an end to gain, the only question with them is, whether they are most likely to succeed by telling the truth or telling lies; either method is resorted to as may best suit their purpose, with a slight preference, perhaps, for the latter.

When they found that, notwithstanding all their descriptions of the fierce and hostile disposition of the people, I was still determined to go, they declared that no tea was grown in this district; being fully persuaded that an Englishman could have no other object in exploring the country than to see the cultivation of his favourite beverage. Indeed, every Chinaman firmly believes we could not continue to exist as a nation were it not for the productions of the celestial empire. It has been stated that his celestial majesty, the Emperor himself, during the war recommended his subjects to use every means in their power to prevent the English from getting tea and rhubarblthe one being what they lived upon, and the other their medicine, without which, his majesty said, they could not continue to exist for any length of time ; and consequently would be more easily conquered in this way than by the sword.

I told the mandarins that I did not care whether there were tea farms on these hills or not; but that, to cut the matter short, I was determined to go and see.

Accordingly, on the following morning I started early, taking the road for the tea hills. The flat

Chap. XX.] MOUNTAIN SCENERY. 381

country through which I passed, between the north side of the city and the moun-tains, is chiefly cultivated with rice, sugar-cane, ginger, and tobacco. On the sides of the little hills, and also for a considerable distance up the loftier ranges, large quanti-ties of sweet potatoes and earth-nuts are grown during the summer season; but as we ascend, the mountains become more rugged, cultivation ceases, and plants indigenous to the country alone show themselves. On my journey over these mountains I came to the conclusion that their native flora was of an intermediate character between those of the southern and northern provinceslthe tropical species of the south being found in the low lands, and the species of more northern latitudes inhabiting the mountains

2000 or 3000 feet above the level of the sea. In the low valleys the *Ficits nitida* attains a large size, and is a great favourite with the inhabitants. It is always seen near villages and temples.

After toiling up one of the celebrated mountain passes, which is paved all the way, and has a house of refreshment about half way up, I reached the summit of the mountain—the highest land in this part of China. A glorious prospect was spread before me: the valley of the Min stretching far across to the other hills; the city of Foo-chow-foo, with its pagodas, temples, and watchtowers standing in the centre of the plain; and the broad river winding smoothly along in its course to the sea; mountain towering above mountain, and

23

SECTION 23

the whole striking the mind with wonder and admiration.

Among these mountains, and at a height of 2000 and 3000 feet above the level of the sea, I found the black tea district, which I was anxious to see, and the existence of which had been denied by my *affectionate* friends the mandarins. Having been in several green tea countries further north, I was desirous to ascertain clearly whether the plant was the same species in both places, or whether, as generally believed, they were different. I have stated in a former chapter that the tea-plant of the northern green tea districts is the true *Thea viridis* of botanists. I was now fortunate enough not only to find an extensive tea district, but also to be present when the natives were picking and preparing the leaves; and I not only procured specimens for my herbarium, but also a living plant, which I afterwards took to the green tea hills of the north, and found, on minute comparison, that it was identical with the *Thea viridis.* In other words, the black and green teas which generally come to England from the northern provinces of China are made from the same species, and the difference of colour, flavour, &c. is solely the result of the different modes of preparation.

In this region I met with no plants which I had not seen before in other parts of the country. I observed the lance-leaved pine (*Cunninghamia Ian- ceolata*) in great abundance; indeed, this species and

Chap. XX.] FLORA OF FOO-CHOW-FOO. 383

the more common *Pinus sinensis* are almost the only trees of any size which grow in this mountainous district. The natives amongst these hills were much surprised at the sight of a foreigner, and came crowding from all quarters to see me; they were, however, much more civil and respectful than their countrymen in the lowlands and at Foo-chow-foo.

On my return from this excursion, I devoted most of my time to the examination of nurseries in the vicinity of the city. They contained some interesting plants. The celebrated *Fingered-Citron,* so common in the shops throughout China, seems to be cultivated in great perfection in this part of the country; in fact, it appears to be its natural locality. The district round Foo-chow-foo seems to be the great Camellia garden of China, and in no other part of the country did I ever see these plants in such perfect health, or so beautifully cultivated. The *Ixoras* and *Hydrangeas* are also particularly well grown and handsome, the latter invariably producing flowers of the deepest blue, much deeper than I have ever seen them in England. They are grown in a fine rich loam, which contains some chemical ingredient which is the cause of their deep colour.

Here, as well as further north, the farmer grows crops of wheat and green vegetables during the winter months. A great part of the low country, at least all that is capable of being flooded, is cultivated with rice during the summer and autumn. The first crop is ripe in July, and the second is planted between the rows of the former, in the same manner as in the northern provinces, and ripens in the autumn. Large quantities of tobacco are grown in the province. The farmers cultivate this plant with very great care, and take every means to have the leaves large and fine. For this purpose all the flowers are regularly picked off, and also all the small and useless leaves as soon as they are formed. Sugar and ginger are likewise grown to a greater extent in this part of China than in any other with which I am acquainted ; and crops of sweet potatoes and earth- nuts abound on the sides of the hills.

Amongst fruits, the plums are good, but inferior to those we have in England; the peaches are curiously formed, but worthless. What may be more properly called Chinese fruits, such as leechees, longans, and wangpees, are, however, excellent, the climate suiting them admirably. When I was here (in July), the leechee trees were covered with their fine red fruit, and were very beautiful, the fruit contrasted so well with the deep clear green foliage. Large quantities of oranges, citrons, and pumeloes are also found in the district of the Min; but none of them were ripe at this season. I saw, for the first time, the tree commonly called the Chinese olive, from the resemblance its fruit bears to the olive of Europe; also the Chinese date, which produces a fruit not unlike the date imported into England.

Chap. XX.]

CLIMATE.

In the fields in the vicinity of Foo-chow-foo, large quantities of the sweet-scented *Jasminum Sambac* are cultivated. It is used to decorate the hair of the ladies, and to garnish the tables of the wealthy. I believe that all the gardens, both in the north and south, are supplied with this favourite flower from the province of Fokien. Various other shrubs, such as *Murraya exotica, Aglaia odorata,* and *Chloranthus inconspicuus,* are grown for their blossoms, which are used for mixing with the tea.

The temperature of Foo-chow-foo appears to be intermediate between that of Hong-kong in the south, and Shanghae in the north. In June, and in the beginning of July, the thermometer ranged from 85 to 95 Fahr., and about the middle of the latter month it rose to 100, which I believe it seldom exceeds. The following table was kept by the late Mr. G. Tradescant Lay: |

1844.Max.Min. 0oAugust -9682September ...9082October ....8671November - 7865December - - - . -75441845. January -7244The weather is generally unsettled and wet about the time the summer monsoon changes, that

is, from April to June, and the district is visited by heavy thunder-storms in July and part of August. Towards the end of August, in September, and in the beginning of October, it is generally very dry. The monsoon now changes again to the north-east, and the weather becomes variable and continues so during the winter months.

During my stay here I received a great deal of kindness from Mr. Walker, of H. M. Consulate. The natives continued to the last troublesome and annoying; and I was very glad when my labours in the district were ended.

Pagoda Hl.md, on the Hirer Min.

Chap. XXI.] ENGAGE A PASSAGE IN A JUNK. 387

CHAP. XXI.

ENGAGE A PASSAGE IN A JUNK. | LEAVE THE DISTRICT OF THE MIN. AN ATTACK OF FEVER RELIGIOUS CEREMONIES ON BOARD THE JUNK. ATTACKED BY PIRATES. SCENE ON BOARD. COWARDICE OF THE CHINESE. | PIRATES BEAT OFF. GRATITUDE OF THE CREW. A SAFE ANCHORAGE!

ANOTHER FLEET OF PIRATES. | ATTACK AND RESULTS. | ARRIVE AT CHUSAN. | INGRATITUDE OF THE CREW. | MODE OF MAKING THEM KEEP THEIR WORD KINDNESS OF FOREIGN RESIDENTS AT SHANGHAE. LARGE PEACHES. | COLLECTIONS PACKED. | LEAVE THE NORTH OF CHINA. | SAIL FOR ENGLAND. | AR-RIVAL IN THE THAMES. | CONCLUSION.

At the time when I visited *Foo-chow-foo,* although it was open to the English as a place of trade and had a British Consul, it was little known in a mercantile point of view. The entrance to the river Min was described as extremely difficult and dangerous, and, consequently, few foreign vessels ventured to touch at this port. When, therefore, my botanical researches were completed, and I was ready to return north to Shanghae, I was obliged to apply for a passage in a Chinese junk, a whole fleet of which were to sail in a few days for Ning-po and Chapoo. Knowing the dislike and jealousy which most of the natives manifest towards foreigners, I had some doubt whether I should be able to induce them to take me as a passenger, and, in that event, I had determined to go down to the mouth of theriver, and, " *sans ceremonie"* get on board, whether they consented or not. I was, therefore, agreeably surprised, when, on sending my servant to make inquiries as to the time when they were likely to sail, he returned, bringing with him the captain and some of the sailors, who were all not only willing, but most anxious, that I should go with them.

The principal part of the cargo carried by the Ning-po and Chapoo junks is wood. This is stowed on deck, and also lashed firmly to the gunwales and sides with large ropes of bamboo which are of great strength. Several hundreds of these vessels may be seen loading at the port of Foo-chow-foo, particularly in the summer season, when the monsoon is fair for their voyage home. The mandarins are extremely jealous of so large a fleet, and will not allow them to carry guns, even for their own defence ; evidently fearing that some day or other these might- be turned against the government. The consequence of this regulation is, that these poor sailors and all they possess on board, often fall an easy prey to the pirates who abound all along this coast.

When the cargo was completed, the captain of the junk came to inform me that he was ready to start, and requested me to come on board. Whilst I was packing up my luggage, he began to examine my fire-arms very minutely, and said to me: " I hope your gun is a good one, and that you have plenty of powder and shot ?" " What is your reason for putting this question ? " said I: " I am sure we shall have nothing to shoot in our voyage

Chap. XXL] LEAVE THE MIN DISTRICT. 389

up the coast." " Oh yes you will," answered he; " we are very likely to be attacked by the *Jan-dous* who swarm outside amongst the islands." " Who are the *Jan-dous ?* " said I, to my servant, never having heard the name before. " Oh! they are pirates," said he, " and we are all very much frightened at them." " Nonsense ! " I exclaimed : " no pirates will attack us; and if they do, they will repent it." At this time I had no idea that the coast was so infested with these lawless characters, and I put it all down to the cowardice of my informants.

As soon as I got on board, we hove up the anchor and dropped down to the mouth of the Min. We here found a large fleet of junkslabout one hundred and seventy saillall like ourselves loaded with wood and ready to start for the northern parts of Ning-po and Chapoo. That evening a meeting of the captains was held on board of our vessel, and a deputation appointed to wait upon the mandarins to request them to send a convoy of war junks to protect the fleet from the pirates. These negotiations were carried on for several days; but the demands of the mandarins were so exorbitant, that the junk people would not comply with them, and it was at last determined to sail without the convoy. Just as they came to this decision, the wind changed and blew a gale from the north for three days, when it veered round to the south, and blew nearly as strong from that quarter, and for the same space of time.These vessels never go to sea in stormy weather, even if the wind is fair; and what with gales of wind and negotiations with mandarins, I was obliged to content myself with a junk life for a fortnight at the mouth of the river.

As long as I enjoyed health I got on well enough ; but the exposure during the past summer, particularly at Foo-chow-foo, had gradually undermined my constitution; and the fever, which was probably kept off for a certain time by bodily exertion, now seized me, and compelled me to take to my cot, where I lay for a number of days insensible at intervals. At times, when consciousness returned, I certainly thought that my travels were drawing to a close, and that my grave would be a lonely one on the banks of the Min. It seemed hard for me to die in a land of strangers, without a friend or countryman to close my eyes, or follow me to my last resting-place; and home, friends, and country, how doubly dear did they seem to me then!

The wind having been fair for several days, and the weather appearing settled, the captain of the junk came down to the place where I lay, and told me they intended to sail on the following morning. He again inquired if I had my gun and pistols in proper order and plenty of powder and ball. Still imagining that they were exaggerating the dangers of the voyage, I laughed, and said: " Do not be afraid, I have every thing in order, and I will undertake to beat off any pirates who may attack us;" nevertheless, I clearly saw that both captain and

Chap. XXI.] RELIGIOUS CEREMONIES. 391

sailors were really uneasy about the voyage, and would have been very glad of another gale to afford a pretext for deferring it a little longer. They had, however, no further excuse for delay, and it was settled that the whole fleet should sail early the next day.

The Chinese sailor never goes to sea without first presenting an offering to the gods to propitiate them, in order that the voyage may be a speedy and successful one. Accordingly, on this day the cabin of our junk was set in order, and the tables covered with dishes of pork, mutton, fruits, and vegetables. Candles and incense were burned upon the tables for a short time, and the whole business had something solemn and imposing about it. The cook, who seemed to be the high priest, conducted all the ceremonies. On other days, as well as this, it was part of his duty to light the candles in the little temple where the gods were kept, as well as to burn incense and prostrate himself before them.

Early on the following morning, the whole fleet was in motion, starting all at the same time, for the sake of mutual protection. The wind and tide were both fair, and we proceeded along the coast with great rapidity, and were soon out of sight of the Min and its beautiful and romantic scenery. The plan of mutual protection soon seemed to be abandoned, and the vessels separated into threes and fours, each getting on as well and as fast as it could. About four o'clock in the afternoon, andwhen we were some fifty or sixty miles from the Min, the captain and pilot came hurriedly down to my cabin and informed me that they saw a number of *Jan-dous,* right ahead, lying in wait for us. I ridiculed the idea, and told them that they imagined every junk they saw to be a pirate ; but they still maintained that they were so, and I therefore considered it prudent to be prepared for the worst. I got out of bed, ill and feverish as I was, and carefully examined my fire-arms, clearing the nipples of my gun and pistols and putting on fresh caps. I also rammed down a ball upon the top of each charge of shot in my gun, put a pistol in each side pocket, and patiently waited for the result. By the aid of a small pocket-telescope, I could see as the nearest junk approached that her deck was crowded with men; I then had no longer any doubts regarding her intentions. The pilot, an intelligent old man, now came up to me, and said that he thought resistance was of no use ; I might manage to beat off one junk or even two, but that I had no chance with five of them. Being at that time in no mood to take advice or be dictated to by any one, I ordered him off to look after his own duty. I knew perfectly well, that if we were taken by the pirates, I had not the slightest chance of escape; for the first thing they would do, would be to knock me on the head and throw me overboard, as they would deem it dangerous to themselves were I to get away. At the same time, I must confess I had little hopes of being able to beat off such a

c c 4

Chap. XXI.] SCENE ON BOARD. 393

number, and devoutly wished myself anywhere rather than where I was.

The scene around me was a strange one. The captain, pilot, and one or two native passengers were taking up the boards of the cabin-floor, and putting their money and other valuables out of sight amongst the ballast. The common sailors, too, had their copper cash or " *tsien"* to hide; and the whole place was in a state of bustle and confusion. When all their more valuable property was hidden, they began to make some preparations for defence. Baskets of small stones were brought up from the hold, and emptied out on the most convenient parts of the deck, and were intended to be used instead of fire-arms when the pirates came to close quarters. This is a common mode of defence in various parts of China, and is effectual enough when the enemy has only similar weapons to bring against them; but on the coast of Fokien where we were now, all the pirate junks carried guns, and consequently a whole deck load of stones could be of very little use against them.

During the general bustle I missed my own servant for a short time. When he returned to me, he had made such a change in his appearance that I did not recognise him. He was literally clothed in rags which he had borrowed from the sailors, all of whom had also put on their very worst clothes. When I asked him the reason of this change in his outward man, he told me that the pirates only made those persons prisoners whohad money, and were likely to pay handsomely for their ransom; and that they would not think it worth their while to lay hold of a man in rags.

I was surrounded by several of the crew, who might well be called " Job's comforters," some suggesting one thing, and some another; and many proposed that we should bring the junk round and run back to the Min. The nearest pirate was now within 200 or 300 yards of us, and putting her helm down, gave us a broadside from her guns. All was now dismay and consternation on board our junk, and every man ran below except two who were at the helm. I expected every moment that these also would leave their post; and then we should have been an easy prey to the pirates. " My gun is nearer you than those of the *Jan-dous"* said I to the two men; " and if you move from the helm, depend upon it I will shoot you." The poor fellows looked very uncomfortable, but I suppose thought they had better stand the fire of the pirates than mine, and kept at their post. Large boards, heaps of old clothes, mats, and things of that sort which were at hand, were thrown up to protect us from the shot; and as we had every stitch of sail set, and a fair wind, we were going through the water at the rate of seven or eight miles an hour.

The shot from the pirates fell considerably short of us, and I was therefore enabled to form an opinion of the range and power of their guns, which was of some use to me. Assistance from

Chap. XXI.] ATTACK OF PIRATES. 395

our cowardly crew was quite out of the question, for there was not a man amongst them brave enough to use the stones which had been brought on deck; and which perhaps might have been of some little use when the pirates came nearer. The fair wind and all the press of sail which we had crowded on the junk proved of no use; for our pursuers, who had much faster sailing vessels, were gaining rapidly upon us. Again the nearest pirate fired upon us. The shot this time fell just under our stern. I still remained quiet, as I had determined not to fire a single shot until I was quite certain my gun would take effect. The third shot which followed this came whizzing over our heads and through the sails, without, however, wounding either the men at the helm or myself.

The pirates now seemed quite sure of their prize, and came down upon us, hooting and yelling like demons, at the same time loading their guns, and evidently determined not to spare their shot. This was a moment of intense interest. The plan which I had formed from the first was now about to be put to the proof; and if the pirates were not the cowards which I beb'eved them to be, nothing could save us from falling into their hands. Their fearful yells seem to be ringing in my ears even now, after this lapse of time, and when I am on the other side of the globe.

The nearest junk was now within thirty yards of ours; their guns were now loaded, and I knew

that the next discharge would completely rake our decks. " Now," said I to our helmsmen, " keep your eye fixed on me, and the moment you see me fall flat on the deck you must do the same, or you will be shot." I knew that the pirate, who was now on our stern, could not bring his guns to bear upon us without putting his helm down and bringing his gangway at right angles with our stern, as his guns were fired from the gangway. I therefore kept a sharp eye upon his helmsman, and the moment I saw him putting the helm down, I ordered our steersmen to fall flat on their faces behind some wood, and at the same moment did so myself. We had scarcely done so when bang, bang, went their guns, and the shot came whizzing close over us, splintering the wood about us in all directions. Fortunately none of us were struck. " Now, mandarin, now, they are quite close enough," cried out my companions, who did not wish to have another broadside like the last. I, being of the same opinion, raised myself above the high stern of our junk ; and while the pirates were not more than twenty yards from us, hooting and yelling, I raked their decks fore and aft, with shot and ball from my double-barrelled gun.

Had a thunder-bolt fallen amongst them they could not have been more surprised; doubtless many were wounded, and probably some killed. At all events, the whole of the crew, not fewer than forty or fifty men, who, a moment before, crowded the deck, disappeared in a marvellous manner;

Chap. XXI.] PIRATES BEAT OFF. 397

sheltering themselves behind the bulwarks, or lying flat on their faces. They were so completely taken by surprise, that their junk was left without a helmsman, her sails flapped in the wind; and as we were still carrying all sail and keeping on our right course, they were soon left a considerable way astern.

Another was now bearing down upon us as boldly as his companion had done, and commenced firing in the same manner. Having been so successful with the first, I determined to follow the same plan with this one, and to pay no attention to his firing until he should come to close quarters. The plot now began to thicken; for the first junk had gathered way again and was following in our wake, although keeping at a respectful distance, and three others, although still further distant, were making for the scene of action as fast as they could. In the mean time, the second was almost along-side, and continued raking our decks in a deadly manner with their guns. Watching their helm as before, we sheltered ourselves as well as we could; at the same time my poor fellows who were steering, kept begging and praying that I would fire into our pursuers as soon as possible, or we should be all killed. As soon as they came within twenty or thirty yards of us, I gave them the contents of both barrels, raking their decks as before. This time the helmsman fell, and doubtless several others were wounded. In a minute or two I could see nothing but boards and shields, whichwere held up by the pirates to protect themselves from my firing; their junk went up into the wind for want of a helmsman, and was soon left some distance behind us.

While I was watching this vessel, our men called out to me that there was another close on our lee- bow, which I had not observed on account of our main-sail. Luckily, however, it proved to be a Ning-po wood junk like ourselves, which the pirates had taken a short time before, but which, although manned by these rascals, could do us no harm, having no guns. The poor Ning-po crew, whom I could plainly see on board, seemed to be very much down-hearted and frightened. I was afterwards informed that, when a junk is captured, all the principal people, such as the captain, pilot, and passengers, are taken out of her, and a number of the pirates go on board and take her into some of their dens amongst the islands, and keep her there until a heavy ransom is paid, both for the junk and the people. Sometimes when a ransom cannot be obtained, the masts and spars and every thing else which is of any value are taken out of her and she is set on fire.

Two other piratical junks which had been following in our wake for some time, when they saw what had happened, would not venture any nearer ; and at last, much to my satisfaction, the whole set of them bore away.

Now was the time for my heroical companions to come from their hiding-place, which they did

Chap. XXI.] GRATITUDE OF THE CREW. 399

with great alacrity, hooting and yelling as the pirates had done before, and in derision calling on them to come back and renew the fight. The stones, too, were now boldly seized and thrown after the retreating junks, reaching to almost a tenth part of the distance, and a stranger who had not seen these gentry before would have supposed them the bravest men in existence. Fortunately the pirates did not think proper to accept the challenge.

With the captain, pilot, crew, and passengers, I was now one of the greatest and best of men in existence. They actually came and knelt before me, as to some superior being, and expressed their deep and lasting gratitude, which, however, did not last long. The sun was now setting in all his glory, behind the hills of Fokien, and many of the more devout amongst the passengers and crew did not fail to bow low in adoration and thankfulness to this supposed deity for their escape out of the hands of the pirates. Shortly after nightfall we arrived at one of the safe anchorages, where the mandarins are too strong for the lawless bands which infest the other parts of the coast.

On the following morning we again got under weigh, and proceeded the whole day without molestation. In the evening we arrived at another safe anchorage, or place of rendezvous; but the security at this place consisted in the number and strength of the junks actually at anchor there, and not in the fear which the pirates entertained for

the government. When we reached this place the night was fine, and as it was nearly full moon, it was almost as light as day. The tide too was just turning in our favour ; and as I was most anxious to proceed on our voyage, I did every thing in my power to induce them to go on. It was of no use, however; for as soon as we reached the anchorage, and found a large fleet of junks, the anchor was dropped and they determined to stay there all night. I felt very much annoyed, but saw it was no use to grumble, and went quietly to bed. In less than an hour from this time, and before I had fallen asleep, hearing a stir upon deck, I inquired what was the cause, and found that we were getting under weigh. This was agreeable news; but as I could not imagine what had caused them to change their minds so soon, I went upon deck to see what was going on. Our people, it appeared, had gone to sleep the moment our anchor was down; shortly after this, the other junks, which, it turned out, were only waiting for the rise of the tide to enter some river in the vicinity, had all weighed anchor and gone off. All on board were now in great consternation, lest the pirates should come down upon us whilst at anchor, and no time was lost in getting it up and proceeding on our voyage, much, of course, to my satisfaction.

On the following day, late in the afternoon, when I was laid up in my bed with fever, the captain came hurriedly down, and informed me that another fleet of pirates were in sight, and

Chap. XXI.] THE PIRATES AGAIN. 401

evidently lying in wait for us. I was obliged to get up, ill as I was, and when I got on deck I could see by the aid of my telescope six junks coming out from amongst the islands under the main land, and evidently bearing down towards us. This time I was not so sceptical as the last. After having once seen these rascally vessels, there was no mistaking others of the same class, as they came sneaking out of the bays. Their clipper- built hulls, the cut of their sails, their raking masts, and the crowd of fellows who lined their decks, all told the business they were after. It was therefore evident that we must prepare for another encounter.

It now struck me that perhaps I might be able to deceive the pirates with regard to our strength, as I was afraid that I might not again be so successful with them, particularly if they found out that there was only one foreigner on board: knowing that they have a great dread of foreigners and their guns, my object was to make them believe that there were a number of us, and that we were well armed. For this purpose I got up all the spare clothes I had, and put them on the least Chinese-looking Chinamen on board. At the same time I desired them to collect all the short levers which they use for hoisting their sails, and which at a distance would look not unlike fire-arms, particularly if the deception was assisted by the report of a double-barrelled gun. Every thing looked promising, and I thought my recruits were likely

to be of some service to me; but when the nearest pirate, who had been coming fast down upon us, gave us a broadside, it was too much for my Chinamen, who were instantly panic-struck, threw down their *arms,* and ran below; and added to this I had again to threaten the men at the helm, who seemed half inclined to follow the example of the others: so I now prepared for the worst.

The pirates came on firing at intervals as the others had done, and I followed my former plan of watching their movements until they were near enough for my gun to tell upon them with fearful precision. Their shot was now flying about our ears and riddling our sails, and they came on in their usual noisy manner, perfectly unconscious of what I had in store for their reception. For the last time the helm of the nearest junk was put down, when we instantly fell flat on our faces and allowed the shot to pass over us. As soon as their last gun was fired, and before they had time to load again, I poured the contents of my gun amongst them fore and aft, as I had done before. This took them completely by surprise ; and as we were still under a heavy press of sail, we were soon a considerable way ahead of them. Two others of the fleet came up and fired some shots at us, but the whole of them evidently imagined that a number of foreigners were on board of our junk, a belief which doubtless had a great deal to do with the success which attended my efforts. At length darkness coming on, they gave up the pursuit and

Chap. XXI.] SAFE ANCHORAGE. 403

bore away from us, and in two hours more we arrived at a safe anchorage. The fever which I had scarcely felt during all this excitement now returned with greater violence, and I was heartily glad to go below and turn into my bed.

During the night I heard a great noise on board, but was too feverish and weak to make any inquiries as to the cause. In the morning my servant informed me that it was occasioned by the arrival of three junks during the night, which had been chased to the entrance of the harbour by the pirates; there had, he said, originally been four in company, but one of them had been taken.

The sailors on board these junks had not been so fortunate as we had been, for several of them were severely wounded, and I was now asked to extract the balls. The wounds were large and ragged, owing to the iron shot which the Chinese use in their guns; I advised the wounded men to hurry on to Chusan, where they would get good medical advice.

Up to nine o'clock in the morning, although the wind and tide were both favourable, there were no signs of the junks getting under weigh ; I therefore sent for the captain and inquired if it was not his intention to proceed. He told me that he had had a meeting with the captains of the other vessels, and that they had determined to get a convoy of war junks from the mandarin before they went on. Being now within eighty or ninety miles of Chusan, I could easily hire a small boat for that distance,and therefore said to the captain, " Very well, then I shall leave you here, as I am very unwell, and anxious to get to Chusan as soon as possible." " Go," said I, turning to my servant, " and engage a boat to take me on to Chusan, and bring it here as soon as you can." When he was about to leave the vessel, several of the crew gathered round him and attempted to persuade him not to go; anxious to serve his countrymen, although at my expense, he loitered about for a little while and then came back and informed me that it was no use going on shore, as I should not be able to engage a boat to take me so far. As I had been informed by one of the shore people who had come on board, that plenty of boats were to be had on hire, I felt annoyed at his deceit, and threatened to punish him if he did not start immediately and bring a boat off. "When he saw that I was determined, he turned sulkily away, jumped into a sand-pan, and procured a boat without the slightest difficulty. The captain and crew now crowded round me, begging me not to leave them, and offering to get up their anchor and proceed at once. Although my destination was Chusan, I had taken my passage for Ning-po, as all the wood junks were bound either for that port or Chapoo ; on their now begging me to stay, I told them that unless they would sail into Chusan harbour and leave me there as they passed, I would proceed in the small boat, as I was anxious to get there as soon as possible, in order to obtain medicine and advice. " Oh," said they, " if you

Chap. XXI.] SAIL FOR CHUSAN. 405

will only go with us, we will run into Chusan harbour and leave you there before we cross over to Ning-po." Upon this assurance I agreed to accompany them.

The captains of the other junks now came to me and asked me if I would undertake to protect them all from the attacks of the pirates; as, if so, they would get under weigh and gowith us also. Upon my telling them that I could not undertake to do this, they told me that they must wait until some arrangement could be made with the mandarins, as they were afraid to proceed alone. We therefore left them at anchor, and proceeded on our voyage. During the day we frequently saw suspicious- looking craft, which were pronounced by the crew to be *Jan-dous;* but none of them were near enough to attack us. Late in the afternoon, as we approached Keto-pointla promontory of the main land near Chusan l we met a large fleet of merchant junks sailing together for mutual protection on their way down. Some of them came alongside us, and made anxious inquiries regarding the *Jan-dous,* and how many of them they might expect to meet with. Our people did not fail to give them an exaggerated account of the number we had seen and fought with, and the news did not appear greatly to delight them. During the night the tide turned against us ; and as the wind, although fair, was light, we were obliged to anchor until morning.

D D 3

When I went on deck at daylight the following morning, I found we were just under Keto-point, and only a few miles from Chusan harbour. The land was well known to me, having been frequently there before. It was the most welcome sight which had met my eyes for many a long day ; and I was thankful indeed to the Almighty for my escape from the pirates.

Whilst the men were heaving up the anchor, my old friends the captain and pilot came below, bolder and in much better spirits than heretofore, and informed me, with the greatest coolness, that they had changed their minds about going into the harbour of Chusan ; and that I must go over with them to Ning-po, from whence I could easily return in a small boat for Chusan. I felt very much nettled at this conduct, which, considering that I had saved their junk from being taken by the pirates on two different occasions, was most ungrateful. I reproached them with this ingratitude, telling them that, as they were now safe from the *Jan-dous,* they imagined that they could do with me just as they pleased. " But you never deceived yourselves more," added I; " you may show as much ingratitude as you please; but I shall take care that you fulfil the promise you made to me yesterday, and take me into the harbour of Chusan, before you go over to Ning-po. Look here: you see this gun and these pistols; they are all loaded: you know what effects they produced upon the *Jan-dous;* take care they are not turned

Chap. XXI.] LARGE PEACHES. 407

against yourselves. Englishmen never allow promises which have been made to them to be broken with impunity. I know the way into Chusan harbour as well as you do, and when the anchor is up, I shall stand at the helm; and if the pilot attempts to steer for Ning-po, he must take the consequence." This threat had the desired effect: and the trembling varlets landed me safely at Chusan in the course of the forenoon.

What with the fever and the excitement of the last few days, I was in a most deplorable condition when I reached Chusan ; but as the greater part of my collections were in the country near Shanghae, I was most anxious to ascertain in what state they were; and, finding an English vessel about to sail for the Yang-tse-Kiang, I immediately crawled on board, and, having a fair wind, we soon reached our destination. I was kindly received by my friend Mr. Mackenzie, and, under the skilful treatment of Dr. Kirk, the fever gradually left me, and I was soon enabled to attend to my collections.

Amongst the more important of the acquisitions which I made in the vicinity of Shanghae, I must not forget to mention a fine and large variety of peach, which comes into the markets there about the middle of August, and remains in perfection for about ten days. It is grown in the peach orchards, a few miles to the south of the city; and it is quite a usual thing to see peaches of this variety eleven inches in circumference and twelve ounces in weight. This is, probably, what some writers call the Peking peach, about which such exaggerated stories have been told. Trees of the Shanghae variety are now in the garden of the Horticultural Society of London.

The whole of my plants from the districts of Foo-chow-foo, Chusan, and Ning-po, being brought together at Shanghae, I got them packed, and, on the 10th of October, left the north of China for Hong-kong and England. As I went down the river, I could not but look around me with pride and satisfaction; for in this part of the country I had found the finest plants in my collections. It is only the patient botanical collector, the object of whose unintermitted labour is the introduction of the more valuable trees and shrubs of other countries into his own, who can appreciate what I then felt.

When we arrived at Hong-kong, I divided my collections and despatched eight glazed cases of living plants for England: the duplicates of these and many others I reserved to take home under my own care. I then went up to Canton and took my passage for London in the ship " John Cooper." Eighteen glazed cases, filled with the most beautiful plants of northern China, were placed upon the poop of the ship, and we sailed on the 22d of December. After a long but favourable voyage, we anchored in the Thames, on the 6th of May, 1846. The plants arrived in excellent order, and were immediately conveyed to the garden of the Horticultural Society at Chiswick. Already, many

Chap. XXI.]

ANEMONE JAPONICA.

of those which I first imported have found their way to the principal gardens in Europe; and at the present time (October 20. 1846) the *Anemone japonica* is in full bloom in the garden of the Society at Chiswick, as luxuriant and beautiful as it ever grew on the graves of the Chinese, near the ramparts of Shanghae.

Anemone on the Tombs.

APPENDIX

THE SECOND EDITION.

METHOD OF TRANSMITTING PLANTS FROM ONE COUNTRY TO ANOTHER BY SEA IN "WARD'S CASES.?'

As many of the readers of this work may have friends in distant countries, who are anxious to send home the beautiful flowers which they meet with in their rambles, the Author has applied to the Council of the Horticultural Society of London, for permission to extract from the Journal of the Society the following paper upon the subject published by him a few weeks ago. He trusts that the directions which experience has enabled him to give will be found useful to those going to, or returning from, foreign countries, in not only affording amusement during a tedious voyage, but in enabling them to enrich one country with the productions of another. For results of this kind, it ought to be generally known that we are mainly indebted to N. B. Ward, Esq., of Wellclose Square, London, who first planned the cases which now bear his name.

" Having been engaged by the Horticultural Society of London to proceed to China for the purpose of examining the Horticulture and Botany of that country, and of sending home such vegetable productions as might be useful or ornamental in England, the Council deemed it

an excellent opportunity for sending out at the same time a collection of living plants and seeds, with the view of ascertaining precisely the effects produced upon such things during a long sea voyage, as well as of introducing to China some of the best flowers, fruits, and vegetables, which are cultivated in Europe. For this purpose they ordered some glazed cases to be prepared, and filled with such kinds of fruit-trees and ornamental plants as were likely to succeed well in the climate of China, and be of use both to the Chinese and to the foreign residents. They were made fast on the poop of the vessel, and we sailed from England on the 1st of March, 1843. The weather during the early part of the voyage was cold, dull, and wet, and the plants grew very little until we reached the latitude of Madeira, which we saw on the 13th of the month. The thermometer averaged 62 Fahr. at this time in the shade, and the plants feeling the effects of the sudden change of temperature, began to grow with great rapidity, completely filling the cases in a few days with young shoots and leaves. This took place before we reached the equator. The vines, peach-trees, and figs seemed quite at home; the roses also grew fast and began to blossom, but evidently in an atmosphere which was too hot and close for their constitution, and in a short time their leaves began to suffer from pressure against the damp glass, in the same manner as we frequently see plants in crowded hothouses in England.

" Aboutthis period,| thatis, when we were in the vicinity of the equator,| the thermometer averaged 77 in the shade, and was frequently higher in the night than during the day. From the condition of the plants at this stage of the voyage, it was evident that a most important point in the preparation of cases is always to select specimens which are strong, healthy, and well-established; weak plants, in many instances, are sure to perish, because the stronger kinds overgrow them, keeping them from the light and air, andAPPENDIX. 413

preventing them from forming stems and leaves for their support.

" We passed the longitude of the Cape of Good Hope in the beginning of May; but, in order to have the advantage of westerly winds, we kept well south in lat. 38, where the thermometer ranged from 55 to 65 Fahr. This change was evidently a most trying one for the plants, which, after having grown rapidly when sailing through warmer climates, and having filled the cases with weak, half-ripened wood, were now suddenly checked by dull weather, and a temperature which was comparatively low. Mildew and other fungi now attacked them, and most of the leaves which were in contact with the glass were rotted by the damp.

" It was curious to remark the similar effects which were produced upon animals and plants by this change of temperature ; both suffered more from comparative than from actual cold. A few weeks before this, the plants began to grow most rapidly in a temperature about the same as that in which they were now suffering from cold; in fact, they grew considerably then ia a temperature several degrees lower. The very same effects were produced upon my own feelings, as well as upon those of the other passengers in the ship. We felt the heat much in lat. 33 or 34 N., with a temperature of 58 and 60, and were then putting on our thin white clothing; while with the same warmth on the south side of the line we felt cold, and were obliged to resume our thick, warm dresses.

" Having kept in the same degree of latitude all along from the Cape until we reached the islands of Amsterdam and St. Paul's, in the Indian Ocean, we then stood northerly, in the direction of Java Head. The temperature, of course, gradually increased as we sailed northwards, but the excitability of the plants was, in a great measure, gone, and even when we reached the Straits of Sunda, where, owing to the proximity of land, it was much warmer than it had been under the line in the AtlanticOcean, still they grew again in a slow and languid manner, and the shoots were weak. It is these rapid changes from summer to winter, and from winter to summer, which destroys so many plants in a long voyage round the Cape, to or from India or China.

" When we reached Hong-kong I found that most of the plants were alive, although some of them were in a very exhausted state. Some olive trees which I took out were as healthy and green as the day we started; vines, pears, and figs also stood the voyage remarkably well. The soil, although it had received no water for four months, was nearly as moist as when we left England, which proved the closeness of the cases.

" Having described what actually takes place during a long sea voyage, I shall now proceed to give some instructions relating to cases, packing, shipping, and general management, which, I trust, will be useful to those interested in such matters.

" *Glazed Cases.* |' Ward's Cases,' or air-tight cases as they are commonly called, are so well known in all parts of the world, that a minute desciiption of them here is unnecessary. They are not, strictly speaking, air-tight, but they are so close that the moisture cannot escape, and therefore if the soil be well watered before the case is closed, the moisture is retained in sufficient quantity to support plants during a voyage to or from the most distant parts of the world. When the sun shines, evaporation goes on in the usual way, but the vapour finding no outlet, condenses on the glass and wood of the cases, as well as upon the leaves of the plants, and in the evening again falls down like dew upon the soil. In this manner the vapour goes on forming and condensing, according to the heat of the weather during the voyage, without much actual loss, providing the cases are tightly made.

" After this explanation, any one will be able to see that it is of the greatest importance to have the cases made of well-seasoned wood, which is not liable to split or openAPPENDIX. 415

at the joints when exposed to the hot Bun of the tropics. If this happens, the plants will either perish from drought, or sea-water will probably be admitted, which is equally fatal to vegetable life.

" Another defect in the construction of many of these cases is the shortness of their feet. The bottom of the case should always be at least six inches raised from the deck of the vessel. Washing decks is the first part of the sailor's business every morning at sea, and they are not generally very particular as to where they throw the water. If the feet of the plant-case are shorter than six inches, there will not be sufficient room for the sailors to dash the water below it, and consequently both the bottom and sides will stand the chance of being washed every morning as regularly as the decks. In the course of a four or five months' voyage, the salt water is certain to find its way into the soil, which it then saturates, and destroys the roots of the plants. I have no doubt that this is one of the reasons why plants generally arrive in such bad condition from India and other parts of the world, for I have frequently seen the soil of such cases in a complete puddle when they come to hand in England.

" *Plants, Soil,* §-c.lI have already noticed the great importance of choosing strong, healthy plants, which are not liable to be overgrown or to damp off during the voyage. I found that grafted plants were also more liable to suffer than others, as one or two of my young scions died, while the stocks remained healthy enough.

" The soil of the cases should be at least nine or ten inches in depth. After the plants are put in, each case should be placed perfectly level, and liberally supplied with water. It is much better if this can be done ten days or a fortnight before the plants are to be sent off, so that they may be well established in their new quarters. During this time they can have frequent waterings; and then, when the soil has filled up all the crevices in the cases and becomes firm, it may be fastened down with

cross bars of wood. A little moss, where it can be obtained, is an excellent thing to sprinkle on the surface, as it both helps to keep the earth down, and at the same time prevents evaporation from going on too rapidly. This mode of packing applies to shrubs and trees; orchids, or air-plants, require different treatment. As the latter do not draw much nourishment from the soil, there is no occasion to have so much of it in the cases; indeed, a large body of damp soil is very apt to rot the plants. Two or three inches is quite sufficient. As these plants are generally found growing upon trees, the best way is to cut the portion of the branch on which the plant grows, and send it home with the plant upon it. In the majority of cases it is a bad plan to pull the root off the wood, if the plants are to be sent in glazed cases and exposed to a sea voyage for five or six months. When I despatched some cases filled with Phalaenopsis from Manila, I had them made with only one glazed side, the other was wood. After packing the bottom of the cases full of plants I nailed a great number to the wooden side, and from the number which arrived in good order in this country the plan must have answered the purpose. It is well known that many of these air-plants require so little nourishment from the soil, that they may be sent home in common packing-cases if the voyage does not occupy more than six weeks, or even two months, such as from the West Indies or South America. The above remarks, with regard to air-plants, therefore, only apply to long voyages, such as from India or China to this country.

" *Ships and shipping Plants.* |When the vessel is about to sail, the cases should be closed firmly, and the joints must be made perfectly tight. Narrow strips of canvass dipped in a boiling mixture of tar and pitch, and put on the outside of the joints, answer the purpose admirably, and should always be used where there is any difficulty in making the joints close. Large vessels with poops are the best for plants, and should always be preferred where

APPENDIX. 417

there is any choice, as their decks are higher, and consequently less liable to be washed by the sea. The poop, either in small or large ships, is the best place for the cases to be placed: in small vessels they should either be put there or not sent at all. The main or mizen top is sometimes recommended; but most captains object to have such heavy articles placed so high above the decks.

" In 1841 or 1842 the Horticultural Society received a case of plants by the ' Emu,' from Van Diemen's Land, the whole of which were dead when they reached this country. As I happened, in 1843, to go out to China by the same vessel, I made some inquiries of one of the officers regarding the treatment this case had received on board during the passage home. He candidly told me that they had considered it too much in the way when on the poop, and had sent it forward near the bows. When, therefore, the vessel was ' on a wind,' or had a heavy head sea to contend with, she shipped a great quantity of water over the bows, and of course deluged the poor plants. This at once accounted for the bad order in which the case had been received. I should, therefore, recommend botanical collectors, and those individuals who are in the habit of sending home cases of plants from the far distant East to their friends in Europe, to obtain a promise from the captain that the cases shall remain upon the poop of the vessel during the whole of the voyage. If they are sent forward, or even placed upon the quarter deck, the contents are sure to be destroyed. It is also the best way to ship the cases in the usual business manner, taking a bill of lading for the same, with the freight payable in England, or in any other place to which the ship may be bound.

" Unless there is some one on board who understands the cultivation of plants, the cases should never be opened from the time they are shipped, until they arrive at their destination. The only directions I was in the habit of giving when I took the plants on board were the following: ' Do not move them from the poop; never allow them to

be opened ; should any accident happen to the glass, repair it immediately, either with glass, or, where Jhat cannot be had, a piece of thin board will answer the purpose; in stormy weather, when there is any probability of spray coming over the poop, throw an old sail over the cases; and, lastly, *never allow the sailors to throw a drop of water over them when they are washing decks in the morning.*' These directions are short, easily understood, and easily acted upon.

" *Treatment during the Voyage.* | When the botanical collector returns with his plants, or when there is any one on board of the ship who understands their management, the cases may be opened and the plants examined from time to time with the most beneficial results. In order that those who are going out or returning from the East may understand how this is best done, I shall detail, shortly, my own practice during the voyage home, and its results.

" Eighteen cases were packed in the manner I have already recommended, and taken on board of the ' John Cooper,' then at anchor in the bay of Hong-kong. As it was in the end of the year, the monsoon was fair down the China Sea, and we reached the island of Java in eleven days. After passing the straits of Sunda, we had variable winds for a week or ten days, and then got into the southeast trades. In these latitudes the weather is generally settled and fine, the sea is smooth, and the vessel is wafted gently onward in her course towards the Cape of Good Hope. In ordinary circumstances, therefore, it is perfectly safe to open the cases frequently during this part of the voyage. Those under my care at this time were made with sliding-doors at each end, so that I could give air and get my hand in, without unscrewing the sides. These slides were drawn out almost every day in the morning *after decks were washed*, and on very fine days the side-sash of each case was unscrewed, and the plants fully exposed. At these times all the dead or damping leaves were removed, and the surface of the soil dressed and cleaned. I always made it

APPENDIX. 419

a rule never to leave any of them open at night, however fine the night might appear to be.

" This mode of treatment was carried on until we began to get near to Madagascar. As bad weather is generally experienced off this island, I made all the cases as tight as possible with putty, and never opened them again until we got round the Cape. After the 'Cape of Storms' is passed, the mariner generally gets again into fine weather, and, with a fair south-east trade wind, runs direct for St. Helena. Knowing that I would be able to procure a supply of fresh water there, I exposed the plants as much as possible every day, in order that all the dampness might be removed, and that the young wood which was then formed on many of the plants might be well hardened. When we anchored at St. Helena, I took care to give the soil as much fresh water as it could take in, and then screwed the sashes down again. The weather continued fine, and the winds fair until we reached the equator. During this time the end slides were generally open every day.

" When near the equator, we again got into variable winds, having run out of the trades, and were frequently deluged with heavy rains. At these times I was in the habit of opening the sashes and allowing the plants to receive a refreshing shower, which did them a great deal of good. In circumstances of this kind, however, great care should be taken that the water does not come down out of some of the sails which have been exposed to the salt spray of the ocean, as it would then be impregnated with salt, and would probably injure or destroy the plants. I notice this more particularly as an accident of the kind nearly happened to myself.

" After coming through the ' variables,' we got what are called the north-east trade winds, and steered for the Western Islands. As the weather was now bad, and the vessel ' close-hauled,' that is, sailing very near the wind, we often had a considerable quantity of spray coming over the deck. Before coming into this weather, I took care tohave the cases again perfectly closed; the end slides now had often to remain closely shut down, not only on account of the spray, but also on account of the saltness of the air, which would doubtless have been very deleterious. After having three or four weeks of this weather, we got at last into smooth water in the English Channel, where, as the weather was fine, I again opened the cases and found them in excellent order. No detention taking place at the docks, the cases were immediately conveyed to the garden of the Society at Chiswick. The following numbers will show the results of this shipment: I

Number of plants put into the cases in China - 250 reported in good condition when landed - 215

which died during the voyage - - 35

" In a communication from Mr. Livingstone of Macao, read to the Society in 1819, and published in the third Volume of the Transactions, it is stated that at that time only one plant in a thousand survives the voyage from China to England, and supposing, on an average, that plants purchased in Canton, including their chests, and other necessary charges, cost 6s. *8d.* each, consequently each surviving plant must have been introduced at the enormous expense of upwards of *3001.* The result which I have given above will show, however, that we have made some improvement in the introduction of Chinese plants since the days of Mr. Livingstone."

A Chinese Funeral.London:

Sfothswoode and Shaw, New-street- Square.

Albemarle Street,

June, 1847.

NEW BOOKS Of The PRESENT SEASON.

l(y Authority of the Lords Commissioners of the Admiralty.

A Voyage of Discovery and Research in the Southern Seas.

Comprising an Account of Kerguelen Island, Van Diemen's Land, Campbell and Auckland Island, New Zealand, The Falkland Islands, Cape Horn, and New South Shetland ; the Discovery of an extensive Southern Continent with Volcanoes 15,000 feet high, in action, and the determination of the South Magnetic Pole.

By Captain Sir James Clark Ross, Knt., R.N.

With 8 Maps, 8 Plates, and 18 Woodcuts. 2 vols. 8vo. 36.

It is with pleasure, amid all the trifling productions and stale and repeated compilations of the season, that we sit down to a work like thisla sterling and solid work, which does high honour to British science, perseverance, and intrepidity. It has added vastly to our general knowledge, and thrown new lights upon some of the most important questions which occupy the researches of mankind."lLiterary Gazette.

Three Years' Wanderings in the Northern Provinces of China.

INCLUDING A VISIT TO THE TEA AND SILK COUNTRIES.

By Robert Fortune.

With Map, Plates, and Woodcuts. 8vo. 15.

" Mr. Fortune's work is characterised by modesty, discrimination, and good sense, as his progress appears to have been by good temper and perseverance. He had a particular object in view, and a more innocent and interesting one cannot be imagined."|*New Monthly Afagazint.*

A New History of Greece.

Containing|

Legendary Greece. .v Is 14

Grecian History To The Reign oP Peisistratus At Athens, f rt

History Of Early Athens, And The Legislation Of Solon. |

Grecian Colonies. I Vols 3 & 4

View Of The Contemporary Nations Surrounding Greece. *f*

Grecian History Down To The Battle Of Marathon. *J*

By George Orote, Esq.

With Maps. Vols. I. to IV. 8vo. 16. each.

" The acute intelligence, the discipline, faculty of intellect, and the excellent erudition, every one would look for from Mr. Grote ; but they will here also find the element which harmonises these, and without which, on such a theme, an orderly and solid work could not have been written. Poetry and Philosophy attend the historian on either hand, and do not impede or misguide his steps."|*Examiner.*

MR, MURRAY'S LIST OF

The Financial and Commercial Crisis

CONSIDERED.

By Lord Ashbuiton.

Fourth Edition. 8vo. 1.

The Story of the Battle of Waterloo.

FROM PUBLIC AND PRIVATE SOURCES.

By Rev. a. R. Gleig, M.A.

Post 8vo. 6.

" The book is a very complete, painstaking, well-arranged, and interesting narrative, embracing all the collateral points of the subject as well as its main features. The arrangement, indeed, is its first excellence. There is a brief and rapid view of the state of Europe after the first downfall of Napoleon, and an equally condensed account of hi? evasion from Elba and march to Paris. The preliminary preparations for the campaign on each side are theu described ; the battles of Ligny and Quatre Bras introduce tie crowning triumph of Waterloo; and the contemporary march of Blucher and the attack of Grouchy upon Thielman at Wavre fall into their proper places in point of time, and support the main story without interfering with it. The subsequent retreat of Grouchy, the entrance into France, the final abdication of Napoleon, and the convention of Paris complete the narrative. More striking accounts of Waterloo, and perhaps of the other battles have appeared, because the author's fulness occasionally runs into ovcr-Jetail on mere military matters ; but we have never met with so complete and well-arranged a view of the Story of the Hundred Days."|*Spectator.*

" This account is instinct with spirit, and many are the striking and touching anecdotes which add to its interest. It is likely to become one of the most popular productions of the very popular series to which it belongs."|*Literary Otaxtte.*

Omoo,
OR PERSONAL ADVENTURES IN THE SOUTH SEAS.
By Hermann Melville,
AUTHOR OP " TYPEE, OR THE MARQUESAS ISLANDERS."
Post 8vo. 6.
We were much puzzled, a few weeks since, by a tantalising and unintelligible paragraph pertinaciously reiterated in the London newspapers. Its brevity equalled its mystery : it consisted but of five words, the first and last in imposing majuscule. Thus it ran :|
' OMOO : By the Author of TYPEE.'
Having but an indifferent opinion of books ushered into existence by such chnrla-tanic.il manoeuvres, we thought no more of' Omoo' until, musing the other day over our matutinal hyson, the volume itself was laid before us, and we suddenly found ourselves in the entertaining society of Marquesan Melville, the phomix of modem voyagers, sprung, it would seem, from the mingled ashes of Captain Cook and Robinson Crusoe. The title is borrowed from the dialect of the Marquesas, and signifies a rover : the book is excellent, quite first-rate."|*Blackwood.*.
NEW BOOKS OF THE PRESENT SEASON.
The Arts of the Middle Ages.
BY THE MONK THEOPHILUS.
TRANSLATED, WITH EXPLANATORY NOTES, AND A NOTICE OF THE PRACTICE OF OIL PAINTINO, PREVIOUS TO THE TIME OF THE TAN VCKS.
By Robert Hendrie.
8vo. 2Is.
" This book is curious as a practical account of the state of the Arts about the time of the Eleventh and Twelfth centuries : and Mr. Hendrie has done good service to this class of literature by the publication of the completes! edition of the work that has yet been given to the world, as well as by the illustrative notes he has appended to it."|
Spectator.
English Hexameters.
CONSISTING OF TRANSLATIONS FROM SCHILLER, GOTHE, HOMER, CALLINUS, and MELEAGER.
Sir John Herschell, I Archdeacon Hare,
Professor Whewell, ' Rev. Dr. Hawtrey,
John G. Lockhart, Esq.
8vo. 9
Verse Translations from the German,
INCLUDING BURGER'S LENORE, SCHILLER'S SONG OF THE BELL, AND OTHER POEMS.
8vo. *If. 6d.*
Autobiography of Sir John Barrow, Bart.,
(late Of The Admiralty). This volume contains|
1. Reminiscences of Early Life.
2. Notices and Observations on China and the Chinese, from Pekin to Canton.
3. Notices and Observations on the Colonists, the Kaffirs, Hottentots, and Bosje-

inans of Southern Africa, from personal intercourse; and on the Natural History of South Africa.

4. Notices of 13 different Administrations, Whig and Tory, of the Navy.

5. Retirement from Public Life.

6. Origin and Establishment of the Quarterly Review.

With Portrait. 8vo. 16.

" Sir John Barrow undertakes his task in a manner which must set every reader at ease. Possessing|not idly boasting|a *meru aana in corpore sano*|bearing testimony, throughout his narrative, to the honourable and healthy influences of work, and to the certainty with which energy and self-improvement will advance the fortunes of one lowly born|we have rarely looked into a record of eighty years which chronicles so much of prosperity and happiness. Nor can we forget that Sir John Barrow's public career lay in the most interesting and varied hemisphere of the official world. That department which is first reached with news of a sea victory, and in which projects for some voyage of discovery are matured, must give play to feelings of more frequent excitement and thoughts of larger enterprise, than find place or occupation in other branches of national service at the desk. In short, here is another pleasant English book, to be added to the Englishman's library.1'|*Aihfnaum.*

MR. MURRAY'S LIST OF

Life of Lord Sidmouth.

ARRANGED FROM PAPERS AND LETTERS LFFT IN THE CARE OF TRUSTEES, FOR THE PURPOSE OF PUBLICATION.

By the Dean of Norwich.

Portraits. 3 vols. 8vo. 42.

"We are sure that few of our readers will be satisfied without making personal acquaintance with a book which, for profound and varied interest, the excellence of its individual subject, and the astonishing importance of the events it commemorates, is exceeded by no work that has appeared within these twenty years, and is as indispensable to the library as the admirable volumes which enshrine the memory of a great cotemporary|Lord Eldon."|*Morning Post.*

Lives of the Lord Chancellors:

FROM THE EARLIEST TIMES TO THE DEATH OF LORD TI1URLOW.

By Lord Campbell.

First And Second Series. 5 Vols. 8vo. *lit.*

" Lord Campbell has, we think, rendered a very acceptable service, not only to the legal profession, but to the history of the country, by the preparation of this important and elaborate work. It contains a great body of interesting and useful information, both on the progress of our jurisprudence, on that of our judicial system, and also on the state of the constitution, and the various events in our civil nnla at different periods of time."|*Law Review.*

Sketches of the History of Christian Art.

By Lord Lindsay,

AUTHOR OF LETTERS ON EGYPT AND THE HOLY LAND." 3 vols. 8vo. 31s. *6d.*

" One of the most laborious and erudite pieces of research on the subject of the Fine Arts that has appeared in the English language, is the work named above. To the true understanding of his subject, Lord Lindsay considers that he has prepared the way by his exposition of the ' Progression by Antagonism,' with its accompanying diagram. His classification of schools and artistslin which there are but "few errorslis, perhaps, the most unique and valuable of its kind that has ever appeared : and proves the extensive knowledge, discrimination, zeal and industry of its author." *Atheiueutn.*

Sketches of German Life.

TRANSLATED FROM THE GERMAN OF VARNHAGEN VON ENSE. By Sir Alexander Duff Gordon, Bart.

Post 8vo. *5s.*

" This is a selection deserving of more than ordinary attention. Though the writer does not take a high rank among the authors of modern Germany, in right either of original talent, or any peculiar charm of style as a narrator, he is easy, circumstantial and trustworthy. He has lived too among distinguished people and in stirring times. His wife, the celebrated Rahel, was acknowledged as one of the intellectual queens of Germany : and her thoughts and opinions were eagerly courted by some of its most learned and most powerful men. It tells us how the writer held colloquy with Richter, took part in the battle of Aspern, and was mingled in the great world of Paris, shortly after the marriage of Napoleon to Maria-Louisa. We mention these passages somewhat disconnectedly, for the purpose of showing the wide range of the book."|A

NEW BOOKS OF THE PRESENT SEASON.

The Sieges of Vienna by the Turks.

CHIEFLY TRANSLATED FROM THE GERMAN.

By the Earl of Ellesmere.

With a Plan. Post 8vo. *I. 6d.*

" Of the manner in which the Earl of Ellesmere has discharged the various duties of translator, editor and author, we can speak in terms of high praise. His style is clear, nervous, rapid : and has the rare merit of combining the freedom and freshness of original composition, with the minute accuracy of German scholarship. The work is a valuable contribution to the history of an important period."|*lthcnaum.*

The Commercial Policy of Pitt and Peel.

1785|1846.

Bvo. 2.

Favourite Haunts and Rural Studies.

INCLUDING VISITS TO SPOTS OF INTEREST IN THE VICINITY OF WIND-SOR AND ETON.

By Edward Jesse, Esq.

With numerous Woodcuts. Post Bvo. 1 '2.

" Mr. Jesse hw added so much more of a various and desultory character to the results of his new pursuit as to render the present volume, like those from his pen which have preceded, a pleasing and popular *omnium gatherum* about interesting architectural remains, the biography of their by-gone inhabitants, country life, rural scenery, literature, natural history, &c."|*Literary Ouzctte.*

The Crisis and the Currency.

WITH A COMPARISON BETWEEN THE ENGLISH AND SCOTCH SYSTEMS OF BANKING.

By John G. Kinnear, Esq.

8vo. 2. 6rf.

Gatherings from Spain.

CONSISTING OP SUCH PORTIONS OF THE " HAND-BOOK OF SPAIN" AS HAVE BEEN OMITTED IN THE SECOND EDITION OF THAT WORK, TO-GETHER WITH MUCH NEW HATTER.

By Richard Ford, Esq.

Post 8vo. 6.

The Emigrant.

By Sir Francis B. Head, Bart.

Fifth Edition. Post 8vo. 12.

" We know not what portiou of Sir Francis Head's volume|speaking of it now solely as a literary production|may not be mentioned with unqualified praise and approval. It is singularly spirited, imaginative, nervous, and philosophical. A more vigorous and fascinating writer does not live."|*Times.*

A History of Germany

FOR YOUNG PERSONS.

On the plan of Mrs. Markham's " Histories."

With numerous Woodcuts. 12mo. *It. 6d.*

" A very valuable compendium of all that is most important in German History. The facts have been accurately and laboriously collected from authentic sources, and they are lucidly arranged so as to invest them with the interest which naturally pertains to them."|*Eraruje Kcal Ma/jazine.*

" This is a well-arranged and clearly-written book. The volume is handsomely printed and profusely illustrated with woodcuts."|*Spectator.*

Correspondence of James Watt,

ON HIS DISCOVERY OF THE COMPOSITION OF WATER. By J. P. Muirhead, Esq., F.R.S.E.

With Portrait 8vo. 10. *6d.*

On English Etymologies.

By H. Fox Talbot, F.R.S.

8vo. 12.

" This is the most interestiug work on the derivation of the English language which has appeared for many years ; and perhaps the most entertaining that has ever been published on the subject. Its author, we need hardly say, is oue whose high scientific attainments have made a name, always honourable, still more widely known throughout Europe. Such a book from such an author is doubly welcome. As an

Etymologist, Mr. Talbot's great merit is to be of no party|to think for himself, and to take a more comprehensive view of his subject than is at all usual."

" All who feel an interest in their own language|and who ought not!|will find such a feast of instruction and amusement as is seldom or never set out for their enjoyment"|*Literary Gazette.*

Allan Cunningham's Poems and Songs.

NOW FIRST COLLECTED. WITH AN INTRODUCTION, AND NOTES.

By his Son, Peter Cunningham.

2-imo. 2. *6d.*

" We congratulate the public on their possessing, in a cheap and elegant form, the works of tlie most tender and pathetic of the Scottish Minstrels who have arisen since the death of Burns. If this little book does not become a favourite, and if it does not speedily make its way, not only into every library, but into every farm-steading in .Scotland,|if the Poems of Allan Cunningham do not become familiar to the lips and as dear to the hearts of our shepherds and our peasantry as those of his great predecessor,|then we shall be constrained to believe that the age is indeed an iron oue ; that the heart of our beloved country has at hut grown cold, and its impulses lese fervid than of yore."|*Blackwood.*

NEW EDITIONS OF THE PRESENT SEASON.

Scropc's Daijs of

Third Edition, with Plates and Woodcuts. Crown 8vo. 20.

UMan ©om&cr'g Kbict to t&e &oman

A eie *Edition,* with Preface and Notes. By W. F. HOOK, I .I .

Fcap. 8vo. 3. *6d.*

iLlnticstgncD rniiuiOaucs in tfjc cOIti antr Jleto &cOtament, a tart of tfieir Ueracttg.

SfCOTitZ *Edition.* 8vo. 12.

AND ON THE EXPEDIENCY OF RENDERING SEPULCHRAL MEMO-RIALS SUBSERVIENT TO PIOUS AND CHRISTIAN USES.

Fourth Edition. Fcap. 8vo. *I. 6d.*

'jS Engtructfonisf in practical

ADOPTED AT THE ROYAL MILITARY ACADEMY, SANDHURST. *Second Edition.* Post 8vo. 7. *6d.*

This Manual is for the use of Young Officers, *Civil and Military Engineers,* Architects, &c., and contains full directions for Surveying, Plan Drawing, and Sketching Ground without Instruments.

Hife anO

A New Edition. With Portrait and Vignette. Royal 8vo. 15.

This Edition is printed uniformly with the Popular one volume editions of Bybon, Scott, and Soi'thet.

A TALE OF AND FOR ENGLAND IN THE YEAR 184|.

Third Edition. 2 Yols. Fcap. 8vo. 12.

Of *tf)t*

IN ITS VARIOUS SOCIAL AND ECONOMICAL RELATIONS.
By O.K. PORTER, of the Board of Trade. *Second Edition.* 8vo. 24.

MR MURRAY'S LIST OF NEW EDITIONS.
&icarto's iiJolittcal
With a Biographical Sketch, and an Index. By J. li. -H'("l.J.OriI, Esq.
Second Edition. 8vo. 16*l*.

riBt Principle of
OR, THE MODERN CHANGES OF THE EARTH AND ITS INHABITANTS.
Seventh Edition. With 100 Woodcuts. 1 vol. 8vo. 18.
Sir Oarlcs JSdl on tfjc &natomg of
AS CONNECTED WITH THE FINE ARTS.
Fourth Edition. With Engravings and Woodcuts. Imperial 8vo. -1.–.

Enctcnt
THEIR PRIVATE LIFE, RELIGION, MANNERS AND CUSTOMS, &c. *Third
Edition.* With 600 Illustrations. 5 vols. 8vo. *41.* 4.
lAankc'0 opcg of llomc.
Translated from the German by SARAH AUSTIN.
TOmJ *Edition.* 2 vols. 8vo. 24.
Uniform with Hallam'i Historical Works, Milman's Gibbon, &c.

Storieg for
SELECTED FROM THE HISTORY OF ENGLAND. *Fourteenth Edition.* With
24 Woodcuts illustrative of English History. 16mo. 5.
CTrokcr'g rofjrcsstbt tT-fOQrapJw for
Fourth Edition, reviled. 18mo. If. 6A
TRANSLATED. WITH EXPLANATORY NOTES, AND GOO WOODCUTS. By
E. W. LANE, Esq. A *New Edition. 3* vols. Post 8vo. 30.
MR. MURRAY'S LIST OF NEW EDITIONS.
HAND-BOOKS FOR TRAVELLERS.
Of Crabel=3Talfc ;
A Series of Dialogues and Vocabularies in English, French, German, and Italian,
intended to serve as an Interpreter for Travellers in Germany, France, or Italy. 18mo.
5s.
" He that travelleth into a country before he hath some entrance into the *language,*
goeth to school and not to travel." I *Bacon.*
(or /3,ortl) ©ermang airtr tfje Ifr&ine.
HOLLAND, BELGIUM, AND PRUSSIA. Map. 12.
for Soutf) ©ermang airtr tfie
BAVARIA, AUSTRIA, SALZBURG, STYRIA, AUSTRIAN AND
BAVARIAN ALPS, AND THE DANUBE. Map. 10.

of fainting.

GERMAN, FLEMISH, AND DUTCH SCHOOLS.
3anti=irooft for
THE ALPS OF SAVOY, AND PIEDMONT. Map. 10.
for jFrance anto tfje
NORMANDY, BRITTANY, THE RIVERS LOIRE, SEINE, RHONE,
GARONNE; FRENCH ALPS, DAUPHINE AND PROVENCE. *New*

Edition, revised. Maps. 1 2.
for Spain.
ANDALUSIA, GRANADA, CATALONIA, MADRID, &c.
New Edition, revised. Maps. 16.
for Nortf) Italg anto jFlorence.
SARDINIA, GENOA, LOMBARDY, TUSCANY, THE RIVIERA, &c.
New Edition, rensed. Map. 12.

for (ffcntrnl ttalj) antr iiomc.
PAPAL STATES, AND CITIES OF ETRURIA. Map. 15.
of ©mfe anlr ISoman anttquttieB.
A COMPANION FOR THE TOURIST AND SCHOLAR. WoodcuU. 10s. *6d.*
ltairt=lioo(; for /Wnltn antr lijr
IONIAN ISLANDS, GREECE, TURKEY, ASIA MINOR, &c. Maps. 15.
for ISgpt.
THE NILE, ALEXANDRIA, CAIRO, THE PYRAMIDS, MOUNT
SINAI, AND THEBES. *New Edition, revised.* Map. 15.

Price Six Shillings, In Cloth,
HOME AND COLONIAL LIBRARY.
CONSISTING or
(Original S&lorks anfc 'Reprints of $jpular
AT THE LOWEST POSSIBLE PRICE.
Volumes already Published. 1. BORROWS BIBLE IN SPAIN. *3-3.* HEBERTS
JOURNALS IN INDIA.
    4. IRBY AND MANGLES' TRAVELS-SIEGE OF GIBRALTAR. 6. HAY'S
MOROCCO|LETTERS FROM THE BALTIC.
    6. THE AMBER WITCH|CROMWELL AND BUNYAN.
    7. NEW SOUTH WALES|BARROW'S LIFE OF DRAKE.
    8. FATHER RIPA'S MEMOIRS|LEWIS'S WEST INDIES.
    9. MALCOLM'S SKETCHES OF PERSIA.
    10. FRENCH IN ALGIERS|FALL OF THE JESUITS.
    11. BRACEBRIDGE HALL. By Washington Irvino.
    12. DARWIN'S VOYAGE OF A-NATURALIST.
    13. LORD MAHON'S LIFE OF CONDE.
    14. BORROWS GYPSIES OF SPAIN.
    15. MELVILLE'S TYPES, OR THE MARQUESAS.
    16. LIVONIAN TALES|MEMOIRS OF A MISSIONARY.

17. SALE'S BRIGADE|LETTERS FROM MADRAS.
18. ST. JOHN'S WILD SPORTS OF THE HIGHLANDS.
19. HEAD'S PAMPAS|SIEGES OF VIENNA BY THE TURKS.
20. FORD'S GATHERINGS FROM SPAIN.
21. SKETCHES OF GERMAN LIFE.
22. MELVILLE'S OMOO; Ob, THE SOUTH SEAS.
23. GLEIG'S BATTLE OF WATERLOO.
Albemarle Street,
June, 1847.
New Books in the Press,
The Court of George the Second and
Queen Caroline.
By Lord Hervey, Vice-Chamberlain.

Edited by the Rioht Hon. JOHN WILSON CROKER.
13 ititrB from tljr Original jW. in Hjc Jam tin 9rd)ffuf nt icfcwortf).

" Boasting of intelligence and professing impartiality are such worn-out Prefaces to writings of this kind, that I shall not trouble my readers nor myself with any very long exordium upon these topicks ; all I shall say for my intelligence is, that I was lodg'd the year round in the court, during the greatest part of these times concerning which I write : and as nobody attended more constantly in publick, or had more frequent access at private hours to all the inhabitants ; I must have been deaf and blind not to have heard and seen several little peculiarity's, which must necessaryly be unknown to tmch of my Cotemporarys as were only acquainted with the chief people of this court in the Theatrical Pageantry of their public Characters, and never saw them when that mask of constraint and hypocrisy essential to their stations, was enough thrown off for some natural features to appear." | *Lord Hervey't Preface.*

With Portrait 2 Vols. 8vo.
The Life, Writings, and Discoveries of Sir Isaac Newton,
From Family Papers recently discovered at Hurstbourne Park, in the possession of the Earl of Portsmouth, and never yet made public.
By Sir David Brewster, F.R.S., D.C.L.
This is an entirely new Biography of Sir Isaac Newton, founded upon materials, of the existence of which neither Sir David Brewster (when he prepared the brief Life for the Family Library) nor any other of his Biographers were aware.
With Original Portrait, &c. 2 Vols. 8vo.
A New Work of Eastern Travel,
By Harriet Martineau.
Post 8vo.
12 MR. MURRAY'S LIST OF
Ranke's History of the Revolution in
Servia,
.-(From Serbian jllcc. aiiti Document.
Translated by MRS. ALEXANDER KERR.
With a Map. 8vo.

Essays on Biography, History, Voyages, Travels, &c.
By Robert Southey, LL.D.
Being a Selection from his Contributions to the "quarterly Review."
Edited by Rev. Charles C. Southey.
3 Vols. 8vo.
A Voyage up the River Amazon,
INCLUDING A RESIDENCE AT PARA.
By William H. Edwards.
Post 8vo.
(For the Dome and Colonial Library.)

Etruria : its Cities and Cemeteries.
By George Dennis, Esq.
The Author has made several Journeys to the Cities and Cemeteries of Etrnria, for the purpose of investigating the existing Etmscan Remains. The book is not only designed for general perusal, but will serve as a Guide to the Local Antiquities.
With Maps and numerous Illustrations. 2 Vols. 8vo.
Lives of the Lindsays.
BEING
A MEMOIR OF THE HOUSES OF CRAWFURD AND BALCAKRES.
By Lord Lindsay.
3 Vols. 8vo.
NEW BOOKS IN THE PRESS. 13
Notes from Life, in Six Essays.
1. HUMILITY & INDEPENDENCE.
2. MONEY.
3. WISDOM.
4. CHOICE IN MARRIAGE.
5. CHILDREN.
6. LIFE POETICAL.
By Henry Taylor, Esq.,
AUTHOR OF PHILIP VAN ARTEVELDE."
Post 8vo.

The Wayside Cross ;
OR, THE BAID OF GOMEZ. A TALE OP THE CARLIST WAR.
By Capt. E. A. MILMAN, 33rd Regiment.
Post 8vo.
For the Home And Colonial Library.

History of the Literature of Europe
DURING THE FIFTEENTH, SIXTEENTH, & SEVENTEENTH CENTURIES.
By Henry Hallam, Esq.
Third Edition, revised. 3 Vols. 8vo.
Boswell's Life of Dr. Johnson.

WITH THE TOUR TO THE HEBRIDES.
By the Right Hon. John Wilson Croker.
A *New Edition,* with Portrait and Vignette. With much additional matter.
One Volume Royal 8vo. Uniform with Byhon, Scott, Crabbb.

Alexander Von Humboldt's Cosmos.
A PHYSICAL DESCRIPTION OF THE WORLD.
Translated under the superintendence of Lieut.-colonel SABINE, F.R.S.

" Je vous autorise, Monsieur, de vous servir en toute occasion, de la déclaration
que la belle Traduction du Colonel Sabine, enrichie de rectifications et de notes très
précieuses, et qui ont toute mon approbation, est la seule par laquelle j'ai vivement
désiré voir introduit mon ouvrage dans la littérature de votre pays."|*Le Baron IIumMilt
à if. Murray, Dec. IS,* 1846.
Vol. II. Post !5vo.
14 MR. MURRAY'S LIST OF
A Hand-Book of the History of Painting. The Spanish and French Schools.
By Sir Edmund Head, Bart.
Post 8vo.
(uniform with Kuoleb's Hand-Books of the Italian and German Schools).

Hand-Book of London,
(Jast anto present.
By Peter Cunningham, Esq.

This work, which is arranged alphabetically, will furnish extended notices of
Remarkable Old Inns, Coffee Houses,
and Taverns.
Town Houses of the Old Nobility.
Places of Public Entertainment.
Old London Sights.
Ancient Theatres.
Ancient Crosses.
The Hostels of Church Dignitaries.

Privileged Places for Debtors.
Old London Prisons.
Places referred to by Old Writers.
The Wanis of London.
The Churches.
Residences of Remarkable Men.
Streets Remarkable for some Event.
Burial Places of Eminent Individuals, &c.
Post 8vo. *(In the Prea.)*
Hand-Book for Northern Europe.

BEING A GUIDE TO DENMARK, NORWAY, AND SWEDEN.

New Edition, rensed. Map. Post 8vo.

Hand-Book for South Italy, Naples, and Sicily.

Post 8vo.

NEW BOOKS IN THE PRESS. *IS*

Catholic Safeguards

AGAINST THE ERRORS, CORRUPTIONS, AND NOVELTIES OF THE CHURCH OF ROME.

Selected from the Works of Eminent Divines.

By James Brogden, M.A., Trinity College, Cambridge.

Vol III. 8vo. *To be completed in Five Volume.*

Life of Belisarius.

By Lord Mahon, M.P.

" A valuable contribution to the history of a most interesting era."|*London Magazine.*

" An able and valuable performance."|*Mvnthly Review.*

" The accurate biography by Lord Mahon."|*Slackwood'i Magazine.*

A New Edition. Post 8vo.

A History of Rome for Schools.

On the plan of Mrs. MARKHAM'S " HISTORIES."

With Woodcuts. 12mo.

A New Classical Dictionary.

By William Smith, LL.D.

Will comprise the same subjects as are contained in the well-known Dictionary of Lempriere, avoiding its errors, supplying its deficiencies, and exhibiting in a concise form the *mults* of the labours of modern scholars. It will thus supply a want that has been long felt by most persons engaged in tuition.

One Volume 8vo.

A Dictionary of Naval Officers.

Detailing the Life and Services of every Living Naval Officer, from the rank of Admiral of the Fleet to that of Lieutenant. Compiled from authentic official and family documents.

By W. R. O'Byrne, Esq.

Royal 8vo.

16 MR. MURRAY'S LIST OF NEW BOOKS IN THE PRESS.

Napoleon at St. Helena.

FROM THE LETTERS AND JOURNALS OF SIR HUDSON LOWE.

Edited and Arranged by Sir Nicolas Harris Nicolas.

This work will contain particulars of all that passed between Napoleon and Sir Hudson Lowe at St. Helena, showing how little foundation there was for the calumnies regarding Sir Hudson, so industriously propagated ; also interesting information regarding the Prussian Campaign of 1813, of Waterloo, and other events in which Sir H. Lowe was concerned, besides Notices of Public Affairs from 1792 to 1814.

3 Vols. 8vo.

CONCLUSION OF

The Lives of the Lord Chancellors.

By Lord Campbell.

Containing LIVES OF LORD LOUGHBOROUGH, LORD ERSKINE, and LORD ELDON.

WITH A TABULAR LIST OF THE LORD CHANCELLORS FROM THE EAR-LIEST TIMES.

2 Vols. 8vo.

The Works of Horace.

With an Original Life. By the Rev. H. H. Milman.

This is an attempt to employ the treasures of ancient Art; of Sculpture, Painting, Gems, Coins, &c., in illustration of the beauties and in elucidation of the meaning of the Classic Poets. The text will be illustrated with Views of the Localities, Vignettes from Antique Statues, Vases, &c., and The Life, with Coloured Borders, 4c.

Crown 8vo.

The Fables of

NEWLY TRANSLATED OR SELECTED FROM THE ORIGINAL.

By the Rev. Thomas James, M.A.

Illustrated with One Hundred Original Designs by John Tenniel.

The existing English Versions of Esop's Fables are dull, pointless, and vulgar. In consequence, a careful translation of the original authors has been made, with the design of rendering this most instructive and amusing of classic authors more popular, and more fitted for the perusal of the young.

One Volume Crown 8vo.

LaVergne, TN USA
14 September 2010

196921LV00005B/80/P